STEFAN HEYM

STEFAN HEYM

A CRITICAL ANALYSIS OF HIS AUTOBIOGRAPHY AND CIRCLE OF ACQUAINTANCES

HUBERT VENEMAN

Precocity Press

Published by Precocity Press, Los Angeles, CA
Editorial Direction and Editor: Rick Benzel
Creative Director and Designer: Susan Shankin
Cover Image of Stefan Heym: Marcel Antonisse / Anefo

ISBN: 978-1-7362174-4-3
Library of Congress Control Number: 2021900464
First edition. Printed and bound in the United States of America

TABLE OF CONTENTS

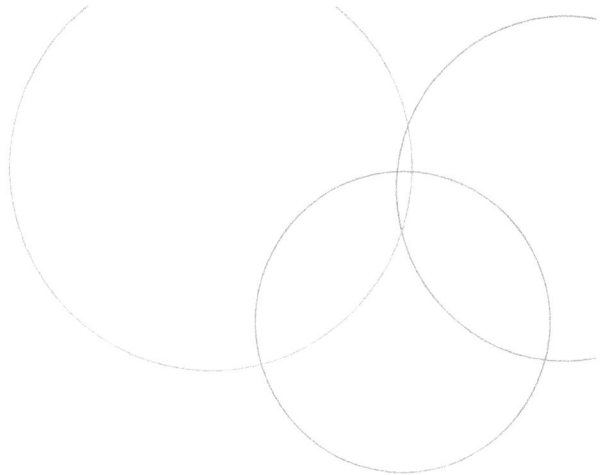

FOREWORD

Hubert Veneman was the firstborn of a family that, previous to his birth, emigrated from Germany to the United States, post-World War II. As was the case for the many thousands who likewise followed this path, their reasons were clear: to attain a better life and the freedoms that America could provide.

Prior to their emigration from Germany, the author's immediate family and relatives experienced many hardships. His grandfather died in a Russian prison camp and his mother and grandmother became refugees, first in the mountains of Germany where they fled then in the former Czechoslovakia. They returned to a newly defined West Germany and eventually found their way to the United States. Other relatives of Hubert Veneman endured similar fates. The author was thus able to learn firsthand from those who experienced so much victimization and inhumanity. In addition, as history has shown, mistruths about political issues, among many other issues, grew exponentially before, during, and after World War II.

This state of affairs led to Hubert Veneman's desire to determine what was and was not true, as well as to gain information and perspective on his family's difficult experiences. He sought to provide clarification by researching a notable figure from that era, namely, Stefan Heym (1913–2001). The research conducted for this book has revealed that Mr. Heym was not merely a novelist and journalist of note, as generally accepted. Mr. Heym was also a political activist with ties to communist organizations established to infiltrate and influence the cultural and political spheres that western democracies share. The author's family wishes that Hubert Veneman's research, as expressed in this book, contributes to the discourse on Stefan Heym, his political activity, and that of his colleagues and acquaintances.

Throughout the book, additional content to provide context for readers appears within brackets. The addenda also includes a glossary of acronyms.

This book has been published posthumously.

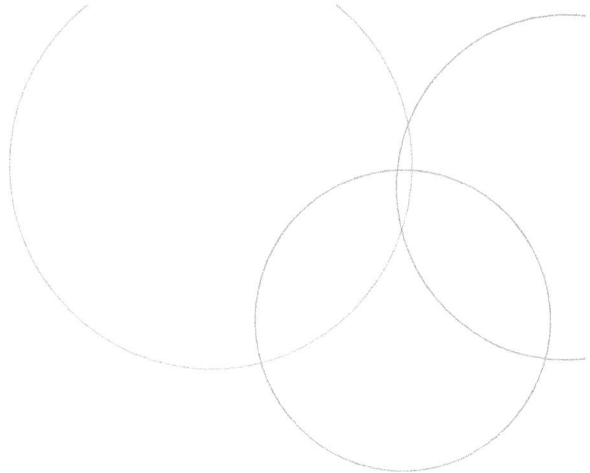

CHAPTER 1

STEFAN HEYM AND THE EARLIEST TIES TO THE KPD

Many attempts have been made during the past several decades to portray Stefan Heym as an independent intellectual who was forced into exile by a reactionary regime. However, a closer analysis of his circle of professional associates reveals something darker.

Heym had been groomed for participation in the communist conspiracy against Christendom from an early age. A converging pattern of facts indicate the conspiracy guided his early career. Also, Heym, or Helmut Flieg as he was then called, was much closer to the inner circles of [communist] power than those who have written of him have yet revealed.

To be blunt, Stefan Heym was a cousin of the Secretary of the Politburo for the KPD [*Kommunistische Partei Deutschlands*, Communist Party of Germany], named Leo Flieg. Heym's autobiography, *Nachruf*, and several other sources state his legal name as Helmut Flieg.

Yet, no one has ever publicly taken notice that his family name is identical to the unusual surname of another notable communist. Investigation shows that both men's fathers were born in Schrimm (today known as Srem) in the once German province of Posen.[1] Over ninety percent of Posen's Jews emigrated during the 19th century when Posen was annexed by Germany, escaping their status as *Ostjuden* [Eastern Jews] further west in Germany or in the United States.[2] Schrimm's population was approximately 5,000 and the possibility that two people of the same ethnic minority with the same uncommon surname were not related seems prohibitively remote. Furthermore, the fathers of both Stefan Heym and Leo Flieg were in the textile trade.[3] Also, Heym's memoir shows he had other relatives also called Flieg in Berlin where the KPD was headquartered.[4]

Heym displayed his capability for igniting controversy as an eighteen-year-old in Chemnitz in 1931. The local socialist newspaper published his satiric poem "Export Business," which decried the sending of arms and military advisors to China. The rhyme is said to have caused such an uproar among local nationalists that Helmut Flieg was forced to leave town.[5]

Affiliation with Leo Bauer

Omitted from Heym's memoir and hitherto published biographical accounts is that Leo Bauer, a German political activist and journalist, also relocated from Chemnitz to Berlin in 1931.[6] Both had grown up in Chemnitz, founded by Benedictine monks in the 12th century, whose market had grown into an important manufacturing city with the nickname "Little Manchester."[7] In defeat and in ruins, it was redubbed Karl Marx Stadt until reunification. Leo Bauer was born in Skalat, Galicia in 1912 while Heym was born in Chemnitz in 1913. Bauer's family moved to Chemnitz during World War I.[8] Heym's *Nachruf* states that he and Bauer had both attended the same synagogue for their religious education.[9] The writer Stefan Hermlin, who was born in Chemnitz in 1913, and in parallel to Heym also lived in the

DDR [*Deutsche Demokratische Republik*, the former West Germany from 1949 to 1990], has also been shown to have written an untruthful memoir.[10]

In 1931, the same year Heym and Bauer moved to Berlin, the *Sozial Arbeiter Partei* [SAP or SDAP, *Sozialdemokratische Arbeiter- partei Deutschlands*, The Social Democratic Workers' Party of Germany] was founded. Bauer became a member and Heym contributed to the SAP's newspaper and was on friendly terms with its editor, Will Schaber.[11] Willy Brandt [West Germany's Chancellor during the 1970s] also joined the SAP and, it may surprise one to learn, never actually left. The branch of the SAP which was exiled in Sweden, as Brandt was, became absorbed into the Social Democrat Party, despite the fact that the SAP's founders had openly become communists.[12] Bauer also became a close advisor to Willy Brandt during his term as Chancellor.[13]

Bauer's affiliation with the SAP lasted only until its disappointing election results in 1932. Bauer then joined the KPD not simply as an ordinary rank-and-file member, but as a participant in one of its secret conspiratorial divisions.[14] At the top of the hierarchy of the KPD's clandestine divisions was Stefan Heym's secret cousin, Leo Flieg.[15]

There are said to have been five such secret divisions, including the M-Apparat, N-Apparat, AM-Apparat, MP-Apparat, and T-Apparat. "M" stood for Military; "N" for "News" meaning intelligence informa- tion gathering; "AM" for Anti-Military which was specifically directed at the militants of rival parties; "MP" for Military-Political; and "T" apparat for Terror.[16] Bauer was part of the AM-Apparat led by an oper- ative named Hans Kippenberger.[17] Leo Flieg was in charge of the ille- gal branches' coordination with the Soviet Union's secret service and was personally in charge of the KPD's passport and document forging operations.[18] Bauer was an acquaintance of Stefan Heym's in Chem- nitz and had moved to Berlin at approximately the same time. He was affiliated with the same obscure splitter party, and, without even an interval, had joined the KPD's secret apparat. It thus seems likely Bau- er's early career was coordinated with, if not actually guided by, the secret apparat's leader, Leo Flieg. When one reviews the progression of Bauer's career, it becomes obvious Bauer was preselected for an elite role and was not simply another pair of fists for street fights.

Bauer's life took many twists and turns as Heym's did. He was arrested in March 1933 and sent to a concentration camp. A schoolfriend from Chemnitz who was also in the SAP helped gain his release.[19] On party orders, Bauer emigrated to Paris. There he worked in contact with Wilhelm Pieck, Walter Ulbricht, Willi Muenzenberg, Gerhart Eisler and, probably, Leo Flieg.[20] These are some of the most illustrious figures of German communism.

Bauer was remembered as bringing files on Nazis to Muenzenberg's office for propaganda exposés and as working with Muenzenberg and Herbert Wehner in sending volunteers to Spain when the Civil War began in 1936.[21] Also in 1936, Bauer succeeded Albert Grzesinski, the former Chief of Police in Berlin, as Secretary of the Central Association of German Emigration. He attended exile congresses in Geneva in July 1936 and London in December 1936.[22] Kurt Hiller, a radical not affiliated with the communist party, recalled a meeting with Bauer in 1933. He called Bauer the commander of communist refugees in Prague and therefore practically the leader of all the refugees there.[23] Bauer already played such a role in his early twenties though he had left Chemnitz because he had not been promoted following his eleventh school year.[24]

Like Heym, Bauer changed his name once in exile and is called Rudolf Katz in memoirs and histories that depict his pre-war exile period.[25] The communists paid him well enough to live in his own apartment in a prosperous section of Paris while other exiles who had been professionals or intellectuals were reduced to sharing apartments, accepting charity, and performing unskilled manual labor.[26] His status as leader of an official exile committee led to his being sent by the League of Nations to occupied Czechoslovakia in 1939 to rescue refugees he deemed merited saving.[27] Also like Stefan Heym, Bauer wrote his memoir in the third person, referring to himself as "Ludwig Bergmann," while Heym called himself "S.H." throughout *Nachruf*.[28]

The rest of Bauer's career merits a summary. Following Germany's invasion of France in 1940, Bauer fled to Geneva and continued as an operative. His activities included an association with Noel Field, an American with the Unitarian Services Committee.[29] Links to Noel Field would have consequences for Bauer and hundreds of thousands of others during the postwar era of East Bloc communist show trials.[30] Bauer's illegal wartime political activity in Switzerland resulted in his imprisonment there from 1942 to 1944.[31] He resumed work with the so-called Free Germany or "Freies Deutschland" movement that the communists were promoting as the new way for Germans.[32] Two other communists from Chemnitz, Hans Teubner and Walter Trautzsch, were among Bauer's collaborators in Switzerland.[33]

Upon return to Germany in 1945, Bauer lead the KPD in Hesse and perhaps in the entire American zone.[34] Bauer and Stefan Hermlin also worked for the newspaper *Frankfurter Rundschau* from its inception, though they were both actually from Chemnitz.[35] In 1947, a car accident in the Soviet Zone seriously injured Bauer a short time after public exposure of his life under the name Rudolf Katz.[36] Later, he was on assignment in Berlin where he led a Soviet radio station in the Masurenallee, an enclave controlled by the Soviets in the British sector. The Soviets soon arrested him and sentenced him to death at a military tribunal as part of the Noel Field purges that swept Eastern Europe.[37] The sentence was reduced to twenty-five years and Bauer was eventually freed from the Gulag in 1956 following the internal admission of gross errors under Stalin. Bauer resettled in West Germany and became an editor at "Stern" and ultimately an advisor to Willy Brandt. He even vacationed with the Chancellor's family in Tunisia in 1969.[38]

Leo Flieg

Of Leo Flieg, he must be considered an historical anomaly. There has been no biography or memoir about him published, as in the case of Heym, Hermlin, Bauer, Muenzenberg and many other KPD figures. There has not even been an article devoted to him in academic journals that specialize in the history of communism. Despite that, the fact remains that he was the Secretary of the KPD's Politburo from 1922 to 1932. In all the memoirs written by German communists, the only portrayal of Leo Flieg longer than a paragraph is found in Margaret Buber-Neumann's *From Potsdam to Moscow*.[39] She was the wife of Heinz Neumann, a German communist who was close to Leo Flieg. Her sister, Babette Gross, was the wife of Willi Muenzenberg, who was communism's leading propagandist until the Second World War and even had the official title "Chief Propagandist of Western Europe."[40]

Frau Neumann described Leo Flieg as having worked in a bank, then having been wounded in the First World War, resulting in being transferred to a desk job on the General Staff in Berlin, before becoming a founding member of the KPD.[41] Flieg was secretary to Leo Jogiches who was the KPD's leader for a brief period after the killings of Rosa Luxemburg and Karl Liebknecht in January 1919, until the assassination of Jogiches in March 1919.[42] Flieg is described as being fastidious, reserved, and well-liked for his unquestioned integrity.[43] It didn't seem possible that he could be the boss of communism's military and terror organizations who routinely sent criminals on assignments and on whose orders robberies of important military officials took place.[44] He is also claimed to have been in charge of the KPD's connection to the OMS, the secret service of the Communist International (Comintern).[45] Flieg was responsible for large sums of money sent to Germany by Moscow and was responsible for renting illegal apartments for leading communists in exile.[46]

It is stated that Flieg did not suffer a demotion in the sphere of his secret operations when his faction, with Neumann and Muenzenberg, was disciplined.[47] Lastly, Margaret Neumann relates that the Swedish-Jewish banker Olof Aschberg advised him not to leave Paris when Flieg received orders to report to Moscow in 1937. Flieg did not want to leave the impression he had absconded with party funds, and so reported and was not seen again.[48]

Additionally, once on return from a trip to Moscow, Frau Neumann was given the task of smuggling contraband by OMS leader

Jakob Mirov-Abramov. Though she hadn't informed anyone of her arrival, a colleague of Leo Flieg's was waiting at Tempelhof Airport for her and her suitcase.[49] The party archives have also made available the short autobiographies that cadres were required to write for the party files. Margaret Neumann, exiled in Paris at the time, refers to Leo Flieg as someone familiar with her circumstances.[50]

Frau Neumann's memoir and party autobiography also note that she was a communist organizer while employed at the Tietz department store concern, which is still among the most prominent in Germany.[51] Coincidentally, but not by mere happenstance, Stefan Heym was well-acquainted with the Tietz family, which he acknowledged in one of his last works.[52] The Tietz family originates from Birnbaum, Posen, which is a town contiguous to Schrimm.[53] As stated, the Fliegs were also in the textile trade and likely there were enduring ties with the Tietzes. Heym also once wrote that the father of a schoolmate in Chemnitz named Furstenberg, later killed by the Nazis, was a general director and large shareholder in the Tietz concern.[54]

Other sources on German communist history do not contradict the description of Leo Flieg in *From Potsdam to Moscow*, except one, which claimed Flieg was already one of communism's leaders in Berlin during World War I.[55] Frau Neumann's account of Flieg's service during World War I is also uncorroborated elsewhere, though it may be due only to the paucity of study on the subject.[56] The only bank mentioned in connection with Flieg was called Sass and Martini. However, this was not an operational bank but merely a dormant corporation purchased for a pittance and then used as a façade for financial swindles. The corporation once exchanged counterfeit foreign notes for genuine German currency but couldn't be prosecuted because of a loophole in postwar German statutes that made the passing of counterfeit German marks illegal but omitted proscribing the passing of false foreign notes.[57] This does support, however, Frau Neumann's depiction of Leo Flieg as being involved in criminal activity.

Leo Flieg was born in 1893 in the Tempelhof section of Berlin.[58] His involvement with the communism is first discernable with his joining the Socialist Youth movement in 1908.[59] Flieg's origins in Posen may have also benefitted him as Rosa Luxemburg, Julian Marchlewski, Leo Jogiches, and Karl Radek, each from Poland, were the leading figures in early postwar German communism.[60] Ernst Toller, who led the brief communist regime in Bavaria, had been born in Posen.[61] Flieg was among the co-founders of the Communist Youth International in 1919.[62] In 1921, he was roommate of another co-founder, Willi Muenzenberg, soon to become the "red" [communist] equivalent of American publishing magnate, [William Randolph] Hearst of Germany.[63] Flieg and Muenzenberg are credited as coauthors of *Die Jugend der Revolution*, published in 1920, which disappointingly strikes one as boilerplate dogma that any functionary could have written.[64] Flieg is noted as attending Youth International conferences in Prague and Luxemburg in 1920. He was arrested and released at some point during this period, and is also noted to have attended a conference in Moscow in 1921.[65]

As stated, Flieg became Secretary of the KPD Politburo in 1922, an office he held until a demotion in the 1932 "conciliator" controversy.[66] As an elite member of the party, he even held a seat in the Prussian Diet from 1923 to 1933.[67] He seems to have been Germany's leading OMS operative and worked closely with its leader, Jakob Mirov-Abramov, who spent much of the 1920s attached to the Soviet Embassy in Berlin.[68] Archives only accessible since the 1990's reveal Moscow transferred 50,000 gold rubles to Flieg to buy weapons for the misfired uprising of 1923.[69]

Flieg is acknowledged to have led the communist's passport forgery workshop called the Pass-Apparat.[70] The false document center is said to have had 170 employees and falsified thousands of documents per year.[71] A courier named Klose was arrested in Vienna in 1929 with a bagful of passports.[72] A raid by the Berlin Police Department in 1932 uncovered evidence that 1,500 false passports had been made in the previous six months.[73] A Soviet trade delegation member, Chubar-Onisenko, was found with five false passports in his villa in Hamburg.[74] The Pass-Apparat had over two dozen offices in Germany and several in neighboring countries and Scandinavia.[75]

Flieg is recorded as having provided a false passport for Italian communist Amadeo Bordiga in 1922.[76] Former KPD Reichstag deputy Nikolaus Thielen was caught by the Nazis with a passport manufactured by Flieg's organization in 1934, which shows Flieg lasted a good while in this nefarious enterprise.[77] Various accounts show communist agents Margaret Neumann, Karl Mewis, Hubert von Ranke, and Abraham Raichmann each used Luxemburg passports without legal entitlement.[78] Franz X. Feuchtwanger, a colleague of Leo Bauer's in the AM-Apparat, also wrote that Leo Flieg was in charge of travel documents.[79] Several of Flieg's staff attained prestigious positions in the DDR, which could have made Heym's return more agreeable, particularly following Leo Flieg's posthumous rehabilitation in 1957.[80]

A high point in Leo Flieg's career was reached in May 1928. He and Hugo Eberlein, also a KPD member of the Prussian Diet, were voted into the Comintern Control Commission.[81] Flieg's live-in girlfriend, Elise Harms, was sister of Eberlein's first wife, Anna Harms. The latter was the mother of Werner Eberlein, who was later a Central Committee member in the DDR.[82] Werner Eberlein even referred to Flieg as "Onkel Leo" in his memoir published in 2002.[83] A post in the Comintern Control Commission made Flieg and Eberlein bosses of the party's internal police, which therefore placed them among the world's most important *nomenklatura*. Hugo Eberlein, incidentally, had also been married to a daughter of Inessa Armand, an intimate of Lenin's who had been granted an aristocratic mansion near the center of Moscow.[84]

Hugo Eberlein also held workshops for young writers. Leo Flieg is generally not mentioned in connection with the numerous renowned intellectuals of the Weimar era. However, a few sources do claim Leo Flieg found posts for writers, presumably including journalists, and he has even been referred to in a reputable work as *verantwortlich fuer Kulturfragen,* meaning "responsible for cultural issues" within the KPD.[85] Recall that Flieg's former roommate Willi Muenzenberg had the official title Chief of Propaganda for Western Europe. Therefore, in

1931, for the young Helmut Flieg, a young communist writer seeking an opportunity, Leo Flieg was in an ideal position.

Leo Flieg played an especially prominent role in KPD party politics from the time of his reelection to the Politburo in 1929 to 1932 when his faction was disciplined and demoted.[86] He is on the record as communicating frequently with Ernst Thaelmann, attending party conferences with him in the Ruhr area in May 1930 and Hamburg in March 1931.[87] Flieg traveled with Thaelman, Heinz Neumann, Hermann Remmele, and Wilhelm Pieck to Moscow to meet with the Comintern Executive Committee three days after the meeting in Hamburg.[88] The same group, without Pieck, was again in Moscow in January 1932 for another meeting with the Comintern executive body.[89]

Within a few months Flieg and his closest colleagues — Muenzenberg, Neumann, and Remmele — lost their status in the official hierarchy. Flieg spent the rest of the Weimar period in Moscow concentrating on his Comintern duties, as if it was known that the Weimar period was concluding.[90] Wilhelm Pieck succeeded Flieg as Politburo Secretary, a post he would hold through his tenure as head of state in East Germany.[91] There is also a report that Walter Ulbricht was Flieg's replacement in the KPD Central Committee in 1932.[92] One researcher found a perceptive article in a Trotskyite paper that wrote of Flieg's transfer as a news story in itself. The article, "Von Flieg zu Pieck," which could be translated as "From Fly to Sting," called Heym's cousin the leader of the Leo Lania Correspondence and all other illegal offices.[93]

Comintern executioner Vittorio Vidali recalled meeting Leo Flieg in his memoir, *Missione a Berlino*.[94] The two met at Comintern headquarters before Vidali embarked on a covert assignment. Flieg supplied Vidali with a passport, money, and a book with a section gouged out to conceal a smaller book; a description which evokes a scene in a spy movie. Vidali was to travel to Germany to find an agent identified as "WB." Likely, Willi Budich, a Serb who had also been an assistant to Leo Jogiches is meant. Budich was a type who actually suffered broken bones and bullet holes in frays with adversaries and had been boss of the military or M-Apparat previously.[95] It is also possible that "WB" could have been Wilhelm Bahnik or writer Willi Bredel.[96]

Vidali wrote he had been under the impression he was to meet with Jakob Mirov-Abramov. The OMS leader may have been busy with other projects in 1933 such as the "Eighth International Sports Base," which was training secret agents for subversion on several continents, or he could have been busy organizing the Amsterdam-Pleyel Conference Against War and Fascism.[97] Amsterdam-Pleyel was so successful that Alfred Hitchcock's film, *Foreign Correspondent* (1940), portrayed it as a meeting of the great men of Europe, except for a few fascist saboteurs, who were trying to avoid war if at all possible; however, the meeting was actually entirely scripted and orchestrated by the Comintern.[98] Mirov-Abramov himself had fallen victim to the Great Terror by the time the film was released.[99] He and millions of other victims went unnoticed in the international media trained to be vigilant against fascists and tolerant of the Soviet experiment.

Another little-remembered episode in which Flieg participated was a conference in Riga, Latvia organized by Heinz Neumann in August, 1933.[100] The event is something of an academic mystery as the only record of it seems to be in Nazi intelligence archives.

During 1934, Flieg and most other KPD functionaries were assigned to Saarbrücken where an important plebiscite was to be held in January, 1935.[101] The Saarland had been administered by the League of Nations from the end of World War I, and the issue of control of its territory and coal reserves was of significance to both Germany and France. Flieg's mission also had the extra purpose of the relocation of the Pass-Apparat's equipment beyond the reach of the Gestapo.[102] The communists campaigned against the option of voting to return to Germany. Street fights were common between Nazis and the KPD, which might have made an impression on Eric Honnecker, then a teenager in the area.[103] However, the KPD's efforts failed miserably with 90% of the vote being for reunification with Germany.[104] Less than five years later, Saarbrücken's population was evacuated in the face of a Moroccan and French invasion, siege, and occupation.[105]

Otherwise, Flieg spent the exile period only in Moscow, Prague, and Paris as far as is discernable from limited sources. The "Mask" intercepts, now available to the public, show Moscow sent a message to Flieg in Paris in October 1934.[106] The year 1935 saw the end of Flieg's term on the Comintern Control Commission but also reacceptance into the KPD Central Committee.[107] He is also noted to have been building contacts to the Czechoslovakian intelligence service in March 1935.[108]

It is very likely that both Leo Flieg and Stefan Heym were simultaneously in Prague at some point from 1933 to 1935. There are also "Mask" documents that show Moscow addressed communiqués to "Alfons," the cover named Flieg used while in Prague during 1935 to 1936.[109] Flieg may or may not be agent "Martini," another addressee in Prague.[110] The code name is likely a reference to the communists' successful Sass and Martini scams.[111]

Flieg's career came to an abrupt end in the spring of 1937 when he was inexplicably arrested by the Soviet leadership he had served long and well. He was taken away from the notorious Hotel Lux apparently within a day of his arrival from Paris.[112] One of his accusers is now known to have been Herbert Wehner who charged Flieg with misusing funds and misleading Ernst Thaelmann.[113] Had Flieg somehow been exonerated, it seems his next assignment would have been to the United States. Stefan Heym was, of course, an editor in New York City by this time.[114] Like his old friend Hugo Eberlein, but unlike most other victims, Flieg was condemned by the highest Soviet military court.[115]This is possibly an indication that both Flieg and Eberlein were in the GPU [*Gosudarstvennoe Politicheskoe Upravlenie,* the Soviet military intelligence service in the early 1920s].

The rest of the clique demoted in 1932 were also liquidated, including Heinz Neumann who was once considered the German closest to Stalin.[116] Muenzenberg, who had also been repromoted to the Central Committee in 1935, was expelled from the party in 1938 for not following Flieg's example of reporting to his elimination.[117] When Germany invaded France in 1940, Muenzenberg fled toward Switzerland where he had sat out World War I with Lenin and other ambitious revolutionaries. He didn't reach Switzerland in 1940 but was found in a remote area a few months later with a broken neck, and a rope attached to himself and a broken tree limb. Some claim it could have been a suicide or the work of a Nazi, but few survived open disputes with Stalin in any case.[118]

Though Stefan Heym never wrote of Leo Flieg, apparently Bertolt Brecht once did. In his play *Happy End,* one of the characters is called "The Fly-the lady in gray." Besides having a claim to the appellation "fly," Flieg is also called an *éminence grise* or *graue Eminenz* [a person with influence or power without an official position] in several works.[119] Leo Flieg is also mentioned, though obliquely, in Alfred Döblin's novel *Karl and Rosa.* In one passage, Karl Liebknecht asks Karl Radek, "Where is Leo hiding?" Döblin adds, "He meant Jogiches," but does not explain that Jogiches' assistant was also named Leo.[120]

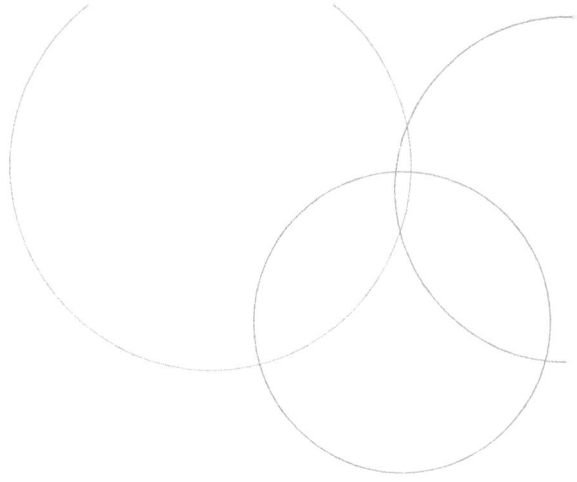

CHAPTER 2

STEFAN HEYM (HELMUT FLIEG) IN BERLIN 1931-1933

H eym's autobiography *Nachruf* discloses that two of his father's sisters shared a floor in an apartment house in Berlin. Heym let a room in their residence and in his book devotes several pages in describing the two, their husbands, and aunts who were married and living in Berlin.[1] Two of the most famous spies of World War II, Arvid Harnack and his American wife Mildred Fish Harnack, also let a room not only in the same building, but within the same apartment in which Heym dwelled.[2]

The Harnacks hosted an informal literary salon in their room, which they occupied from 1932 to 1934.[3] The Harnacks' soirées are neither mentioned in *Nachruf* nor is there mention of Heym in public recollections of their discussions. Arvid Harnack used the meetings to expand his own network of contacts while Mildred Harnack became prominent among Americans living in Berlin. She became a close friend of Martha Dodd, daughter of the U.S. Ambassador to Germany [William Dodd Sr.].[4]

Shortly before they moved into Heym's relative's apartment, Arvid Harnack helped found a Soviet-front organization called ARPLAN [*Arbeitsgemeinschaft zum Stadium der Sowjetrussichen Planwirtschaft*, the Society for the Study of the Soviet Russian Planned Economy].[5] It was intended as a subtly controlled club with a communist founder and a few other agents to be among its leading members. ARPLAN was set up with the help of a Soviet economic official named Sergei Bessonov who was connected with its trade delegation. He became a frequent guest in the Harnack's room in the Flieg apartment.[6] Bessonov was later promoted to a position in the embassy and organized a trip to Moscow for 23 ARPLAN members including the Harnacks.[7] Arvid Harnack met important executives in the Comintern such as Otto Kuusinen and Osip Piatntski, the latter often a contact for Leo Flieg.[8] Bessonov was later recalled and sentenced to fifteen years during the purges, but it doesn't change the startling coincidence of yet another important Soviet in propinquity to Helmut Flieg (Stefan Heym).

As is well known, the Harnacks were among the leading members of the Red Orchestra [the anti-Nazi resistance movement] during the war. The Nazis discovered the group, and the Harnacks and dozens of others were arrested in 1942.[9] Arvid Harnack was executed in December 1942 and Mildred Harnack in February 1943.

To anyone familiar with Heym's memoir, along with Leo Flieg's career, and the many volumes on the Red Orchestra, the idea of Soviet agents visiting and living in an apartment where several people are named Flieg simply stretches the idea of happenstance too far. Curiously, no one has ever deduced what was plainly apparent, in print at least.

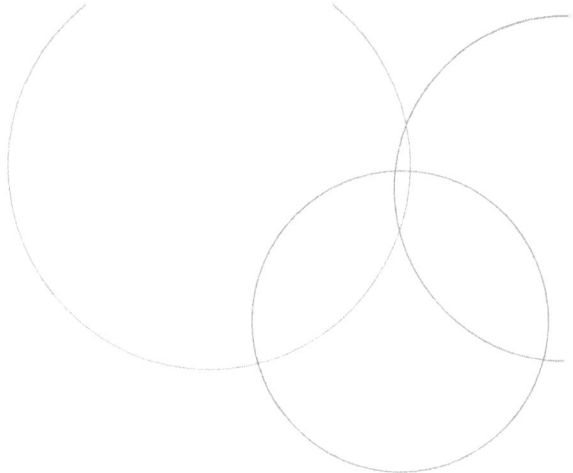

CHAPTER 3

EGON KISCH AND THE PRAGUE ANTEBELLUM YEARS 1933-1935

One of the last people Heym mentions seeing in Berlin before the Reichstag fire [an arson attack on the German Parliament building in 1933] was the Prague-born writer Egon Erwin Kisch.[1] Both were among the attendees at a Marxist writers workshop. His encounters with Kisch must have had some significance for Heym as he made the Kisch residence in Prague his destination after a clandestine night border crossing into Silesia.[2] It is also true Kisch knew nearly everyone important among communists and was the most well-known reporter in Berlin at the time.[3]

The name Kisch is taken from the German spelling of a town near Karlsbad/Karlovy Vary in the Sudetenland.[4] The family evidently settled in Prague by the 17th century. An Abraham Kisch (1725–1803) became the first Jewish physician in the Austrian Empire. Numerous relatives gained notoriety in many fields and even include a British General, Frederick Kisch, an advisor to Lloyd George at Versailles.[5]

Kisch Street in Tel Aviv is said to be named for him.[6] A Hermann Kisch was Postmaster of India. Enoch Heinrich Kisch (1841–1918) was the 19th century's leading authority on balneology, quite a distinction in an era when cures were popularly sought at mineral spring spas. Kurt Weil had a sister-in-law named Rita Kisch.[7] There are still, in 2006, at least six thoroughfares named for Egon Kisch in the former East Germany.[8]

Egon Kisch's mother Ernestine Kuh, who hosted Helmut Flieg in his first day outside of Germany, was from a family active in journalism. Oskar Kuh (1858–1930) was founder of the *Prager Montagblattes*.[9] Anton Kuh (1890–1941) was the main rival of the renowned Viennese commentator Karl Kraus.[10] Frederick Kuh was the United Press International correspondent at the Reichstag fire trial.[11]

Particularly interesting was Egon Kisch's great uncle, Dr. Samuel Basche, who was personal physician to Kaiser Maximilian, the Habsburg who ruled Mexico during the 1860s on behalf of France. Kaiser Maximilian became impotent during his reign, and his wife, Empress Carlotta, bore a child by a Mexican general. The child was raised in France and later became General Weygand who served the Vichy government for a brief but interesting period. He was the same General Weygand whose name is dropped by Peter Lorre as "Ugarte" in *Casablanca* (1942). The entire episode would be even more obscure except that Kisch enjoyed recounting it. One wonders whether Kaiser Maximilian's worries were despite or because of Kisch's great uncle and whether Egon Kisch met many people who had the courage to ask him such questions.[12]

Kisch's career seems as though it was coordinated by the dark powers behind the thrones and intelligence departments of Europe. He gained notoriety as a young reporter on the eve of World War I, breaking the story that the head of Austrian intelligence, Colonel Redl, had committed suicide after having been found betraying military information to Russia. Kisch learned of the tragedy as if by accident. A defender on his amateur soccer team failed to appear for a match.

Following the expected defeat, Kisch contacted his missing teammate who was a locksmith and was told of his emergency call and presence at the scene of Redl's death.[13]

Kisch spent the war in Austria's press service under Robert Musil, the gifted writer and inventor from Klagenfurt.[14] In the wake of Austria's defeat, Kisch became a front line revolutionary making heated speeches, storming newspaper offices, and publishing his own "red sheet."[15] One is not supposed to ask what light this places on Uncle Basche's care in Mexico or the breaking of the Redl story.[16] Two other of Kisch's Vienna comrades of 1918, Gerhart Eisler and Karl Frank, also went on to long careers fomenting subversion.[17]

The success of Kisch's cause of blatantly leftist activist journalism is, ironically, illustrated by a forgotten anecdote. When Governor [Alvan] Fuller of Massachusetts visited Berlin shortly after the Sacco-Vanzetti verdict, Kisch organized a leftist demonstration outside his hotel room.[18] Can one imagine the decades of indignation that would have followed had it been [Nazi minister of propaganda Joseph] Goebbels who howled at the visiting American?

Kisch never held an official party office following his activities in Vienna in 1918. However, there are many indications he wielded power of a sort. He seems to have once chosen the editor for Muenzenberg's newspaper, *Arbeiter Illustrierte*.[19] He is quoted as denying on behalf of the party that Trotsky had made attempts on Stalin's secret fund.[20] He chose the office space for the periodical *Die Neue Weltbuehne* in Prague after the journal left Berlin.[21] In Paris, while seated with KPD commissar Johannes Becher, Kisch is recalled as telling Alfred Döblin that a request to have another writer attend a conference was "out of the question."[22] Another KPD writer, Walter Schoenstedt, is said to have given the appearance of being Kisch's *adjutant* [an officer who is an assistant to a more senior officer] noted so in the memoir of a DDR cultural minister.[23]

Kisch was also the closest friend of Otto Katz from their youth in Prague, to their time in Berlin in the last years of Weimar, to their parallel role as exiles in Paris, to Katz' leadership of the Soviet "news" service, Agence Espagne, during the Spanish Civil War. They then went to the U.S.A. and Mexico, and following the war, were again in Prague.[24] A cynic might say Kisch was the power behind Katz' colorful career, which made a deep imprint on both sides of the Atlantic Ocean and helped shape Zionist history.

Kisch is even noted wreaking havoc in Shanghai in 1932, attempting arms deals, breaking into police files, and founding a Soviet front organization.[25] Muenzenberg sent him to Australia for several months in 1934–1935, which seems like a loose thread in his career.[26] Heym's memoir notes only one meeting with Kisch during Heym's 1933–1935 stay in Prague.[27]

Egon Kisch's wife, whom the Hungarian British novelist Arthur Koestler called "horse-teethed" and a GPU Soviet military intelligence agent, was named Gisela Lyner.[28] In her earlier years, she had been secretary to Clara Zetkin, one of the KPD's leaders during the 1920s, and also *Aelterspraesident* of the Reichstag, which is a special distinction in the German parliament for its eldest representative.[29] Gisela Lyner married Egon Kisch in 1938 though they had known each other for thirty years.[30] Her sister Rosl was married to communist Erich Jungmann who had been the youngest member of the Reichstag in 1932 at age twenty-five.[31]

Like Egon Kisch, she seemed to hold some extraordinary secret status. Egon Kisch is quoted as calling her "Lenin's widow" in the memoir of Elisabeth Poretsky who was the widow of the Soviet operative Ignace Reiss.[32] Frau Kisch is likely the title character of a 1948 book about the Cold War called *Gisel contre Gilda* [Gisel Against Gilda]. The name "Gilda" refers to Rita Hayworth's character [in the film *Gilda* (1946)], but explicit discussion of the identity of "Gisel" was apparently too dangerous to clarify, though the film's title at least leaves a trace of the era's concerns.[33]

Gisela Kisch also played a special role in the postwar purges of anyone who had met American relief worker [and spy for the Soviets], Noel Field. She and her husband had known Field longer than any of those who were condemned. Their acquaintance began during the

Spanish Civil War while others who were banished or executed met him during World War II or shortly thereafter. Field paid a special visit to the Kisches in Mexico following the war and attended Egon Kisch's funeral in Prague in 1948, shortly before things became ugly again among the communists. Somehow, Mrs. Kisch was able to implicate others while remaining immune from scrutiny.[34] Nothing has been written of her life following the Field purges [of local communists in Czechoslovakia, Hungary, and East Germany].[35] Stefan Heym did not note her in his autobiography, so no notice of having met her has yet entered the historical record.

"Prague, the Prague of that time, with its people — Czechs, Jews, emigrants — is today like a dream," wrote Stefan Heym in *Nachruf* in its section on his asylum there from 1933 to1935. He omits Germans who had been one-third of the population during the 1860s and were still a significant minority, especially in the older more storied districts, as of 1933. All the famed writers of Prague, including Egon Kisch and his acquaintance Franz Kafka, wrote in German.[36] Heym wrote two novels, *Hostages* and *The Eyes of Reason* set in Prague, but still preferred conveying the inaccurate impression that the occupiers of 1939–1945 were the only Germans to have lived in Prague.

Flieg/Heym enjoyed passing some of his free time at the Café Continental where exiles gathered.[37] The companions mentioned include Wieland Herzfelde and F. C. Weiskopf (1900–1955), who were communists, like Heym.[38] Herzfelde and Weiskopf were married to women who were sisters, which is disclosed in *Nachruf*.[39] Weiskopf, a Czechoslovakian citizen, is mentioned later in the autobiography as having become an ambassador. He is one of several artists and writers who became part of the Czechoslovakian diplomatic corps. This fact was mentioned in connection with Heym's meetings with the ambassador to France who was a former caricaturist, ironically named Adolf.[40]

Weiskopf was plenipotentiary for his government in Washington for a brief transition period following the war and became ambassador to China from 1950 to 1952.[41] He spent the last few years of his life in East Germany. His diminution was likely in connection to the Slansky trials where those who had appointed him were executed. There is documentary evidence from 1936 that Weiskopf was a Comintern agent.[42]

Another acquaintance from the Café Continental was someone Heym claimed he knew only by his alias, "Konrad."[43] Heym, portraying himself as the *ingénue*, had long discussions with the mysterious operative who made statements that the young writer only fully understood years later. One of the leading members of Leo Flieg's document forgery center, Hermann Duenow or Dynow, also used the same cover name.[44] Following the war, he became an inspector with the "Vopo," short for *Volkspolizei*, East Germany's Gestapo.[45] If the "Konrad" at the Café Continental was not Duenow, some of the confusion could be attributed to Heym. However, one really shouldn't believe he was never able to discover his companion's identity in all the years he spent with his fellow exiles, including the years behind the Iron Curtain.

Contrarily, Heym candidly volunteers that a researcher once sent him a copy of a Czech intelligence report of March 1935 that lists Heym as one of seven dangerous German communists who merited the police's attention.[46] Heym only disputes that the report lists him as a worker in Muenzenberg's *Internationale Arbeiterhilfe* [Workers International Relief], which he denied.[47] It is true that no evidence connects Heym to this organization, which putatively operated as a charity. The only other name on the police list disclosed by Heym was Walter Ulbricht, misspelled by the Czechs as "Ulbrich," who was noted straightforwardly and without irony to have been traveling on a false passport.[48]

There was a power struggle, or more accurately, a communist coup, at an influential periodical in Prague in 1934 that benefitted Stefan Heym and his Stalinist comrades. *Die Neue Weltbuehne*, well-known simply as *Die Weltbuehne* in Weimar Germany, had in late 1933 printed articles authored anonymously by a German communist that severely criticized the Soviet Union's immigration policy. In early 1934, it published a series of articles by the dreaded Leon Trotsky. The editor, Willi Schlamm, was denounced repeatedly by Stalinist sympathizers who worked in the Prague German-language press. The Stalinists were able to inveigle the owner, a widow who had inherited a controlling interest, to join the campaign. In an attempt to reestablish his authority, Schlamm traveled to her residence in Zurich and tendered his immediate resignation. The bluff backfired as she announced that the new editor, Hermann Budzislawski, was in the adjoining room.[49]

Die Neue Weltbuehne suddenly dropped all criticism of Stalin's policies.[50] Stefan Heym became a regular contributor though he hadn't had a byline during Schlamm's tenure.[51] A few years later when Heym became an editor, the name Hermann Budzislawski would be included on the list of contributors printed on the stationery of [the German-language weekly] *Deutsches Volksecho*.[52] This was not the only instance of communists asserting control over an apparently unaffiliated periodical. Commissar Johannes Becher sent an enforcer to literally shut down the presses at *Neue Deutsche Blaetter* in Prague when it didn't toe the party line. Stefan Heym wrote poems and a review for the publication while it was under Soviet control.[53]

CHAPTER 4

HEYM'S ASSIGNMENTS IN CHICAGO 1935-1936

S tefan Heym attended the University of Chicago for the 1935–1936 academic year. His memoir is quite open in disclosing that his scholarship to attend found him rather than through his own feverish searching or pleas to aid agencies. An acquaintance, referred to as "Comrade Jacobsen," found him at a public place and informed him of this opportunity. Heym accepted the arrangement of study abroad, with the tuition paid by a Jewish academic organization.[1]

In his approximately one and a half years in Chicago, Heym attended classes, received a degree, and also worked odd jobs as a salesman, night school instructor, and even as a dishwasher.[2] He also met James Farrell, Laurence Lipton, and Richard Wright who are, perhaps, American examples of proletarian writers.[3] Heym was still in his early twenties but had already worked with several writers and actors who would attain popular renown. While still in Chemnitz, he had already met with Hans Soehnker to discuss a theatrical project. Soehnker became a leading man in German and international cinema.[4]

While in Prague, Heym wrote and attempted to produce a play in which an actor named Voskovec starred. Likely, this was George Voskovec, a Czech who had a minor Hollywood career that included roles as an East German attorney in *The Spy Who Came in from the Cold* (1966) and as an East Bloc defector who was shot down in the street by the communists in an episode of the TV series "Johnny Staccato," which aired in 1960.[5] Although Heym was not able to remain in his birthplace, he wasn't always an outsider.

Heym's connection to power is palpable in two letters he sent to Johannes Becher in 1936. Heym tells the head of the German section of the Soviet Writers Association to "get things going at that lame outfit" and that Becher's organization was "the only source of annoyance — late in corresponding, imprecise and unfulfilled promises made."[6] In the second letter, he writes "maybe Bredel knows [where his manuscript is]," and that he won't be able "to make propaganda" unless he is published.[7] It is explicit that he had previously met Becher. By informally referring to Bredel by his last name alone, the phrasing would be inappropriate in writing to Becher if he did not know him. These instances of berating Johannes Becher, as though the lyricist of East Germany's national anthem was an inept slacker, leads one to deduce that Heym felt he belonged to a more powerful branch of the Soviet hierarchy.

Stefan Heym also wrote for the local communist German-language publication *Volksfront*.[8] In *Nachruf*, the publication's editor Erich von Schroetter is referred to as an "independent scholar."[9] In a letter to a relative, Egon Erwin Kisch once wrote of von Schroetter on the occasion of the death of von Schroetter's grandmother in Vienna in 1917.[10] The tone of the letter is a bit disrespectful and condescending. Erich von Schroetter is referred to as a lecturer at the University of Chicago. The university, however, does not have record of von Schroetter as a professor there, although Kisch does seem to have the city right. By itself, the mention of von Schroetter in a letter of Kisch's would be insubstantial. However, in a continuing string of such coincidences, it merits recording.

Heym's writing career made an important step when he was published in the June 27, 1936 issue of *The Nation*. His article, "Youth in Hitler's Reich," was intended to debunk reports that Germany's economy was improving under Hitler. The article marked Heym's first known work in English. There is no mention of his minor triumph in the immodest *Nachruf*, although it is stated in a later section that he had contributed to American periodicals. Up to this time, he had only written in German and, except for the *Prager Tagblatt*, had only written for communist-controlled publications. Public criticism of *The Nation* being so sympathetic to Moscow that it could be called communist was many years away. He was able to follow up with a second article that appeared in the openly communist *New Masses* in September 1936.[11] Also omitted from his memoir was that he taught German at the Academy for Adults in Chicago from June to August 1936. He found the position through the placement office at the university.[12]

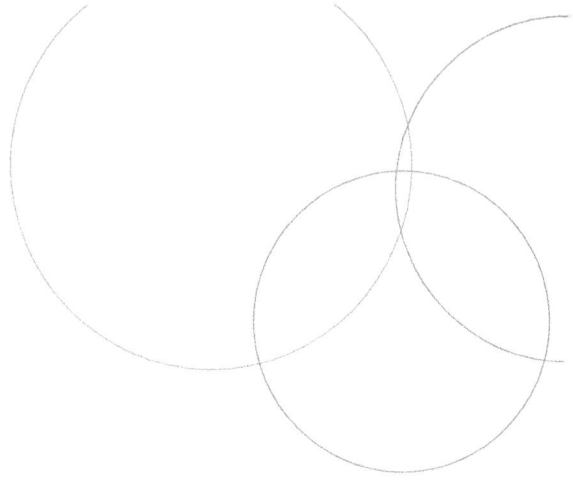

CHAPTER 5

OFF TO NEW YORK 1936-1937

S tefan Heym dissembled in describing how he next became a newspaper editor in New York City. According to his autobiogra- phy, he was enjoying apple strudel at the von Schroetter residence during Christmas when a letter from Kurt Rosenfeld (1879–1943) arrived.[1] Rosenfeld is described as a former Prussian Justice Minis- ter but not as co-founder and chairman of the *Sozial Arbeiter Partei* (SAP). He was also co-founder of the party's newspaper for which Heym had been a contributor in Berlin four years earlier.[2] Rosenfeld was also a veteran Soviet agent with decades of radical activity in his record.

Rosenfeld joined the SPD in 1898 because the KPD was not yet in existence.[3] He regularly defended revolutionaries and became Rosa Luxemburg's attorney and intimate friend.[4] Rosenfeld remained with the SPD following World War I and became associated with its far left wing known as the USPD [*Unabhängige Sozialdemokratische Partei Deutschlands*, The Independent Social Democratic Party].[5]

It is forgotten that the KPD was led by Ernst Thaelmann, Walter

Ulbricht, and Wilhelm Pieck, who were all also renegade SPD members previous to World War I, no less radical than Rosenfeld. It was possibly because he served briefly as Prussian Justice Minister under a short-lived postwar red regime, and possibly because he remained a well-known defense attorney that he refrained from openly joining the KPD during the Weimar era.

In 1920, he publicly supported the proposal that all center parties accept dictatorship of the proletariat on the basis of the Soviet system.[6] He bore public humiliation in 1922 when, on a pilgrimage to Moscow, he and Karl Liebknecht's brother Theodor were jeered and called betrayers of Lenin.[7] A memoir recalls that he smuggled a letter from Stalin to a communist client in jail in 1924.[8] He also worked with Willi Muenzenberg's *Internationale Arbeiterhilfe* in 1924 and at some point during the Weimar period became attorney for the Soviet Embassy in Berlin.[9] Other prominent clients included writer Ernst Toller, editor Karl von Ossietzky, and KPD Reichstag deputy Ernst Torgler.[10] In 1925, Rosenfeld attempted to intercede in Horthy's prosecutions against communists in Hungary. Rosenfeld visited the Soviet Union again in 1928 when it was securely under Stalin's control.[11]

Rosenfeld founded a periodical *Das Klassenkampf-Marxistische Blaetter* in 1927 with Max Seydewitz, who was also Rosenfeld's partner in founding the SAP in 1931.[12] Both were also members of a Muenzenberg front group called "Friends of Soviet Russia."[13] Seydewitz openly joined the KPD in exile in 1934 and Rosenfeld finally joined by 1938, leaving the SAP, which still existed in exile, abandoned by its founders.[14] Approximately coinciding with Seydewitz' switch to the KPD, he authored a book advocating support for Stalin, titled *Stalin oder Trotzki?* [Stalin or Trotsky].[15] Communists, of course, weren't simply able to write a book about Stalin without very high authority, and Seydewitz was, probably, like Rosenfeld, a communist all along. The SAP was then Stalin's second party in the Reichstag, the KPD being his primary supporter. It is true the SAP never held many seats, but it did siphon off members and support from the SPD during the key period of the last two years before Hitler came to power.

Seydewitz spent exile in Scandinavia and was imprisoned in Sweden in 1942 for engaging in political activity contrary to the terms of his asylum. Following the war, he became President of the province of Saxony in East Germany. His sons, Frido and Horst, spent exile in the Soviet Union and were arrested during the Great Terror in 1938. They were, perhaps uniquely, released in 1948 while all or nearly all surviving inmates of the Great Terror were not released until Stalin's death.[16] Max Seydewitz became curator of Dresden's museums in 1955, and his wife wrote the DDR's literature on its impressive collection.[17]

It's been long forgotten that Rosenfeld cross-examined Adolf Hitler in court in 1932 and cornered Stalin's rival into a contempt of court citation that carried a fine of approximately $250. Hitler refused to respond to an interrogatory regarding whether a Czech industrialist had contributed to the Nazi Party.[18] The incident was carried in U.S. newspapers and could be considered part of the media build-up in which Hitler was typecast as the unreasonable villain.

In Rosenfeld's first year of exile, he co-founded a press agency called *Inpress* with future Red Orchestra leader Alexander Rado.[19] He traveled to the United States with Willi Muenzenberg in June 1934 for the Reichstag fire Counter-Trial propaganda tour, which included a stop in Madison Square Garden.[20] Through his involvement in the staged counter-trials, he became acquainted with the American radical attorney Arthur Garfield Hays who traveled to Europe to work with the communists' defense and publicity campaign. Rosenfeld later shared office space with Hays in New York City.[21] An FBI report claims Rosenfeld immigrated with the help of Congressman Sam Dickstein, who has been shown to have accepted bribes from Soviet agents.[22]

Also omitted from Heym's memoir is that both he and Rosenfeld wrote for Muenzenberg's *Der Gegen Angriff* between 1933 and 1936.[23] Budzislawski, who is said to have run free ads for Rosenfeld in *Die Neue Weltbuehne,* had the favor returned in the *Deutsches Volksecho.*[24] Rosenfeld, who sat on many communist front committees, was the New York envoy for the *Weltbuehne Volkerbund* while Willy Brandt [future Chancellor of Germany after World War II] was its Oslo representative.[25]

The KPD was based in Paris during the period the *Deutsches Volksecho* existed, from February 1937 to September 1939. Its surviving files in the French National Archive show that the KPD considered Rosenfeld one of their own operatives in several documents.[26] Another source states Rosenfeld joined the KPD in 1938.[27]

The other sponsor of Heym's editorship of the *Deutsches Volksecho* was Alphonse Goldschmidt, who was also a prominent figure among German leftists. Goldschmidt had also visited Russia in Lenin's time and his account helped form the budding debate on the nature of communist government.[28] He was involved in several of Muenzenberg's committees and founded the *Marxistische Arbeiterschule* [Marxist Workers School, abbreviated as MASCH] at which Heym recalled seeing Egon Kisch days before the Reichstag burned.[29] He spent part of his career as a professor in Mexico where several Berlin communists and the Kisches later spent the war years.[30] Goldschmidt also authored *Whither Israel?* with [a foreword by] Albert Einstein, [published in 1934].

France's *Deuxième Bureau* [the external military intelligence agency] considered Goldschmidt a communist insider to whom couriers reported to in the early 1920s when von Seekt had placed too much pressure on the ordinarily designated functionaries.[31] In an American source, he was the fellow in Whittaker Chambers' [book about Soviet spies in America], *Witness*, who claimed at a social gathering in New York City that he had seen Chambers before in Russia and that Chambers identified himself as "Karl" at the time.[32] This anecdote is unknown in German sources while information on Goldschmidt is scarce in American sources. The encounter between Chambers and Goldschmidt in New York, described in *Witness*, may have occurred near the time Heym traveled from Chicago to accept the post as editor of the *Deutsches Volksecho*.

CHAPTER 6

DEUTSCHES VOLKSECHO
1937-1939

A nother intersection between *Nachruf* and Whittaker Chambers is the communists' intended infiltration of a German-language New York City newspaper, *Neues Volkszeitung*. In 1933, an agent from the NKVD [*Naródnyy Komissariát Vnútrennikh Del*, the Soviet Interior Ministry, which was also a secret police organization] known to Chambers as "Herman" discussed expropriating an American newspaper.[1] Chambers learned from an editor at *Neues Volkszeitung* who was an ex-communist that it was his newspaper which was the object of the NKVD's efforts. *Witness* relates that the Soviets succeeded in removing Chambers' contact from his editor's post.[2] However, they were not able to seize control of the newspaper.

In 1936, the editor of the *Volkszeitung* was Gerhart Henry Seger, a former Social Democrat representative in the Reichstag who had been interned in Oranienburg concentration camp.[3] One day a young man who identified himself as "Hans Weber" visited Seger's office. "Hans" proposed that *Volkszeitung* work more closely with, and drop opposition to, the communists.[4] The communists' Popular Front strategy of that era called for the appearance of cooperation with less extreme leftists.[5] Its rather cynical aims were to infiltrate other leftist's organizations and to coerce them to drop opposition to Stalinism.

Seger did not wish to become embroiled in an intrigue but told the young intruder he would consider the proposal. The so-called "Hans Weber" recalled, fifty years later, that the tone was less than friendly.[6] In 1937, the fellow who posed as Weber, actually known as Stefan Heym, became editor of the *Deutsches Volksecho* and unabashedly began to make overtures again to Seger. Seger, disgusted and not willing to abandon opposition to Stalin, publicly exposed Heym as having previously proposed an alliance while using a false name.[7]

Heym also omits that, although "Hans Weber" sounds merely like a typical German name, there was an actual German communist named Hans Weber who had been, against Moscow's wishes, elected to the KPD Politburo in 1925.[8] Weber was expelled from the party in 1928, likely due in great part to the unsanctioned promotion in 1925.[9] Whether the actual Hans Weber was an enemy or rival of Leo Flieg's, and whether that could have been a reason for Heym's usurpation of Weber's identity, are, of course, topics Heym the memoirist would not address. He did, upon his exposure by Seger, complain publicly that Seger had betrayed his alias to the fascists.[10]

It is also a dark coincidence that another editor and writer for the *Neues Volkszeitung* was named Rudolf Katz.[11] Heym's classmate from Chemnitz, Leo Bauer, was at the time, using the same name as another leading member of the *Neues Volkszeitung* staff in New York. Perhaps, Gerhart Seger's fault was not in exposing Heym, but in not revealing the full extent of the abuse being committed.

The first issue of the *Deutsches Volksecho* is dated February 20, 1937.[12] Heym's memoir notes there were congratulatory messages from "Prag, Paris, Zurich, Moskau."[13] Yet, noted in *Nachruf*, and printed in bold lettering in the *Deutsches Volksecho* are greetings from Egon Kisch and "Rudolf Breda, alias Otto Katz."[14] Kisch's message states, "Finally did it! Break a leg and neck. Congratulations." The next message, which was from Paris, states in the truncated manner of a telegram, "Overjoyed at publication of broad People's Front newspaper. Stop. Send editorship *Deutsches Volksecho* heartfelt greetings and good luck." signed Rudolf Breda. The name "Rudolf Breda" was itself also an evil joke of Otto Katz. Breda, a city in the Netherlands, had been hometown of Marinus Van der Lubbe, the executed arsonist behind the Reichstag fire.[15] Katz traveled to Hollywood, gathered prominent film stars and officials, and raised money on the pretense of being a heroic resistance fighter named Rudolf Breda. The money itself was perhaps secondary to wielding the power to make dupes of America's most important media celebrities.[16] The phenomenon of a community of celebrities was, of course, unknown a few decades earlier. Stefan Heym does not acknowledge knowing personally the founder of the Hollywood Anti-Nazi League during the 1930s and omitted that Katz was Egon Kisch's closest friend.[17]

Revealingly, the good luck wishes of Georg Bernhard, editor of the *Pariser Tageszeitung*, appeared immediately below those of "Rudolf Breda." Georg Bernhard was founder of the *Pariser Tageszeitung,* which he created out of the *Pariser Tagesblatt* where he was already editor. In 1936, while Bernhard attended a Popular Front conference in New York, his writers and co-conspirators falsely claimed on the front page that Bernhard had been unjustly fired.[18] Through their unity, the group was able to enforce their lie for a time, took over the journal, and renamed it. In 1938, the rightful owner, a Jewish pro-tsarist exile, was able to win a court judgment as Bernhard could offer no proof of his discharge.[19] However, for two years, Bernhard and, it has recently come to light, Willi Muenzenberg were able to control the assets and opinions of the journal. The *Pariser Tagblatt* was, therefore, a much more successful attempt by the Soviets than their efforts against the *Neues Volkszeitung*.

Heym's use of Bernhard's endorsement illuminates the time he pretended to be Hans Weber. The communists were simply out to take what they could from non-Stalinist leftists in Paris, New York City, and in Spain where their death squads executed thousands of Republican troops for not following the Communist Party line.[20]

Heym, his biographer, and some historians, claim that the *Deutsches Volksecho* was an independent journal but its close affiliation to the Communist Party is easily shown.[21] The *Volksecho* was a successor to *Der Arbeiter,* which was openly bonded to the Communist Party. *Der Arbeiter* had as its subtitle, until 1934, "Official German Organ of the Communist Party."[22] Its last weekly issue, dated February 13, 1937, encouraged its readers to subscribe to the *Volksecho.*[23] The first exemplar of the "new" *United Front* newspaper under Stefan Heym is dated February 20, 1937.[24] The *Volksecho* even took over the physical premises of *Der Arbeiter* according to government documents.[25]

There is also indication that Heym himself admitted the *Volksecho's* subsidiary status to the party during a time when it appeared he would remain permanently ensconced behind the Iron Curtain. An East German book on exiles in America included a contribution by a writer named Jurgen Schebera. At the beginning of one paragraph, it is stated the *Volksecho* was financed by the CPUSA [Communist Party USA] and its associates. There are a few sentences more about the *Volksecho* and a footnote at the end of the paragraph.[26] The listed source is a 1972 interview with Heym by Schebera.

One can ask oneself whether a non-communist weekly would have printed more than a few of the following articles, which is only a small but representative selection from the *Volksecho's* contents. (Dates in parentheses are for the relevant issues of the *Deutsches Volksecho.*)

- an article by Ilja Ehrenburg on a communist sympathizer who named his son Komsomol (February 20, 1937)
- an article in memory of the passing of Sergo Ordzhonikidze that claims 750,000 marching in his procession next to a picture showing Russian workers with their hands raised described as a protest gathering against Trotsky (February 27, 1937)
- approving coverage of the Show Trials in Moscow (February 20, 1937; April 3, 1937; July 3, 1937; July 10, 1937)

- a protest against the confiscation of the Spanish Republic aid ship *Mar Cantabria* (March 13, 1937)
- a report from Madrid in March 1937 by Otto Katz, again under the alias Rudolf Breda (March 20, 1937)
- greetings from KPD cultural commissar Willi Bredel from Moscow (March 20, 1937)
- a summary of Stalin's speech on the Show Trials without criticism (April 3, 1937)
- the suppression of the P.O.U.M. [The Workers' Party of Marxist Unification, a Spanish communist political party] in Barcelona depicted as a Trotskyite revolt (May 15, 1937)
- the poem "Batterie Thaelmann" supposedly written in the trenches (May 22, 1937)
- democracy praised in the "Volga German Republic" (June 12, 1937, June 26, 1937)
- a reprinted essay by Walter Duranty in support of the Soviet Union (July 3, 1937)
- "Ludwig Renn in USA" full-width front page headline (October 9, 1937)
- "Before the Russian Vote" full-width headline on page 5 (October 16, 1937)
- an article by Lion Feuchtwanger in defense of the Soviet Union and an article with Rudolf Feistmann's name above the title on the same page (October 30, 1937)
- excerpts from Andor Gabor's *Die Sammlung* [a literary magazine]
- serialized novels by Upton Sinclair and Rudolf Leonhard
- a photo of a union organizer allegedly being beaten up by "hoodlums" hired by Henry Ford with the caption "Das ist Fordismus!"
- an article by Michael Gold (January 1, 1938)
- Josef Stalin's thoughts on Lenin (January 15, 1938)
- an article headline "Stalin's Call to the Workers of the World" (February 19, 1938)

- an article on new Soviet Show Trials which uncovered a Trotskyite conspiracy and the murder of Gorky, which ends by doubting whether Gerhart Seger really is a friend of the Soviet Union (March 5, 1938)
- an article headline, with dateline Moscow, "Trotskyites and Fascists—the Conspiracy Against the Workers' State" (March 12, 1938)
- an Erich Weinert report from Republican Barcelona—a very subjectively written anti-Franco article. (April 20, 1938)
- a warning that Nazis are seated in the highest places in America, repeating an assertion by former Ambassador William Dodd (June 11, 1938)
- "Die Bank von Spanien-Ein Fester Turm" by Alfons Goldschmidt; the article cites vast gold reserves which, however, had already been stolen by Soviet agents and moved to Moscow (July 2, 1938)
- Erich Weinert on the last march of the International Brigade (March 18, 1939)
- an advertisement for *Das Wort,* Kusnetski Most, 18, Moscow (April 8, 1939)
- an advertisement for "Internationale Literatur" Kusnetski Most, 18, Moscow (May 13, 1939)
- an advertisement for *Deutsche Volkszeitung,* a Paris-KPD publication (May 13, 1939, June 3, 1939)
- a photograph of the opening of the Soviet Pavilion at the World's Fair in Flushing, Borough of Queens, New York City (May 20, 1939)
- "Der Politische Dichter" by Johannes Becher; on same page an advertisement for "Internationale Literatur;" and a small article "Paul Robeson fuer die Spanische Demokratie" (July 15, 1939)
- Molotov on the Soviet Union's politics of peace (September 9, 1939)
- reference to Walter Krivitsky as Samuel Ginsburg and actually saying he was wrong in predicting a Hitler-Stalin alliance

since what was signed was termed a non-aggression pact (September 16, 1939)

Occasionally, the *Volksecho* made token attempts to appeal to a wider readership. Former *New York Post* foreign editor Johannes Steele was hired to write a series of columns.[27] The German *Paris-Soir* correspondent Curt Riess had his syndicated apolitical "Hollywood in Uproar" column included in the back pages of the *Volksecho*. Riess, however, was also a friend of Otto Katz' and was a witting attendee to his Breda charade in Southern California.[28]

The *Volksecho* once ran a short work by Hermann Hesse, but only once.[29] Heym also interviewed Thomas Mann upon Mann's arrival in New York, one of the best scoops a German writer could have made.[30] However, Mann grew gradually closer to the communists while in exile and even became a contributor to Otto Katz' Orwellian-named *Freies Deutschland* during the war.[31] In another instance, the *Volksecho* ran an article by an ostensibly ordinary reader who traveled to Moscow and had his impressions printed in his local paper as though this proved everything was honest and straightforward.[32]

The surviving documents of the KPD archives for this period are available to scholars in the French National Archive in Paris. There is conclusive and explicit evidence that the KPD considered the *Deutsches Volksecho* its own newspaper and that Heym, Rosenfeld, and others on the staff were KPD operatives. There are several Paris-to-New York and New York-to-Paris missives from 1937 to 1939 that show the KPD exerted authority on its New York agents.[33] There are also several reports from New York usually not signed by the writer's legal name but under code names such as "Jonny" that give account of the status of their efforts.[34]

There exists a typed seven-page report on the subject of the *Volksecho* from New York with "The Editor" typed at the close instead of a signature.[35] The editor was, of course, Stefan Heym. In October, 1938, "EJ" wrote from New York to Paris that "the DV [*Deutsches Volksecho*] was almost due solely to the effort of the editor St. H."[36] "EJ" is likely Erich Jungmann who was married to Gisela Kisch's sister. It seems through Heym's early career, the Kisches were never far away.

It is also clear from the records that the *Volksecho* was used as a mail drop by the communists.[37] Incidentally, the U.S. government was aware that the *Volksecho* received mail from Moscow during this period.[38] Interestingly, the KPD was often critical that the *Volksecho* was too orthodox in its communism and not promoting the Popular Front guise well enough. There exists a complete letter written to Earl Browder by the KPD on this subject.[39] Likely, it was hoped that Browder would exert influence on Stefan Heym. It has also been noted that Heym concealed membership in the CPUSA during 1936 to 1939, which includes the period of the *Volksecho's* existence.[40]

It should not be forgotten that millions were slaughtered during the *Volksecho's* thirty-one month subsistence. Despite, or rather, because the *Volksecho* had correspondents in the U.S.S.R., the outrage of the Great Terror was muted. To their disgrace, Americans were more likely to believe Rudolf Breda's pleas for resistance against the regime in Germany, which Breda claimed had created 5,000 victims. In Spain alone, the regime for which Otto Katz was press agent murdered more than that number of Catholic priests. Stefan Heym's *Deutsches Volksecho* was part of Stalin's successful campaign in promoting the ideals of communism and throttling exposure of its macabre realities.

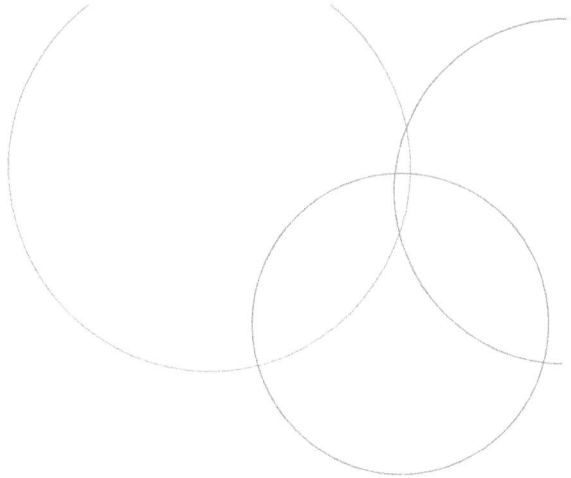

CHAPTER 7

THE FBI FILES IN CONTRAST TO NACHRUF

Leo Flieg is never mentioned in the pages of the *Deutsches Volksecho* but this is only consistent with other KPD publications. If Stefan Heym felt anguish due to Flieg's imprisonment and execution, it was kept hidden. There is one New York to Paris message in the KPD's files stating that the KPD must look for a new editor for the *Volksecho*. Whatever the difficulty was, it was resolved without further mention.[1] The exact date of Leo Flieg's sentencing was March 14, 1939 and one can only conjecture on whether Heym received word of the legal proceedings during that year. Many other relatives of victims were never informed as to the fate of those trapped in the Kafkaesque Soviet judicial system.[2]

In addition to Heym's unsuccessful infiltration of the *Neues Volkszeitung*, he confronted Fritz Kuhn's Silvershirts. Kuhn was convicted of converting several hundred dollars of party funds to personal use. The accusation was headlined on the front page of the *Volksecho* at an early stage.[3] From the German Nazi perspective, Hitler had not allowed the New York fascists to affiliate themselves with the German Nazi party and therefore never conceded that Kuhn's fall affected their interests. Kuhn's debacle, occurring just previous to the war, was a signal that the far right was "out" domestically and could have made a Democrat administration's road to intervention a bit smoother. Heym also must have felt satisfaction at hindering Hitler's sympathizers, as his father had committed suicide under Nazi harassment in 1936.[4]

From a clinical viewpoint, when two marginal parties on opposite ends of the political spectrum engage in public conflict and both receive publicity, both benefit. Since both parties confessed loyalty to a foreign power, open activity is likely to arouse interest, if not suspicion, from local authorities. It was during the *Volksecho* period that the FBI began checking on Heym's activities through informants. However, there is no available evidence showing that he was directly followed by Hoover's agents.[5]

An informant observed Heym at the 10th Annual Convention of the Communist Party, USA, on May 26, 1938 held at Madison Square Garden. Heym is said to have spoken to [Ella Reeve] "Mother" Bloor [a labor organizer and communist activist] "whom he seemed to know very well." He spoke to Illinois delegates and greeted Michigan delegates warmly. Heym was recalled as saying most of the communist auto workers were from Flint and Pontiac.[6] Another report simply cites the *Daily Worker* that Heym was sponsor of the Yorkville Anti-Nazi League and would speak at the August 5, 1938 meeting of the German Workers Club in Yorkville.[7] He attended the September 25, 1938 meeting, also at Madison Square Garden, of the "Save Czechoslovakia Committee" that, according to the FBI, was "completely under communist sponsorship and management."[8] Not noted, or possibly no longer part of the file, are several other speaking engagements that were promoted regularly in the *Volksecho*.[9]

Heym and Kurt Rosenfeld were each briefly subjects of news coverage during the *Volksecho* period. In March 1937, one of those odd one-paragraph items appeared in journals around the country stating that there were numerous reports that Leon Trotsky had been spotted in New York City. The police cleared up the matter by determining that the figure mistaken for Trotsky was actually Kurt Rosenfeld.[10] One can speculate as to whether Rosenfeld was the object of a practical joke. From 1934 to 1942, Rosenfeld was quoted in the *New York Times* on several occasions on matters pertaining to Germany as a resident expert exile.

Stefan Heym became an ancillary figure in a New York City Councilman's attempt to get his party's bills out of the committee process in order to be put to a vote. Robert Straus of the idiosyncratic local Fusion Party received coverage in the *New York Times* for his letter to Stefan Heym, editor of the *Deutsches Volksecho,* suggesting enforcement of the local city charter that gave a group of five councilman the right to demand action from the mayor when votes had been delayed beyond a certain period.[11] The story shows Heym was not completely ignored by local government and media. His appearance on the *Times'* affiliated radio station, WQXR, to discuss the "decline of culture in Nazi Germany" was printed in the paper's listings.[12]

An FBI disclosure which may be startling to many is that Heym edited a second publication contemporaneously with the *Volksecho.* The offshoot, named *Underground News,* is called "a propaganda sheet" by the feds.[13] The existence of the publication is verified by the catalogue of the New York Public Library that shows it was published weekly exactly one hundred times from October, 1937 to September, 1939. Only approximately fifteen issues, all from 1939, are available on microfilm. The copies remaining extant show *Underground News* with the subtitle "from opposition sources in Germany today" could be described as a leaflet and only two sides of one 8 1/2" x 11" sheet of paper long. Also written on the masthead is "issued weekly by American Committee for Anti-Nazi Literature." It was noted as being located in Suite 302 at 20 Vesey Street in Manhattan, while the *Volksecho* was in Room 303. Neither Stefan Heym nor anyone else is listed as an editor or writer. The issue number is typed at the top of each issue. No price is listed, so perhaps the sheet was tucked inside the *Deutsches Volksecho* or distributed as a free leaflet or made available only at selected newsstands. Each issue covers two or three stories on new developments from Germany such as workers, called S.S. or S. A. Men, striking when told their factory was to be relocated. Other examples are stories on coffee hoarding, extension of working hours for coal miners, and S.S. men being sent to Benito Mussolini's Libya.[14] *Underground News* is not mentioned in Heym's autobiography *Nachruf,* nor, aside from government files, anywhere else in connection with Heym.

Affiliation with Louis Gibarti

The Committee for Anti-Nazi Literature also published *Nazis in USA*, which could be called a book or pamphlet, and considered as Heym's first credit as an author. The organization's name sounds like one of the many communist fronts set up by Willi Muenzenberg in the 1920s and 1930s such as the League Against Imperialism or the All-German Society of Friends of Soviet Russia.[15] In fact, Muenzenberg's leading associate, Louis Gibarti, worked in New York City with Stefan Heym on *Nazis in USA*. The association of Gibarti and Heym was first mentioned in print in the first edition of Stephen Koch's *Double Lives,* which appeared in 1994. Koch even mentioned the pairing to Willi Muenzenberg's widow, Babette Gross, who was aghast at the news. She presumed that since Gibarti worked with Heym, it meant Muenzenberg's veteran cohort was therefore working for the GPU.[16] The implication of her understanding of Heym's affiliation is clear. Babette Gross was not uninformed as to her husband's career. During this period of exile in Paris, she ran her husband's publishing house, Editions du Carrefour.[17]

The primary source for the determination that Louis Gibarti worked with Stefan Heym is a transcript of an interview that a Senate committee held with Gibarti's ex-wife, Helen Konieczny, in 1952.[18] It is now corroborated by the report of an FBI agent who once phoned the *Volksecho* office and spoke with Gibarti instead of Heym, who had stepped out of the office.[19] Helen Konieczny was once one of the scores of typists employed by the Muenzenberg concern in Berlin. She testified that she had seen Heym in Berlin during the latter part of the Weimar era, though she did not specifically state she had seen him at KPD headquarters, which was the Karl Liebknecht House where she worked.[20]

Louis Gibarti (1895–1967), a Hungarian whose legal name was Ladislas Dobos, fled Hungary when Béla Kun's communist regime was overthrown in 1919.[21] It is, so far, not known what type of role he played during the eleven-month red regime that precipitated his flight. There were hordes of brutal young commissars who terrorized the so-called "class enemies" during the thankfully brief reign of Kun. In exile, they scattered around the world and became Comintern agents, as if in prelude to the KPD of 1933.[22] Gibarti had a brother, of whom even less is known, who emigrated to work in an industrial area of Ohio.[23] His legal presence gave Gibarti a convenient pretext to visit the U.S. in the 1920s.[24] He visited and operated in the U.S. several times between 1921 and 1938.[25]

As Willi Muenzenberg's top aide, Gibarti helped establish and administrate the most famous and influential front committees and conferences of the era such as the League Against Imperialism. In the U.S., his work on the American Committee to Aid Spanish Democracy and his post as director of Soviet motion picture importer Amkino are examples of his attempts to exercise influence in as many spheres as possible. In Cologne, in 1927, he announced an Arab Freedom Conference to be held in Mecca which, however, never came to fruition.[26]

Though little known to the public, he involved Jawalaral Nehru, Ho Chi Minh, Madame Sun Yat Sen, and Albert Einstein in his committees.[27] Romain Rolland is one of the few intellectuals to have left record of their acquaintance. One must scour sources to find Gibarti was once secretary to Henri Barbusse [French novelist and communist].[28] Gibarti wrote articles occasionally for periodicals within the Muenzenberg concern.[29]

In 1934, Gibarti traveled to Spain and several members of parliament convened with him.[30] He was listed on a legal document as business manager of the *Deutsches Volksecho*" though Heym wrote that the actual business manager was named Curt Loewe.[31]

Stephen Koch is apparently the only writer to attempt to research Gibarti. Koch found Gibarti was involved in Kim Philby's earliest assignments for the Soviets in Vienna upon Philby's graduation from Cambridge in 1934.[32] The Hungarian also collaborated with Alexander Orlov in Vienna only a few years previous to Orlov's notorious reign of terror as chief NKVD commissar in Spain.[33] Koch also found Gibarti was behind the Oberfohren forgery, an attempt to distort the newsreader's perception of events in Germany, in 1934.[34] He was also in New York City the same year with a *mandat*, a sort of Comintern power of attorney, which gave him authority over local *apparatchiks* [communist party members], even Earl Browder.[35]

January 1935 found Gibarti in Chicago with Erich von Schroetter, holding rallies on the Saarland plebiscite while most of the other important German propagandists were in Saarbrücken itself.[36] He left Chicago after a month or six weeks, thus more than a month before Heym's arrival. Heym wrote in *Nachruf* that the circumstances of his first meeting with von Schroetter were "not reconstructable" (*nicht mehr zu rekonstruieren*) but the pairing must have been intended as a complement to Gibarti's efforts by the Comintern's administrators.[37]

Gibarti worked from September 1937 at the *Volksecho* office at 20 Vesey Street until he departed the U.S. in July 1938, according to the testimony of his former wife. She stopped in several times for brief greetings and though she did not testify that she saw Stefan Heym there, he undoubtedly was at his office regularly, which is known from his memoir and the simple fact that he was editor of the newspaper.[38] As stated, both worked on communist publicity with Erich von Schroetter in 1935 and Helen Konieczny, as Mrs. Dobos testified to an acquaintance with Heym in Berlin. Therefore, it seems likely Helmut Flieg also knew Louis Gibarti prior to 1937, though documentary evidence unequivocally stating so is not available.

The KPD files in Paris do not mention Gibarti in connection with the *Volksecho*. He is cited as having formed an emigration committee and as being Second Chairman of the *Liga fuer Menschenrechte*, the League for Human Rights, in Prague.[39] Another note includes him on a list of those suspected of disloyalty.[40] The suspicion could have derived from the fact that the KPD could exercise only very limited jurisdiction over the Hungarian outside of Germany. Note also that baseless, alleged suspicion was rampant during the period of the Great Terror.

There is an acknowledgment in *Nazis in USA* stating, "I wish to acknowledge the assistance of a friend whose factual data and comprehensive knowledge of Nazi activities has proven invaluable. – Stefan Heym."[41] The anonymous friend was likely Louis Gibarti. His wife also testified that he was working on an anti-Nazi pamphlet at the same time he frequented the *Volksecho* office. Heym's memoir gives no details on the writing of *Nazis in USA*. There were also two other assistants working on the pamphlet not associated with the *Volksecho*, William Dodd Jr. and the obscure Dero Saunders.[42] Dodd Jr. who lived in Berlin from 1933 to 1937, son of the American Ambassador to Germany, was the titular head of the American Committee for Anti-Nazi Literature which published *Nazis in USA*.[43]

Gibarti returned to Paris in mid–1938 and helped launch a new periodical of Muenzenberg's called *Die Zukunft* [The Future]. The magazine was in existence from October 1938 to May 1940 and was to be completely independent of the party, though Muenzenberg insisted publicly he was still a revolutionary and still employed Gibarti.[44] Another connection between Gibarti and Muenzenberg that is relevant to Stefan Heym is that Gibarti organized the tour to the U.S.in which Muenzenberg and Kurt Rosenfeld took part.[45] By 1936, Muenzenberg's status in the party was diminished, or it was decided he would be more effective as a revolutionary opponent. Moscow sent a representative to dispossess him of his corporations and committees.[46] Muenzenberg refused orders to report to Moscow, which saved his life temporarily, but he was soon officially expelled from the Communist Party.[47]

As with the American Committee for Anti-Nazi Literature, Gibarti's status at *Die Zukunft* was unofficial, but this didn't stop him from holding himself out as a representative.[48] Arthur Koestler and

Alexander Wirth were two of Muenzenberg's more prominent co-ex-ecutives at the magazine and its associated party. Koestler's novels, memoirs, and political essays are still popular. Wirth had been Chan-cellor of Germany when the Treaty of Rapallo was signed and had ambitions of leading a government-in-exile. There are several note-worthy correspondences and compositions in the files of *Die Zukunft* that have still escaped the attention of academics.[49]

Gibarti used *Die Zukunft* to send reports to U.S. government offi-cials and to solicit responses. Harold Ickes is an example of an official in the Roosevelt administration who replied to the Hungarian's letter campaign.[50] Others did not respond, or else the files have been dis-creetly purged during the intervening decades. Ickes and several other famous Americans of the left also contributed articles to *Die Zukunft* in a special issue devoted the worker's movement in the U.S. Gibarti also seemed to have been in communication with the U.S. Embassy in Paris. In a letter to U.S. civil rights lawyer Gardner Jackson, he calls Mssrs. Murphy and Thompson of the embassy "obliging gentlemen" and claims to have an appointment with Mr. Bullitt. He also contacted Mr. Barnes, the embassy's press secretary several times, but conclusive evidence of reciprocation from anyone in the embassy is lacking.[51]

In June 1939, Gibarti sent an apparently unsolicited report on eco-nomic conditions in Germany to Winston Churchill. Within a week, he received the following note:[52]

Dear Sir,
I am desired by Mr. Winston Churchill to thank you for your let-ter of June 10, together with the enclosure. Mr. Churchill would be very glad to receive further communications from you.
   Yours faithfully, K. Hill Private Secretary

Gibarti sent another report on German economic conditions on August 3, 1939. He wrote again on August 12, 1939 asking Churchill to spend fifteen minutes with "Alfred Thomas" during his visit to the Maginot Line [a line of fortifications and weapons installations along France's border with Germany]."[53] The name may be an alias for Gibarti or another Soviet spy.[54] The timing is obviously interesting, being only a few weeks from Churchill's rejoining the staff of [British Prime Minister] Chamberlain and Great Britain's declaration of war. At the time of Gibarti's letter, Churchill was a "backbencher" in the House of Commons. It is as if Gibarti knew the rise of Winston Churchill was forthcoming.

Like many foreigners, Gibarti fled France with the outbreak of the war. He went to Italy and is listed as having worked as a cinematographer on a film there. The Nazi-Soviet Pact and perhaps Muenzenberg's acquaintance with Benito Mussolini [founder of Fascist Party and Prime Minister of Italy, 1922–1943] could account for the unusual circumstance. Most forget that, as a Socialist prior to World War I, Mussolini attended the same conferences as Bolshevik-supporters, including Muenzenberg.[55]

The Freedom of Information Act reports on Gibarti show he was arrested in Madrid in May 1941. Following the war, he worked for the World Federation of Trade Unions continuing his career in service to Soviet front organizations.[56] Two U.S. senators, Willis Smith (D-North Carolina) and Homer Ferguson (R-Michigan), and U.S. Senate Special Counsel Robert Morris interviewed the Hungarian expatriate in Paris in 1951.[57] The last tidbit that reached publication, though not including in former Iron Curtain countries, is that Gibarti moved to West Germany in 1959.[58] All one can say about Gibarti, one supposes, is that he was someone Winston Churchill and U.S. senators wanted information from, but someone historians try to ignore. All the committees formed by Muenzenberg and Gibarti may seem esoteric and moot today, but a walk through any European city shows a Europe which looks as if it is run by the League Against Imperialism, rather than by traditional concepts such as the nation-state.

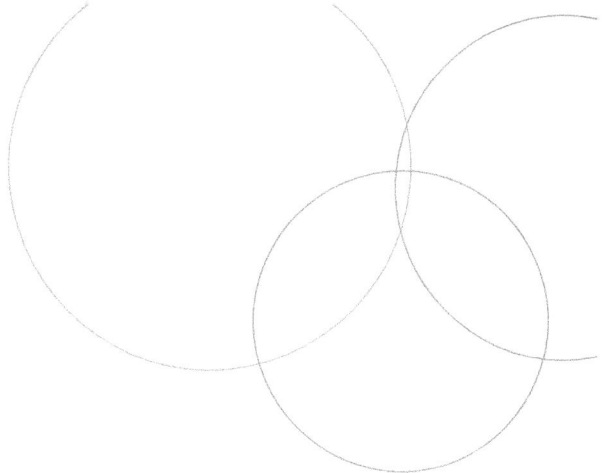

CHAPTER 8

KPD HANDS IN NEW YORK

Louis Gibarti was not the only Comintern agent in the *Volksecho* office. The name Martin Hall often appeared in its pages as an author and in advertisements for speaking engagements.[1] His cover name is described as a "*nom de guerre*" in *Nachruf*, while his actual name, doubtlessly known to Heym, was Hermann Jakobs.[2] He had worked in the Communist Youth International headquarters in Berlin in 1921 and was, presumably, known to Leo Flieg, given that Jakobs rose to an executive position in the same organization in 1924.[3] Jakobs/Hall became an editor at the *Neues Zeitung* in Munich in 1927 and was an editor in Chemnitz shortly before or shortly after Flieg/ Heym's departure.[4] Certainly, they must have had many acquaintances in common, even if their own paths didn't cross previous to 1937. In not revealing his actual name and background, Heym creates a mystification in order to conceal the fact that both had careers guided by the same force behind communist power.

Jakobs is noted by Franz Feuchtwanger as a Comintern press instructor in Switzerland during the early exile period.[5] He became based in the Midwest and, as Martin Hall, was also listed next to Erich von Schroetter as editor of *Volksfront* in 1939.[6] His wife once wrote to the KPD in Paris to ask them not to send mail under the name Jakobs to Von Schroetter's office as she felt it was a security breach.[7] He made many public appearances in New York City, Chicago, and other major towns, mostly in the Midwest. Many of those towns had sizable German-speaking populations and German language dailies with circulations in the tens or even hundreds of thousands.[8]

The other member of his staff whose name Heym pretended not to know, "Hans oder Otto," or "Fleischer, Gerber oder Schroeter," was actually called Johannes Schroeter (1896–1963).[9] The obfuscation was cleared up by Wolfgang Kiessling in *Partner im "Narrenparadies"* which is, apparently, the only other work that expands upon the official story of Heym's career.[10] Both Heym and Kiessling note that Schroeter wrote in the *Volksecho* under the name Alfred Langer.[11] However, another source states Alfred Langer was an alias for Hans Kippenberger, another leader of the KPD's secret divisions who, therefore, would have been a close associate of Leo Flieg.[12]

Alfred Langer is quoted, prior to the exile period, as having written that "one of the most important preliminaries to the fight is tireless, obstinate, systematic work shrinking from no terrorism, within the armed forces and the bourgeoisie, a continuous revolutionary education of the soldier masses," and "in dealing with outspoken opponents of the revolution it is necessary to apply the severest revolutionary discipline and even terrorism. The degree to which terrorism is to be adopted is purely a question of expediency. This also applies to the question of hostages."[13] It's all a bit odder if Kippenberger was also "Langer," as Kippenberger had been sentenced to death in Moscow even before the *Volksecho* began publication and was executed in October 1937.[14] If so, the above quote would not have been part of the complaint against him.[15]

When the *Volksecho* and *Underground News* disbanded following the Molotov-von Ribbentrop Pact and the collapse of the façade of the Popular Front, Schroeter and his wife, Dr. Reni Begun, moved to Mexico.

Wolfgang Kiessling actually interviewed Dr. Begun in Mexico in 1981. She revealed Schroeter had been a Comintern agent in exile and received a regular stipend from the CPUSA while in New York.[16] Further, following the Reichstag fire but before exile, Schroeter worked in the communist underground with Hugo Eberlein.[17] While in Paris, Schroeter received a false passport, delivered with a message from Wilhelm Pieck.[18] The false passport and work with Eberlein, of course, suggests a connection to Leo Flieg. Begun also claimed to Kiessling that she, with Schroeter's help, authored part of a book for Muenzenberg's Editions du Carrefour, though they were not openly credited as authors.[19] An FBI report called Schroeter a GPU agent and noted he was familiar with Hannes Eisler, composer of the East German national anthem. Heym also stated Schroeter had contacts in the entertainment and financial realms.[20]

Many other prominent German leftists also spent the war years in Mexico such as the Kisches, the Katzes, Bruno Frei, Ludwig Renn, Alexander Abusch, Bodo Uhse, and Anna Seghers. There were also a few who were no longer with the KPD, such as Babette Gross, Gustav Regler, Otto Ruhle, and Heinz Gutmann. Schroeter again became involved with German newspapers and in 1946 replaced the ill-fated Rudi Feistmann as editor of Mexico City's *Demokratische Post*.[21] In 1947, Feistmann became foreign editor of the DDR's official newspaper *Neues Deutschland*. Through little fault of his own, he became implicated in the Noel Field affair and was found poisoned to death in 1950.[22] The exiles who had been based in Moscow used the Field affair to consolidate their power, but Schroeter was cleverer to stay in Mexico.

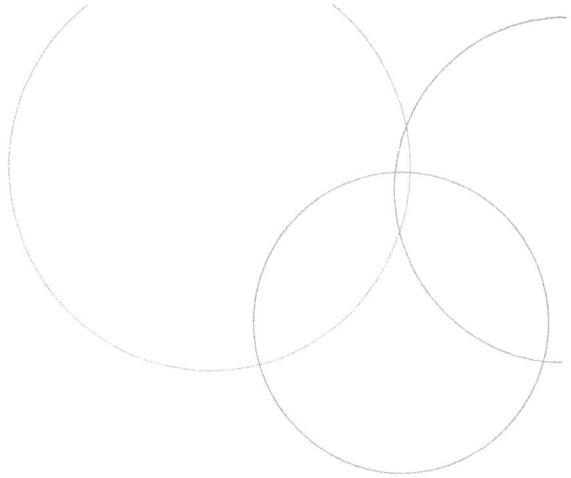

CHAPTER 9

WILLIAM DODD JR.

Another Soviet agent who frequented the *Volksecho* office at 20 Vesey Street was William E. Dodd Jr., son of the U.S. Ambassador to Germany from 1933–1937.[1] As stated, Dodd was nominally chairman of the American Committee for Anti-Nazi Literature, which published Stefan Heym's *Nazis in USA* and the weekly leaflet *Underground News*. The committee occupied the same office space as the *Deutsches Volksecho*."[2] William Dodd Jr. was recruited by the Soviets while in Berlin by 1935.[3] The KPD archives in Paris call him an active participant in the Soviet front *Rassemblement Universelle Pour la Paix* [Universal Association for Peace]; other archives confirm this.[4] He even convinced his father to help solicit funds for the organization while he was still *en poste*, against normal standards of diplomatic behavior.[5]

Dodd Jr. traveled to Shanghai and Moscow in 1936 under the auspices of his Soviet controllers.[6] His father's tenure as ambassador ended in December, 1937 and Dodd Jr.'s position in Vesey Street began upon, or very soon following, his return to the U.S. He ran and lost in the Democratic primary a bid for Congress in Virginia, later in 1938, on a "100 percent pro-Roosevelt" platform.[7] He married in 1940 and briefly worked for the U.S. government during the war.[8] The Venona intercepts show that the Soviets were interested in hiring him to work at the TASS news service. His job at TASS ended after a short while when his sister, the notorious Martha Dodd Stern, purportedly complained that his openly Soviet position harmed her covert efforts.[9] He moved to the West Coast and passed away in 1952, well before the family name became front page news again.

Dodd Jr. is omitted from *Nachruf,* although his sister and brother-in-law are noted in connection with the 1939 dissolution of the *Volksecho.* According to the autobiography, Heym was without means of support and requested help from the American Guild of Cultural Freedom.[10] The trust was run by Hubertus von Loewenstein, who had aided and abetted Otto Katz' chicanery in Hollywood, as if Loewenstein wanted to make his role with Breda/Katz more authentic.[11] Loewenstein became a Social Democrat representative in the Bundestag in West Germany and never seems to have had his work with Muenzenberg and Katz exposed during his career. Fittingly, Heym's description of his request for funds is also deceptive, having been made in July 1939 while the *Volksecho* was still a going concern, and not in September 1939 when the Pact was announced.[12] A letter of Heym's requesting a reference reveals the actual time.

Heym exhibited falseness in yet another way in September 1939 when he joined the public excoriation of Walter Krivitsky.[13] As head of the Western Bureau of the Comintern, Krivitsky must have been a familiar acquaintance to Leo Flieg.[14] Heym, cloaking his own identity, joined those who exposed Krivitsky's legal name, Samuel Ginsburg.[15] Even though Krivitsky was either murdered or driven to suicide in 1941, Heym seems to have maintained an antipathy toward him, with a character named "Krivitsky" in his short story "A Good Second Man." The character is derided for an ineffectual appearance: "his most impressive feature was his nose and even that didn't have any character." It is difficult to accept seriously Heym's disapproval when so much is concealed.

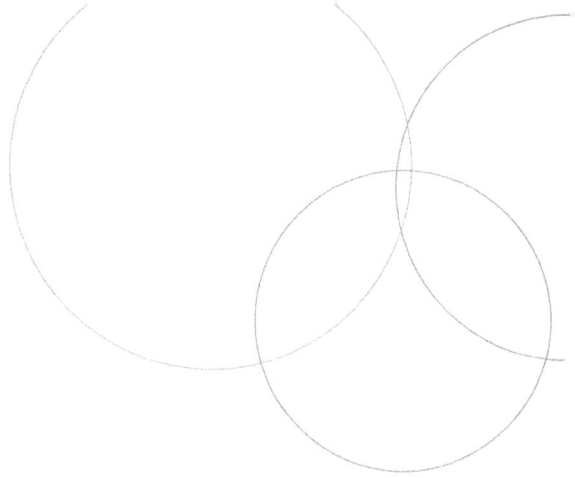

CHAPTER 10

MARTHA DODD STERN AND ALFRED STERN

I n *Nachruf*, at the point of the chronology when the *Volksecho* ended publication, Heym wrote the only thing Johannes Schroeter left him was the acquaintanceship of Alfred Stern. Then, in describing Stern, he notes that Stern married Martha Dodd, daughter of the American Ambassador to Germany [William Dodd Sr.].[1] William Dodd Jr, Martha's brother, is simply omitted, though it is more logical that Heym met Dodd's sister and brother-in-law through him, as he worked in the office. A swarm of coincidences make it obvious that Heym's acquaintanceship with the Sterns was not simply the work of Schroeter but prepared and prearranged by communism's administrators.

While in Berlin from 1933 to 1937, Martha Dodd was best friend of Heym's former apartment sharer, Mildred Fish Harnack.[2] Dodd grew up on the campus of the University of Chicago where her father was a history professor and where Heym was a student from 1935 to 1936.[3] Also, Alfred Stern, who was a fairly well-off banker's son, became a millionaire due to his previous marriage to Marion Rosenwald, daughter of the major shareholder of Sears, Roebuck and Company, Julius Rosenwald.[4]

Rosenwald was also a significant, if not the leading benefactor of the University of Chicago.[5] The Fliegs seem to have been close to the Tietz family, who owned Germany's leading department store concern previous to and following the Nazi regime.[6] Heym disclosed this fact in one of his last books. No amount of dissimulation will convince a sensible person that such circumstances occur by happenstance, especially in a case where the subjects are all Stalinist agents. One cannot find a better illustration for the hypothesis that communism is oppression by great capital.

Martha Dodd became a Soviet agent in Germany in 1934 or 1935 in conjunction with her affair with Boris Vinogradov, First Secretary of the Soviet Embassy.[7] At the University of Chicago, she had already been the girlfriend of Robert Morse Lovett, who designed the curriculum for the secret school of the CPUSA.[8] Newspapers ran a wire service photo of her posing by the airplane portal when she took an excursion to Moscow in 1934.[9] Apparently, the Comintern archives in Moscow give irrefutable indication of Martha Dodd having been a witting Soviet agent while her father was ambassador. The archives include her reports to superiors on her espionage efforts.[10]

She also traveled to Warsaw in November 1937 in order to bid goodbye to Vinogradov who had been transferred there.[11] He was killed in the purges a short time later. Earlier, in September 1937, she made a trip to Geneva on behalf of *Rassemblement Universelle Pour la Paix* and met with Otto Katz and Louis Fischer, who were leading figures in the Spanish Republic's press, and Juan Negrin, the republic's president.[12] Fischer's presence is interesting for several other connections. He was employed by *The Nation*, which, like the *Volksecho*, was located at 20 Vesey Street, one floor above the *Volksecho* office.[13] *The Nation* had printed an article by Heym in June 1936, as noted earlier.

Fischer often took his meals with Katz and Negrin during the Spanish Civil War.[14] Fischer's and Negrin's children also attended the same school in Moscow together with other elite communists such as Svetlana Stalin and Markus Wolf.[15] Eleanor Roosevelt was so enamored of Fischer's children, she had them sleep over at the White House while Winston Churchill was a guest.[16] Martha Dodd once volunteered to marry Fischer if the Soviets wished.[17]

The Soviets made arrangements to have an operative in New York City meet with Dodd when she returned to the U.S. in December 1937.[18] Her brother began working at the American Committee for Anti-Nazi Literature, attached to the *Volksecho* office, at approximately the same time. It is a very unusual circumstance that an ambassador's family can be proven to work on behalf of another country's government. Curiously, the Dodds didn't seem to operate secretly and received more than the usual amount of press coverage. Objectively, how does it appear when the power the Dodds colluded with, the U.S.S.R., later allied with the U.S. in war against Germany?

One would expect that the appointment [of William Dodd Sr. as Ambassador to Germany], which received so much press attention between the two most powerful combatants of the previous war, was very carefully planned. Consider also that Franklin Roosevelt was of aristocratic ancestry and had traveled to Germany several times in his youth, including attendance at a German school.[19] As part of his duties with the government, he also visited the U.S. occupation area in Germany following World War I. In 1933, the relationship with Germany was among America's highest international priorities, yet William Dodd Sr. was appointed without any experience in the State Department. Dodd had studied three years at the University of Leipzig prior to World War I, but as a history professor had written only on U.S. history and specialized in history of the South. His closest brush with the subject of German history was that he had edited a work on Woodrow Wilson's papers.[20]

There was even talk in Washington that President Roosevelt had chosen the wrong Dodd.[21] In Chicago, there was also a prominent attorney and author named Walter Dodd. The President of Princeton University, a position Woodrow Wilson once held, was named

Walter Dodds. Following the war, columnist Westbrook Pegler wrote that Mrs. Roosevelt, though a "ruddy friend" of Martha Dodd, called Martha the daughter of the President of Princeton in a book plug.[22] Additionally, Pegler could quote former Roosevelt aide Ed Flynn, also a Bronx party boss, who told the story of the Dodd mix-up in his memoir *You're the Boss*.[23] Dark forces are said to have caused Flynn to later disavow his version [of the mistaken Dodd], but the fact of Eleanor Roosevelt's ostensible confusion, Flynn's original story, and the unusually unqualified appointee remained.[24]

However, since Roosevelt had so many other communists in his administration, it isn't the most logical supposition that he accidentally sent a family that was amenable to being used as Soviet agents. Defenders of the administration such as Mrs. Roosevelt and Ed Flynn were left to obfuscate about the matter when Martha was indicted as a spy. The explanation that Roosevelt intentionally appointed communists makes more sense than the proposition that Roosevelt was too uninformed about Germany to worry about the appointment.

Recall that the Reichstag fire and subsequent suspension of civil liberties in Germany occurred only a few days before FDR's first inauguration on March 4, 1933. The idea that the ambassadorship to Germany was a matter to be glossed over and forgotten is simply unrealistic. Better is another account suggesting that Colonel House, the plenipotentiary who wasn't really a colonel, was influencing Roosevelt in the appointment of Dodd. House, without an official title, held great influence over Woodrow Wilson and was still a force in the Democrat Party in 1932 when Roosevelt was elected. It is also claimed House was behind selecting Chicago as the venue for the party convention in 1932.[25]

Alfred Stern

As stated, Martha Dodd returned to America toward the end of 1937. By June 1938, she was engaged to Alfred Stern whom she married, dressed in black, at her father's Virginia estate in September.[26] She may have met Stern in Germany where he is noted to have given the under-ground communists financial support.[27] He had attended Harvard and married Sears Roebuck heiress Marion Rosenwald in 1922. They were divorced in 1937, as if in preparation for Martha Dodd's return. He had been in charge of the Rosenwald Trust, which made a University of Chicago connection among Heym, Stern, and the Dodds unmistakable.[28] The university had been investigated before and following World War II because of indications that faculty members had been communists. Westbrook Pegler called it "red as a bloody nose."[29] Stern had increased his personal wealth during his first marriage according to later accounts. Significantly, he had two children with Marion Rosenwald, making the liaison one that could not be casually written off.[30] Marion Rosenwald was also a financial supporter of the left and financed her second husband, Max Ascoli, in founding the periodical *The Reporter*. She also helped fund the liberal New York City daily called *PM*.[31]

Noted in *Nachruf*, Stern and *Volksecho* writer Johannes Schroeter planned to erect an anti-Nazi offshore shortwave transmitter. Heym wrote that the project wasn't feasible due to technological limitations.[32] The KPD files in Paris mention Stern as a supporter of the splinter faction *Neu Beginnen* [New Beginning] led by Karl Frank, a veteran of Kisch's attempted putsch in Vienna who had also been in the SAP in 1931.[33] Heym noted gratefully that Stern had once lent him $1,000 in 1940 or 1941 when Heym needed to show means of support to comply with immigration legalities.[34]

If part of Martha Dodd Stern's mission was to cause dissent between Germans and Americans, she scored a minor coup by having polarizing comments on German women carried in a syndicated story of April, 1939. She is quoted as complaining "the middle class woman [in Germany] is poorly dressed, doesn't fix her hair attractively, doesn't wear lipstick because it is frowned upon" and added, "she hasn't been able to keep her femininity with all the physical training she has been subjected to," and "she looks more like a big healthy animal than an attractive woman."[35] It is easy to see that these sorts of generalizations approach the race propaganda that the Nazis themselves were accused of. Another example of a member of a diplomat's family making a public statement that an inhabitant of their host nation resembled an "animal" would be difficult to find. The fact that these comments were printed also show she was regarded as something of a public figure, while at the same time she was likely an occasional visitor to the *Volksecho* office.

The Sterns were known for their numerous parties for important leftists and society types. The affairs were possibly a prototype for the "radical chic" scene of the following generation.[36] They had a large apartment at 115 Central Park West, only a short distance from Heym's apartment in 1939 and 1940.[37] Alfred Stern once set up a record company to be used as a Soviet front with Hollywood producer and music score director Boris Morros as the chief operating officer.[38] Morros, who had directed music scores for over a hundred films, became an FBI informant in 1947.[39] The Venona intercepts show the company lost Stern's $130,000 investment.[40] Morros and Stern did have one hit with the awful "Chattanooga Choo Choo."[41]

Stern made headlines briefly when he led a "rent march" on the state capital, Albany, New York, in 1946. The couple also supported Henry Wallace's candidacy for president in 1948.[42] Scrutiny of the couple's activities increased with the onset of the Cold War. Martha Stern recruited, paired, and organized agents, including Jane Foster Zlatovski.[43] The couple, apparently afraid to be called in front of the U.S. House Un-American Activities Committee (HUAC) [the committee charged with investigating communist threats in the U.S.] or a grand jury, relocated to Mexico in 1953.[44]

The couple traveled to Moscow in 1956, which automatically aroused suspicion, perhaps justifiably, during that era.[45] In 1957, the Sterns were called to testify in the trial against Myra Soble and Jacob Albam. They fled fearing extradition to the United States.[46] An indictment against the Dodds that followed included a charge of treason, punishable by death.[47] A guest at their parties, Vassili Zubilin, who was an official at the Soviet Embassy, had put the friendly couple in the orbit of atomic spies, which the U.S. government was determined to punish.[48] The dreaded arrest warrant was signed by the same judge who had presided over the Rosenberg spy case.[49]

Alexander Korotkov, who had been controller of the Harnacks in 1939, was named as an unindicted co-conspirator.[50] President Eisenhower considered the matter important enough to order Ambassador White to meet personally with Mexican President Ruiz-Cortines on the matter.[51] The charges had not been filed sooner, possibly because of Morros' value as a counterspy. It was only when it became obvious that the KGB had discovered Morros was an FBI informant that the investigation concluded and prosecutions began.[52] The Sterns hired William O'Dwyer (1890–1964), former Mayor of New York City and former Ambassador to Mexico, as their defense attorney.[53] O'Dwyer had remained in Mexico City since the end of his term as ambassador in 1952.

A contempt of court fine for the Sterns of $50,000 was ordered in New York in May 1957. The couple fled on August 20, abandoning a partly constructed $70,000 home in Cuernavaca.[54] They traveled widely in the Soviet sphere, lived in Castro's Cuba for a short while, and never returned to the U.S. though the charges against them, except the contempt of court fine, were dropped in 1979.[55] Their first stop behind the Iron Curtain and the city they resided in for most of the next decades was Prague.

Boris Morros wrote a memoir called *My Ten Years as a Counterspy*, which was made into the motion picture called *Man on a String* (1960).[56] The identity of the Sterns was changed to the name "Benson." The screenplay depicted "Mrs. Benson" as spying for the Soviets in postwar Berlin without mentioning that she had been the daughter of the U.S. ambassador. Though Martha Dodd may not have even been in Berlin again until her defection, her activities made clear she was a Stalinist even when there were no fascists to oppose.[57]

William O'Dwyer and the Sterns

The association of William O'Dwyer with the Sterns seems a very curious circumstance. O'Dwyer, born in Ireland, attended seminary in Salamanca, Spain before emigrating. He became a New York City police officer and attended law school in the evening. He was elected Brooklyn District Attorney in 1939 and had several notable organized crime figures put to death in the era of "Murder Incorporated" [rampant Mafia killings in New York City].[58] However, the November 1941 death of an informant while in custody allowed a major gangster to gain acquittal, which cast suspicion upon O'Dwyer.[59]

In July 1944, while still Brooklyn D.A., William O'Dwyer was called to a meeting with President Roosevelt and appointed to the Allied Control Commission in Italy with the rank of Brigadier General.[60] He had broad powers over the economy in Allied-occupied Italy and met with leaders of the Italian government; a coalition of anti-Mussolini parties including the Communist Party of Italy.[61] In January 1945, following a personal meeting with President Roosevelt, he was named Executive Director of the War Refugee Board.[62] O'Dwyer worked with Count Folke Bernadotte of Sweden to bring food and medical supplies from Switzerland to numerous concentration camps in the final months of the war.[63] The War Refugee Board was also responsible for cooperating with many other relief agencies including, as mentioned specifically in O'Dwyer's memoir, the Unitarian Services Committee, headed in Europe by Noel Field.[64]

On New Year's Day in 1946, William O'Dwyer was sworn in as New York City's 100th Mayor succeeding Fiorello LaGuardia.[65] He was portrayed on the cover of *Time* magazine on June 7, 1948. He oversaw the construction of the United Nations building and met often with Trygvie Lie [first Secretary-General of the U.N.].[66] He was easily reelected to the mayoralty in 1949. O'Dwyer, a widower, married fashion model Sloane Simpson whose father had been an officer with Teddy Roosevelt on San Juan Hill.[67] She was shown on the cover of *Life* magazine on May 29, 1950 as the epitome of the glamourous hostess among the rich and powerful.[68]

Yet, O'Dwyer resigned in August 1950 to become U.S. Ambassador to Mexico.[69] Abandoning a position as mayor so soon after reelection was unheard of. O'Dwyer claims he needed the change of climate for health reasons, though this was contradicted by his recent marriage to a younger woman. O'Dwyer's autobiography states the sitting ambassador was leaving his post anyway. This, too, is contradicted by the following statement by the embassy attaché, Samuel Montague: "The current ambassador, who was very popular at the time, was Walter Thurston. People thought he was being railroaded out to make room for this political newcomer. There was a lot of resentment."[70]

Also, President Harry Truman's leading biographer lists O'Dwyer as having supported a "Draft Eisenhower" effort to deprive Truman of the Democrat nomination in 1948.[71] Not then known to the public was that O'Dwyer would be called to answer questions at the Kefauver Committee Hearings to combat organized crime.[72] O'Dwyer indeed returned from Mexico to answer questions about whether he remembered receiving an envelope filled with cash several years ago and whether he knew that friends of criminals had been hired by the city.[73] The potential allegations did not seem to be of a magnitude to cause someone of O'Dwyer's stature to flee the country.[74] If the allegations were serious, then it was still very odd that a president would appoint someone who was subject to investigation.

Then there is the odd coincidence of O'Dwyer having been a seminarian in Spain and marrying the daughter of an officer who fought in the Spanish-American War just before the appointment to a former Spanish colony. At the time, Spain was being ostracized from the Allied-dominated U.N. and was excluded from the Marshall Plan.[75] O'Dwyer's circumstances were such that they would endear him to Mexicans and slight the Spanish.

O'Dwyer held his post in Mexico City from 1950 to 1952 and seems to have been unusually popular with Mexicans.[76] His term ended routinely with the elapsing of Truman's presidency. His marriage dissolved, as if it also expired with the Truman administration. A bit unusually, both stayed on in Mexico.[77] O'Dwyer lived in a large room of the Prince Hotel in Mexico City and opened a law office branch in partnership with his notable brother Paul O'Dwyer.[78]

Sometime later, his ex-wife Sloane O'Dwyer was named "Ambassador of Fun" in Mexico by Braniff Airlines. In 1954, she hosted a syndicated radio show and interviewed celebrities, including Vice President Nixon.[79] Upon her return to New York, she appeared on the stage including, once, Broadway, as well as one film role and local and national television.[80] William O'Dwyer retired to New York City in 1960 without repercussion from his unique departure or the Stern case.

William O'Dwyer as an Irish cop who rose to District Attorney, General, Mayor and Ambassador to Mexico, did not have the background of a communist or even a leftist. However, he was willing to make the necessary compromises with the powerful red forces in New York to further his career. His younger brother Paul, who represented the Sterns before a judge in New York, was openly a leftist and took positions and made statements consistent with the communist line of his era.

William O'Dwyer was guest of honor at a dinner of the American Committee for the Protection of the Foreign Born in 1943, spoke at the National Council of American Soviet Friendship in 1946, had a list of such associations, as the saying went, "as long as your arm," and explicitly refused to repudiate communist support when he received it.[81] He also claimed to have represented in Mexico several others on the run from the House Un-American Activities Committee.[82] However, he also once led an effort to deprive the Democrat nomination from Benjamin Davis, the openly communist city councilman from Harlem.[83]

His presence in Mexico and abandonment of the mayoralty are still conundrums. His career from 1940 to 1960 demonstrate a unique role in events of the highest importance, though they remain unnoticed except in his own rather obscure memoir. Odd also is that his career path intersected with Martha Dodd and Noel Field, and also included Cuernavaca, as though part of his life was molded in reference to Stefan Heym's.

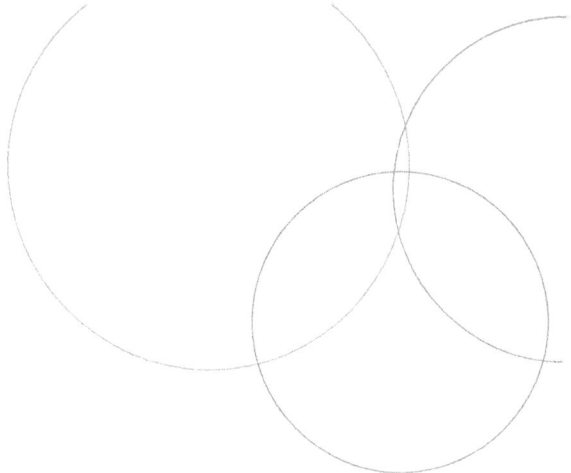

CHAPTER 11

THE EARLY WAR YEARS, STATESIDE

Heym suffered a reversal following the closure of the *Volksecho* when he fell ill following dinner at a Manhattan eatery. His sickness, though not life-threatening, necessitated repose at a hospital beyond a full week.[1] Unable to save much of his editor's salary, he was impecunious and could not afford medical care. It has since come to light, though nearly sixty years after the fact, that the League of American Writers (L.A.W.), an organization properly called a communist front, settled the medical bill.[2]

Upon recovery, Heym obtained ordinary employment as a sales-man of printing services.[3] The Army's security investigation into this period determined his employer was Prompt Press or New Union Press, 119 Fourth Avenue, from September 1939 to May 1941 where he earned $40 per week.[4] He later accepted a better offer at Herald Square Press, further downtown on Spring Street.[5] Once he regained his health, the closure of the *Volksecho* was perhaps a relief, as he earned substantially less as an editor.[6]

Heym was able to take time off from May to August 1941 to write his successful first novel, *Hostages*, then represented Herald Square Press until October 1942.[7] Among Heym's clients were The Society for Ethical Culture, The Federal Council of Churches, Lavanburg Homes, and a periodical called *Standby*, published by the American Federation of Radio Artists.[8] Apparently, he was able to bring these accounts to his new employer, which was part of the reason for his improved salary.[9]

Heym lived at four different addresses in Manhattan from his arrival in 1937 until induction in the Army in 1943. *Nachruf* mentions his poorly furnished apartment on 73rd Street and 7th Avenue while editor of the *Volksecho*.[10] The address was actually 171 West 73rd Street.[11] 73rd St. and 7th Ave. does not exist. The hypothetical street corner would be within Central Park where there is no residential housing. The U.S. government discovered Heym first lived at 46 or 48 Barrow Street in Lower Manhattan for the first several months he lived in New York. The best record of his stay there is from February to November 1937.[12]

Heym mentioned his apartment at 425 East 17th Street, which is accurate, but omits having lived at 1 Rutherford Place.[13] Even the records of the government background investigation do not give a precise description of time spent at each address, but it is clear he also resided at 1 Rutherford Place, which is at the corner of East 15th Street, a few blocks walk from the apartment on East 17th Street.[14] Coincidentally, his acquaintance from Prague, F.C. Weiskopf, resided at 306 East 15th Street.

Heym's connections from his Prague period seem also to have influenced his interest in Hanussen, the mystic or charlatan who is said to have foreseen the Reichstag fire.[15] Before writing *Hostages*, Heym acknowledged writing two unproduced plays: *Deadline*, set in a newspaper office, and *Hanussen*. Another KPD author, Bruno Frei, wrote a book on Hanussen in 1934 while interest in the Reichstag fire was high. The work was published in Strasbourg, France, and Egon Kisch happened to have written the introduction.[16]

Nachruf mentioned Frei as an editor in Berlin known to the youthful Helmut Flieg.[17] Frei's own memoir is one of the few that admits having seen Heym in Prague in the 1933 to 1935 period.[18] Frei had been one of the communists stranded in Casablanca, following what is called the Fall of France in 1940. Frei then found himself in New York, detained by immigration authorities who threatened to return him to Europe as he did not have a valid entrance visa. Somehow, Kurt Rosenfeld, as Frei wrote, had strong connections to the U.S. Justice Department and was able to wrangle the necessary papers for his passage to Mexico, where Frei claimed he intended to go all along.[19]

Frei became part of the retinue of former Muenzenberg-men under Otto Katz and E. E. Kisch. He contributed to their publications and once produced a radio show on the tenth anniversary of the Reichstag fire Trial.[20] Following the war, Frei did not rejoin his comrades in East Berlin or Prague but resided in Vienna. This is perhaps why his memoir, *Die Papiersaebel*, recalls Heym and Rosenfeld who are elsewhere omitted.[21]

Kurt Rosenfeld

Incidentally, Kurt Rosenfeld is claimed also to have militated to keep dissident communist Gustav Regler out of the U.S.[22] With the outbreak of the war, Rosenfeld founded another newspaper called *The German-American*, a very generic-sounding name for a strictly pro-Soviet screed. The co-founder of the newspaper was the notorious Gerhart Eisler, who had Moscow's authority over American communists as well as the exiles. *The German-American* was run without the *Volksecho* writers, as many party veterans were now at hand. Heym avoided the new paper and no connection between him and Gerhart Eisler is documented even from available government papers.[23]

Rosenfeld was very busy at the forefront of exile politics. He founded the German-American Emergency Conference as a complement to the newspaper in an attempt to create an exile organization that would be able to influence politics in postwar occupied Germany.[24]

He kept in contact with Otto Katz' organization in Mexico and contributed to Katz' *El Libro Negro del Terror Nazi in Europa* and to the Stalinist Mexico City publication *Freies Deutschland*.[25] Rosenfeld, a prominent attorney, was also consulted in a plan to return property to dispossessed Jews. Katz, Kisch, and other Jewish communists had founded a *Tribuna Israelita* and concerned themselves with potential postwar Jewish questions including reparations and a Zionist state.[26]

Rosenfeld is recorded as traveling to Mexico to speak at a Stalinist function and brought back communiqués for Gerhart Eisler.[27] He also attended, apparently as a delegate from Germany, an early United Nations conference in support of Russian war relief.[28] Over one hundred countries were represented at the meeting. Kurt Rosenfeld was in an advantageous position to be a leading postwar figure, but he suddenly died in September 1943 before his more ambitious plans could be realized and is therefore much less renowned now than he might have been.[29]

There is also a provocative anecdote of Rosenfeld's that has never been the subject of analysis. The Army intelligence service did a background check on Stefan Heym and wrote its reports in May 1943, as noted in *Nachruf*. On April 16, 1943 there was a meeting of German Stalinists in New York City. Several people were present, but the only ones named in a published account are Kurt Rosenfeld and F. C. Weiskopf. The revolutionaries were discussing how best to ensure that the next government of Germany would be Stalinist. Someone suggested organizing uprisings by linking with underground groups already in place. Another suggested that America would crush a revolt. Rosenfeld's reply was transcribed by an intelligence service only said to not be the FBI, and so, it is possibly the Army intelligence service investigating Heym. The transcription is as follows:

Rosenfeld: That worry, my friend, certainly is a naive one. It indicates a surprising forgetfulness of Stalin's stature. Do you think for a moment that Roosevelt could do anything that is contrary to Stalin's wishes? Haven't recent events proven that? And if Roosevelt should ever try to oppose Stalin's wishes, you can rest assured Stalin has ways and means to force Roosevelt to respect his wishes. Mark my words.[30]

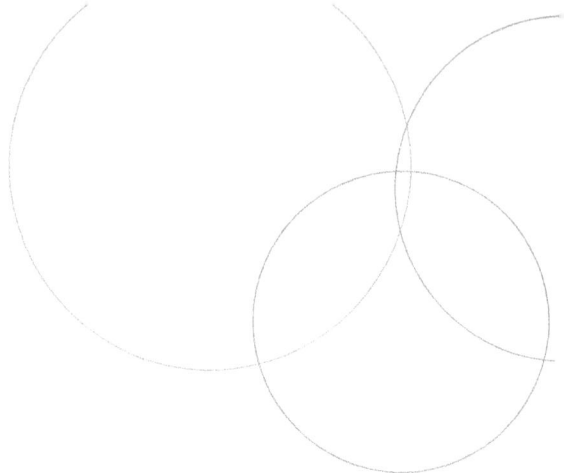

CHAPTER 12

OSTENSIBLY ALOOF

nother curious omission in *Nachruf* is the apparent absence of
contact between Heym and other German communist exiles
from the beginning of the war in 1939 until early 1943 when
Heym entered the Army. Alfred Kantorowicz, Albert Norden, Max
Scheer, Hans Marchwitza, Max Schroeder, Albert Schreiner, Horst
Baerensprung, and Phillip Daub each spent the war years in New York
City.[1] Gustav Regler stayed in the New York area for a time before set-
tling in Mexico, where he became a dissident.[2] Heym's acquaintances
from Prague, Wieland Herzfelde and F.C. Weiskopf, were also in town
for over five years. Weiskopf's apartment at 306 East 15th Street was
literally just around the corner from Heym's apartment at 1 Rutherford Place.[3] Weiskopf had been an editor for Muenzenberg's *Berlin am
Morgen* until 1933 and for Muenzenberg's *Arbeiter Illustrierte Zeitung*
in exile, and also had a by-line in the *Volksecho* more than once.[4]

Egon Kisch, Otto Katz, and their wives lived in the New York area
for approximately a year from 1939 to 1940.[5] According to one source,
Egon Kisch was helped to immigrate by the League of American

Writers.[6] FBI records show Kisch claimed upon his arrival on December 28, 1939 that he was to be guest of former Ambassador William Dodd Sr.[7] Diary excerpts indicate he contacted *Volksecho* writer Oskar Maria Graf, and Reni Begun, wife of *Volksecho* writer Johannes Schroeter, during his first days in the U.S.[8] An associate of Otto Katz noted Kisch, weary from reproach of the Hitler-Stalin Pact, would stop in at F.C. Weiskopf's apartment to catch his breath.[9] Two of his cousins from Prague, Bruno and Guido Kisch, were also in New York in 1939 to 1940.[10] Though there is no explicit mention of a meeting between Egon Kisch and Stefan Heym in New York with the mention of L.A.W., William Dodd, Reni Begun, and F.C. Weiskopf; it is as though Kisch moved with Heym as a reference point.

Otto Katz wrote *J'accuse the Men Who Betrayed France* in New York during this period under yet another pseudonym.[11] Katz' books were not written to impress historians, but attempted to mold or shake the public's convictions at particular points during the era. His sensationalist titles such as *The Nazi Conspiracy in Spain* were written under the pseudonyms of O.K. Simon, Franz Spielhagen, Rudolf Breda, and the name under which he became a Czechoslovakian government official, André Simone.[12] In the United States, Katz was armed with a warm letter of reference from Eleanor Roosevelt on White House stationery, which irritated the FBI.[13] There's an odd anecdote about Mrs. Roosevelt in *Nachruf*. Heym claimed he accidentally crossed paths with her once in Greenwich Village. Mrs. Roosevelt said, "I didn't recognize you," to which Heym rejoindered, "Mrs. Roosevelt, you don't know me."[14]

In October, 1940, Katz and Kisch took their enterprise to Mexico.[15] It is claimed by two sources that Katz made illegal trips to Hollywood to continue forming and organizing party cells.[16] They remained in Mexico for the duration of the war. As at their previous stations, they published journals, held conferences, corresponded with other exile centers, and produced a program for shortwave radio.[17] Katz, Kisch, and other Jewish exiles also became involved in the Zionist movement, an interest that is not discernable in their previous activity. They founded another journal, as mentioned, called the *Tribuna Israelita* [Israeli Tribune] and contributed to the local *Loge Spinoza* yearbook.[18]

Stephen Wise and Nahum Goldmann visited them in Mexico. Eduard Benes, a visiting professor at the University of Chicago during the war, offered Kisch a government post in 1944.[19] Katz had worked for the exiled Czechoslovakian government while in Paris and was a close friend of the projected foreign minister, Vladimir Clementis.[20] Katz and Kisch stopped in New York for two months before sailing to Europe on the *Queen Elizabeth* in 1946.[21] Oddly, fittingly, or both, the ship suffered a serious fire shortly after docking in Southampton, England.[22]

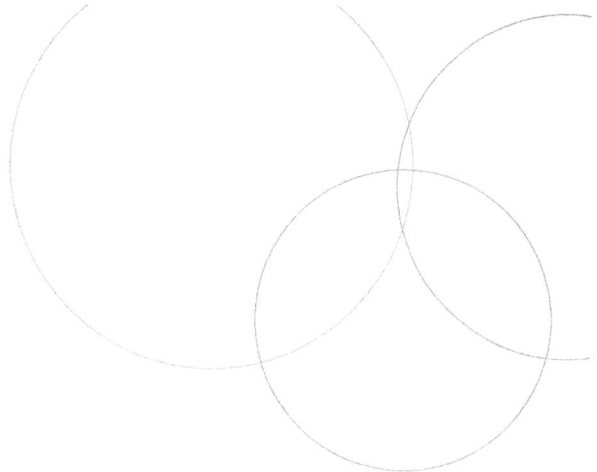

CHAPTER 13

HEYM'S WRITING PROJECTS

U.S. government files notice another project of Stefan Heym's not included in his autobiography. An FBI report states he actively directed a cooperative publishing house of German authors, called Die Tribuene. It was organized in New York in May 1942, perhaps while Heym was finishing his novel, *Hostages*. The FBI files also cite an October 1942 article in the German-Jewish weekly *Aufbau*, which stated that Hollywood director Berthold Viertel hosted an evening in honor of Stefan Heym. The item called the event an evening of the Tribuene. It is also stated that Thomas Mann, Albert Einstein, and Paul Robeson were leaders of the Tribuene's "honorary committee."[1] However, the Tribuene never went beyond its initial meetings.

There was a later cooperative publisher called Aurora Verlag, led by Heym's acquaintance Wieland Herzfelde, which combined the efforts of about a dozen leading exiles. If there was a connection to Heym's prospective firm, it has never been noted. More information on the writing of *Hostages* has been made available due, ironically, to the Army's background check of 1943. *Nachruf* claimed Heym became acquainted with a literary agent named Max Pfeffer, also an exile, who advised Heym to write a novel. Heym is supposed to have told Pfeffer he had never written one before. Pfeffer purportedly replied that it was alright as he'd never sold a novel before.[2]

Army investigators interviewed the agent who sold *Hostages*. His name is yet deleted but one can surmise that it is likely the same agent, Pfeffer, as named in *Nachruf*. Heym's fiduciary took credit for advising Heym to make his story of occupied Prague a novel rather than a play, which, by implication, is how *Hostages* was originally pondered.[3] Also, comments of the Eastern story editor of Paramount Pictures indicate that the studio bought an option on the project at an early stage of its authorship.[4] Heym and Paramount's editor met several times during the writing of the novel to ensure the studio would approve of the plot line. Heym was rewarded as the studio exercised the option for, according to one source, $30,000.[5]

In addition to the pre-completion movie deal, *Hostages* also had other marketing advantages. The U.S. government bought 50,000 copies of the novel to send to military personnel domestically and overseas.[6] The book was excerpted in *Reader's Digest* with its broad respectable middle-class readership.[7] Large ads were taken out in *The New York Times* in October 1942, featuring a rave review by the literary critic from the *Philadelphia Inquirer*. In December 1942, shortly before Heym first reported for military service, he was interviewed by influential publisher Bennett Cerf on radio in New York.[8] *Hostages* also became a radio play on *Treasury Star Parade*, and featured Heym and actor Joseph Schildkraut who had earlier expressed interest in Heym's dramatization of the Hanussen affair. It aired on several occasions in the New York area between March and October 1943 on a variety of stations.[9] It is apparent that a coordinated effort was made to bring *Hostages* to the public on as many media outlets as possible on behalf of the war propaganda campaign.

Heym's memoir notes he met his future wife, Gertrude Gelbin, in 1942 as he was beginning work on *Hostages*. Heym acknowledged she worked for Metro Goldwyn Mayer's publicity department.[10] Further research shows she wrote movie summaries in story form that were syndicated in small markets around the country.[11] One wonders as to the reactions of the impressionable who read her versions of *Pride and Prejudice, Barnacle Bill,* or *We Were Dancing* from 1938 to 1942 when it was later learned in 1953 she had defected behind the Iron Curtain to East Germany. Disarmingly, Heym is candid about Gertrude having been a communist, and even stated she had been in the same party cell as the notable OSS [Office of Strategic Services, the wartime U.S. intelligence agency] agent Joe Gould.[12]

Jurgen Kuczynski, who was, it seemed, a nearly untouchable member of the German underground, could deliver documents to the front door of the Soviet Embassy in Berlin in 1936. He later recruited atomic physicist and spy Klaus Fuchs, knew William Dodd Sr. before he was posted in Berlin, and maintained contact with Martha and William, Jr. for many years after their departures from Berlin.[13] Kuczynski, who became an OSS officer in London during the war, worked with Joe Gould in preparing to send paratroopers as underground agents within Germany once the Normandy invasion succeeded in 1944.[14] Heym's mention of Gould, whose civilian job was, incidentally, as a publicist for United Artists, blatantly dares the reader to notice the pattern of coincidences.

Nachruf also admits that Heym applied to the *Organisation Donovan* [predecessor organization to the CIA], seeking to infiltrate the foreign intelligence agency, apparently before it was even known as the OSS.[15] He was turned away possibly because he wasn't yet an American citizen. The fact was that Heym, whose legal name remained Helmut Flieg until 1943, saw himself as an intelligence agent and not merely an exiled scribe attempting to survive the term of an enemy regime. Like Martha Dodd, he remained a Stalinist for years beyond the defeat of Hitler. For them, anti-Nazism was a convenient guise to make the Stalinist extremists seem like caring liberals. It is reasonable to assume Heym visited the Donovan office on behalf of the same interests that instigated his charade as "Hans Weber."

The success of *Hostages* sent Heym on speaking engagements to Town Hall and Carnegie Hall in New York City, as well as to Boston, Pittsburgh, and a book signing in Chicago.[16] In early February 1943, he was feted at the Czechoslovakian Embassy with a reception hosted by the ambassador's wife, Mme. Vladimir Hurban.[17]

Heym reported for military duty a few days later on February 9, 1943.[18] He could not have yet been sent to a severe boot camp, as on February 15 he spoke to promote concern for Czechoslovakia during United Nations Day conference.[19] Czechoslovakian government minister Jan Papanek was also to speak and the event was carried on local radio station WMCA.[20]

If a "United Nations Day" in 1943 seems premature, do not forget that the international body already existed as a signed document on President Franklin Roosevelt's desk during the war.[21] The United States of America, due partly to Roosevelt who had been president since 1933, never joined the League of Nations [the international diplomatic organization formed after WWI], which became moribund as a result of World War II. Its corporation and properties in Geneva were simply absorbed by the new U.N. organization at the end of hostilities. Many *New York Times* headlines during the war refer to the armies of the U.S., U.K., and U.S.S.R. not as "the Allies" but already as "the United Nations." One can leaf through old issues from 1943 to 1945 and see the term "United Nations" in the headlines nearly every day.[22]

On February 16, 1943, Heym and Mrs. Herbert Lehmann, wife of the New York state governor, spoke at the United Jewish Appeal's Emergency War Campaign at the Biltmore Hotel in Manhattan. This is possibly the earliest event at which Heym appeared on behalf of a Jewish cause.[23] Following the war, Heym and Gertrude Gelbin, who married on March 4, 1944, the same date as the eleventh anniversary of Roosevelt's first inauguration, spoke frequently on behalf of the Jewish Agency.[24]

Other basic biographical details of Gertrude Gelbin include that she was over ten years older than Stefan Heym, having been born in 1900.[25] The FBI noted that the age difference of the couple was less onerous as Heym looked much older than his listed age. Biographical synopses and *Nachruf* state she wrote for magazines under the name "Valerie Stone."[26] She did speak at banquets held by the Jewish Agency under her pseudonym, but one is left wondering where she was actually published in another name than as Gertrude Gelbin.

Heym's mother, as noted in his autobiography, was able to flee to New York in mid 1941 on the last scheduled liner to take Jews out of Germany.[27] Between the time of Heym's father's death in 1936 and 1941, she had remarried. She is referred to as Elsa Primo Flieg Fuchs in FBI documents.[28] Her second husband was a rabbi in Argentina. There is no indication of contact with Heym's step-relatives in the FBI reports. Incidentally, Mrs. Fuchs maiden name, Primo, means "cousin" in Spanish, making her actual name "Cousin Flieg." Apparently, *Nachruf* was not perused by a wide enough Spanish-speaking readership. Though Heym first reported for duty on February 9, 1943, Army records show he wasn't inducted until March, 1943.[29] During his time at Fort Dix, Heym edited the base's newspaper.[30] Gertrude visited him in Fort Monmouth, New Jersey where a childhood friend owned a vacation home directly across from the military facility's entrance.[31] Heym, apparently, challenges the reader to conjecture on the reasons for the apparent serendipity, which one can't help but feel was eerily contrived. Gertrude also visited Heym at Camp Crowder in Missouri in May, 1943.[32]

Heym's memoir refers several times to the background investigation of FBI agents Cody and Robinson in the section devoted to his training for the Army. The investigation recommended Heym not be allowed to serve in military intelligence or have access to secret materials and that he be placed in the category of those suspected of disloyalty or subversive activity.[33]

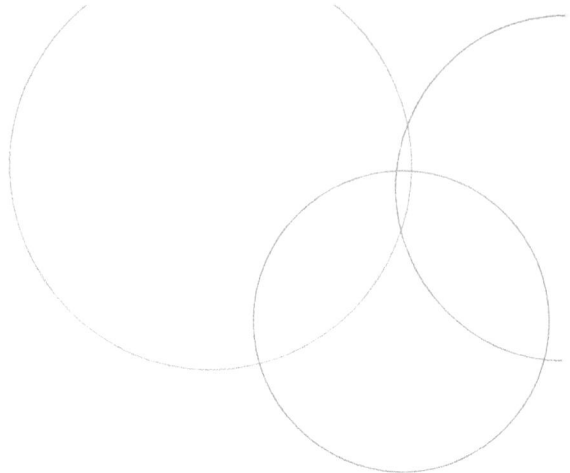

CHAPTER 14

BREDA MOVIE PROPAGANDA

Heym's novel *Hostages* was made into a motion picture in 1943 starring William Bendix and [German-American actress] Luise Rainer. Newspapers had speculated that the [French-American actor] Charles Boyer would star in the film.[1] Lester Cole, then vice president of the Screenwriters Guild, was hired by Paramount to write the screenplay. The assignment could not have been adverse to Cole's status, as he became president of the Screenwriters Guild in 1944.[2] Cole was a communist and in his autobiography, *Hollywood Red*, he claimed the film's director, Frank Tuttle, was also a communist while they were acquainted.[3]

The production of *Hostages* in all its formats—including the 50,000 book copies bought by the government, Paramount's option of the then-uncompleted first novel, and the serialization in *Reader's Digest* — developed as though it was ordered from a very high level of the American hierarchy to promote the war effort. As in most projects of the Roosevelt administration, the number of communists involved seemed to be maximized, rather than minimized.

During the era of the Hollywood blacklist, it was entirely forgotten that Lester Cole had been hired to write the screenplay for FDR's personally commissioned *President's Mystery* (1936) during his first term in office.[4] It is a telling, if ignored, coincidence that Cole's ex-wife became the spouse in 1984 of Alger Hiss [the American government official accused in 1948 of spying for the Soviets during the 1930s].[5]

One of the characters in both the novel and the film *Hostages* is named "Breda." The character, as one could guess, is one of the heroic local resistance fighters in the plot. Otto Katz, who also used the same name in Hollywood as an alias, was also born and raised in Prague.[6] *Hostages* therefore also served to extend the "Breda" fiction from communist *agitprop* [political propaganda] to mainstream wartime propaganda. It was put over on the public with such coordination of efforts as though it had been planned so, including complicity with Stalinist agents, all along. There was also a character named "Reinhardt" in the story; this was the alias used by an assistant to Otto Katz named Alexander Abusch. It was also used, with a slightly different spelling, as the same surname of an FBI agent who became familiar to Louis Gibarti during the *Volksecho* period.[7]

Watch on the Rhine was also one of the propaganda films of 1943. It starred Paul Lukacs as a brave resistance hero seeking support in Washington but meeting instead threats from Nazis in the American capital. It is now known that the author, Lillian Hellman, based the character on Otto Katz, whom she knew, and his "Breda" charade.[8] Lukacs won the Academy Award for Best Actor, and additionally played "Reinhardt" in *Hostages*, as if cast to infuse more of Katz' presence on the screen. Further, there was also a character of a small boy named "Bodo" in *Watch on the Rhine*. Coincidentally, the German communist writer Bodo Uhse stayed with Otto Katz in Los Angeles during 1939. Doubtlessly, the character name was some sort of inside joke among the Stalinists. Uhse moved to Mexico in 1940 and actually wrote an article on Stefan Heym in 1943 for *Freies Deutschland*, a publication founded and managed by Otto Katz.[9]

Hangmen Also Die opened on theater screens about two months before *Hostages* was released. Both stories are about the resistance to the German occupation of Prague. Bertolt Brecht wrote the screenplay and Fritz Lang directed *Hangmen Also Die*. Otto Katz once wrote a letter to Fritz Lang thanking him for loaning Brecht $80 per month while Brecht was awaiting Hollywood offers.[10] Brecht and Katz were good friends, likely from the Weimar era when Katz was manager of Erwin Piscator's theater and a Soviet film executive. They are said to have shared a mutual cynicism and a fascination with the power of lies.[11] While Katz played a confidence game as "Breda," Brecht upset Americans by saying "the more innocent they are, the more they deserve to be shot," referring to Moscow's purge victims. Letters of Brecht to Katz have also been published. Katz, to whom communists turned to for financial help, made the travel arrangements for Brecht's return to Berlin and helped him recover his Czechoslovakian royalties at the end of the war.[12] One wonders whether Katz had anything to do with the pairing of Lang and Brecht.

Artistically, *Hostages* was rather undistinguished. It is notable for having been Luise Rainer's last film. Rainer, born in Vienna in 1909, won the Academy Award for Best Actress in 1936 and 1937 but hadn't appeared in any films from 1938 until *Hostages* in 1943. After, she made no other films but appeared occasionally on television. Astoundingly, she again appeared in movies released in 1997 and 2003.[13]

Hostages also seems to have been produced in conjunction with two much better known films in 1943 that were also attempts to influence political opinion toward the left, namely *Mission to Moscow* and *For Whom the Bell Tolls*. Actors Michael Visaroff, George Sorel, and Leonid Snegoff appeared in all three films. Altogether, eleven of the cast of *Hostages* appeared in *Mission to Moscow*, which came under scrutiny following the war for embracing Stalinism. The names of the other eight actors were Louis V. Arco, Ivan Triesault (his film debut), Richard Ryen, Noel Cravat, Marie Melish, Peter Michael, Felix Basch, and Brecht's cohort Oskar Homolka. Eight of the cast of *Hostages* appeared in the adaptation of Hemingway's *For Whom the Bell Tolls*.

The remaining five were Eric Feldary, Michael Rasumny, Arturo De Cordova ("Breda" in *Hostages*), John Mylong, and Katina Paxinou who won the Academy Award for Best Supporting Actress in her film debut at age forty-three.[14]

Additionally, eight of the cast appeared in *Hangmen Also Die*, seven appeared in the adaptation of Anna Seghers' *The Seventh Cross*, six of the cast appeared in *The North Star* (1943), another film that attracted Congressional investigation. Six of the cast of *Hostages* appeared in *The Mask of Dimitrios* (1944), which was not war propaganda but did feature Katz and Kisch friend, Peter Lorre, and FDR's daughter-in-law, Faye Emerson.[15] Twelve of the cast also appeared in *Action in the North Atlantic* (1943), though all in uncredited bit roles.[16] With so much of Paramount's wartime output connected with open members of the KPD and CPUSA, who can blame HUAC for investigating?

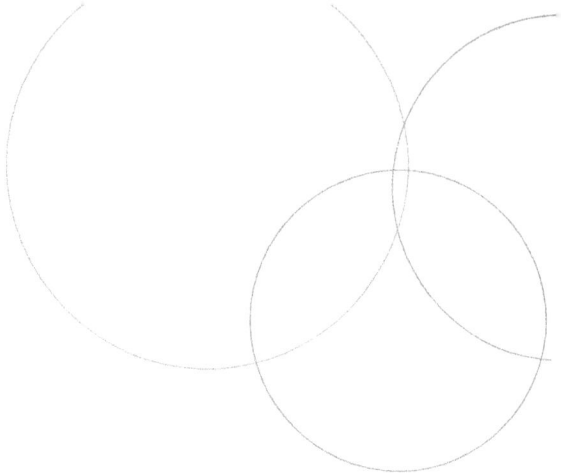

CHAPTER 15

WRITING DURING ACTIVE SERVICE

Stefan Heym was able to write two more short novels before the invasion of France in June 1944. As described in *Nachruf*, his *No Turnpike Gates* was not actually published, because the lead character's similarity to Clare Booth Luce caused the publisher to fear a libel suit. Orville Prescott of *The New York Times* evaluated the manuscript, which caused an effective halt to the story's printing.[1] Somehow, the *Times* printed a notice of Heym's upcoming second novel mentioning the title and giving a brief summary of the plot.[2] Presumably, the item was written before the project was shelved. Of course, a conflict between Stefan Heym and Clare Booth Luce would have been typical of the Cold War period, which was inevitable following the defeat of the Axis.

His next novel, *Of Smiling Peace*, reached the publishing house shortly before D-Day. It depicts intrigue in North Africa where American forces had landed in fall 1942. It failed to receive as much praise as *Hostages* had. It was reviewed in *The New York Times* in October

1944, which was obviously a high point of U.S. involvement in World War II.[3]

The communist Germans in Mexico City attempted to publish one of Heym's novels through their own publishing firm called El Libro Libre. The U.S. censorship office, which apparently read most of the letters sent from Mexico to the U.S. during the war, found a leaflet of June 1943 that listed Stefan Heym as one of the prospective authors of El Libro Libre.[4] Another letter of December 1943 noted eight books that were ready for publication in Spanish, including one by Stefan Heym.[5] However, a May 1944 FBI report from San Francisco noted that a confidential source advised that El Libro Libre found it impossible to publish Heym's book.[6]

Another development in his literary career during the war itself was that an article he wrote appeared in the November 1944 issue of *Freies Deutschland* in Mexico.[7] His own byline as "Sgt. Stefan Heym" was printed in the September 10, 1944 and December 3, 1944 issues of *The New York Times*.[8] The two articles, as others of his next few *Times* contributions, appeared in the Sunday supplement magazine section. The second article, titled "The Germans Hear a New Masters Voice," referred to Germans as "a spineless people who know no law except force."[9]

Heym's next *Times* article was published in the January 20, 1946 issue of the Sunday magazine and titled "But the Hitler Legend Isn't Dead."[10] The issue of how a legend could possibly be a threat to the Allies, who controlled the entirety of military force, against a spineless people, is, of course, not explained. At this point, Heym had only four weeks earlier ended his brief term as editor of the official newspaper of the U.S. occupation called *Neues Zeitung*. Heym claimed that his superior, a Colonel Powell, is supposed, by happenstance, to have been a friend of the *New York Times'* publisher.[11] Colonel Powell is purported to have sent Heym to be introduced to the executive. This doesn't explain his articles published in 1944 or his earlier appearances on radio station WQXR, which was managed by a relative of the same family that owned the *Times* and was later acquired by the newspaper.

It's not possible to ignore that the title of his memoir, *Nachruf*, is a reference to his own listing in the obituary file of *The New York Times*. Heym reemerged on the pages of the *Times* again in the 1970s, as though he had stayed in touch with, or at least was remembered by, the editorship.

Heym's military service in the Army's department of psychological warfare brought him in contact with two other well-known writers, Hans Habe and Peter Wyden. Habe, born Janos Bekessy, of Hungarian-Jewish ancestry, was a journalist in Vienna, and fled Germany's annexation [of Austria] in 1938.[12] His father, Imre Bekessy, founded the Viennese journals *Die Borse, Buehne,* and *Die Stunde.*[13] Imre Bekessy had an unsavory reputation as a blackmailer who extorted bribes in exchange for suppressing information that was unfavorable to business concerns.[14] As a twenty-year-old, Habe made news in being the first to note that Hitler's father's name had actually been Schicklgruber.[15]

Habe first met Heym at what Habe called a "hush hush camp" in Maryland.[16] Heym mentioned Maryland only to say he had been married there without giving away that he had undergone training.[17] Their personalities clashed, and Habe later wrote a couple of unflattering anecdotes on his subordinate, which were not of a directly political nature.[18] In the postwar era, Habe founded over a dozen West German newspapers.[19] The stature of his accomplishment depends on one's assessment of the quality of journalism in the BRD [*Bundesrepublik Deutschland*, meaning West Germany].

Habe also wrote dozens of novels and has several postwar film credits for stories and screenplays. Politically, he was openly much more conservative than the majority of exiles who worked for the U.S. authorities. Peter Wyden (1923–1998), born Weidenreich in Berlin, was a more sympathetic companion for Stefan Heym. He also became a successful author with over a dozen titles and one movie credit. Wyden's *Stella* contains a photo of Heym, Wyden, and Habe together in uniform while in the U.S. Army.[20] Wyden's comments regarding

Heym are polite and diplomatic. In 2006, his son, Ron Wyden, is a U.S. Senator representing Oregon.

A lingering complaint against Heym, although it isn't even widely written about in Germany itself, is that he broadcast executions as a tactic to intimidate the German populace. The charge was made in print as recently as 2001.[21] The victims were alleged to have been German spies. Such topics do not receive much attention when the victims were on the side of the Axis and the perpetrators were Allied supporters. For example, the postwar purges in France and Italy, where there were over 100,000 killed in supposed revenge, remain a taboo subject except for the familiar scenes of women forced to have their heads shaved for having been consorts of Germans. Those scenes are even more disturbing when one discovers that the hard truth is far bloodier.[22]

An issue that has been dormant for half a century involves FBI comments concerning an alleged Army associate of Stefan Heym, named Walter Schoenstedt. Not mentioned in *Nachruf*, Schoenstedt had been active for the KPD in literary and political affairs in Prague, Paris, and New York.[23] The FBI expressed its suspicions of Schoenstedt in the endnotes of the transcript of the statement by Helen Konieczny, as follows:

> Schoenstedt was given an Army commission despite a derogatory report from the FBI. During the war, he sought and obtained one of the most sensitive positions in the Pentagon, namely in the office for Psychological Warfare. As a result, Schoenstedt succeeded in placing approximately half a dozen former secret German Communists in key spots in General Omar Bradley's 12th Army Group Psychological Warfare unit. These men — some of whom have since been publicly exposed by Congressman George Dondero — after the German surrender obtained *the* key spots in directing our American propaganda organs (newspapers, magazines, and radio) to influence the German people. It has

been stated on the floor of Congress that the blame for turning a large portion of the German public opinion against the United States and making them ripe for Russian propaganda was due to the 'ineptitude' of the American propaganda media referred to above. One of these officers was the Stefan Heym mentioned previously by Mrs. Dobos in her testimony.[24]

Schoenstedt (b.1909) had been a prototypical working class writer who had published novels during the 1930s while he was in his twenties. Editions du Carrefour published his *Auf der Flucht Erschossen*, one of the more sensational anti-Nazi works of 1934.[25] Alexander Abusch noted Schoenstedt accompanying Egon Kisch in Paris and described his bearing as that of an "Adjutant."[26] Two other novels, *The Cradle Builder* and *In Praise of Life,* were published in English by 1940.[27] The KPD archives show he was at a party meeting in New York in 1939.[28]

Klaus and Erika Mann, who were fellow travelers but not altogether uncritically, recalled staying at the same hotel in Manhattan as Schoenstedt and crossing paths on the way to speaking engagements in the Midwest.[29] Schoenstedt appeared in secondary towns such as Oshkosh, Wisconsin and Lowell, Massachusetts as well as Chicago and Cleveland from 1938 to 1940. He was accused in print of using his public forums for peddling worthless bonds with the proceeds sent on to the Communist Party.[30] There has been absolutely no analysis of his activities or service in the Army in histories of the era, despite a supposed hysteria concerning communist infiltration.

While in the U.S., Schoenstedt married Christine Grauthoff, an actress who was the widow of Ernst Toller and daughter of the German translator of Romain Rolland [a noted French novelist].[31] He stayed on in the U.S. following the war but simply vanished at some point in the early 1950s.[32] One supposes the disappearance was under communist aegis, as they never complained that Schoenstedt had vanished and they published new editions of some of his works in the 1970s, indicating he was not in disfavor.[33] Whether he was a purged agent who was rehabilitated following the death of Stalin, or continued his life secretly behind the Iron Curtain or under a new identity elsewhere, is simply not anywhere disclosed.

It should be noted that the single statement in the FBI files that Heym and Schoenstedt served together is not definite proof that the two were in contact. Schoenstedt's story is, however, interesting enough to mention in any case. Another question worth considering is that since Heym and Schoenstedt belonged to the same conspiracy, can they be considered collaborators even if they never met?

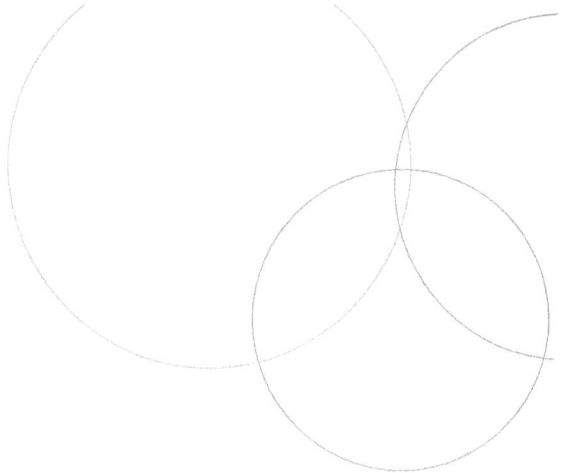

CHAPTER 16

OCCUPATION EDITOR

Following the conclusion of the war, Stefan Heym became editor of the American military's official German-language newspaper, the *Neues Zeitung*. The publication, which in its initial stage was printed twice per week, used the same facilities as the Nazis' *Volkische Beobachter*, which somehow had not been bombed.[1] The first issue appeared in October 1945 though the war had ended in May. The front page of the debut issue features a column by Stefan Heym titled "Der eigene Magen" [Your Own Tummy] beginning on the upper left corner, while General Dwight David Eisenhower's statement on the purpose of the new publication is centered, lower on the page.[2] Heym's association with the *Neues Zeitung* lasted only until December. The U.S. authorities discharged him for refusing to be critical of the U.S.S.R., as noted in *Nachruf*.[3]

For his approximately ten week tenure, Heym had a regular column, "Weltpolitische Rundschau," [Panorama of World Politics] that gave him a forum to comment on the many regime changes taking place in Europe and beyond. His only openly pro-Soviet statement occurred in the November 4 issue when he appealed for understanding for Stalin's Russia. A page one article in the same issue was titled "Vorwarts und nicht Vergessen," [Forward and Do Not Forget], recalling a Bertolt Brecht stanza from the Weimar era. The conflict that led to Heym's dismissal may have already been brewing, as his column did not appear in two issues during that month.[4]

Heym once took a position on the postwar Palestine question not in his own words but by quoting an article from the *London Times* that called for a "middle way" between Palestinians and Jews. It also stated that the matter was no longer for the British to administrate but for the U.N.[5] The term "middle way" seems too vague to mean anything specific. Somewhat surprising is that a British paper was already calling for Britain to unilaterally relinquish its control over such an important matter.

Heym's indifference to non-Jewish German refugees was shown by dryly citing the statement of Czech minister Fierlinger that 3,000,000 Germans were expected to be deported from their native regions. Heym also reported on elections held by Soviet authorities in Konigsberg and Tilsit without any criticism, as well as without noting that the few remaining Germans in East Prussia were being mistreated and forced to flee.[6] The Americans' "White List" of acceptable German authors was printed in the *Neues Zeitung* during Heym's brief term as chief editor.[7]

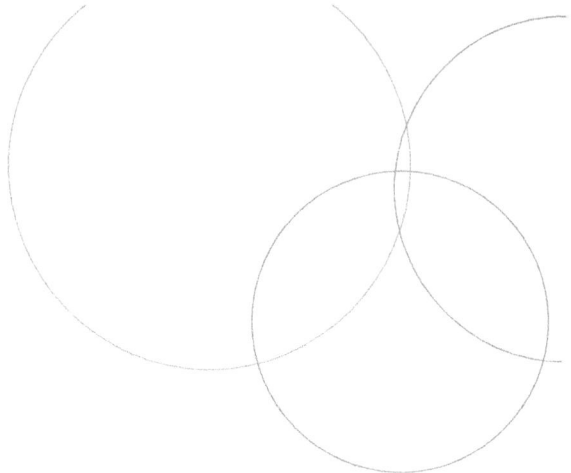

CHAPTER 17

DEMISSION, NEW YORK, MEXICO, RETURN TO PRAGUE 1945-1949

H eym left the U.S. military in late December, 1945. The conference with Colonel Julius Ochs Adler probably occurred in January 1946.[1] The meeting resulted in Heym's next articles for *The New York Times*. The first was in print by the end of the month. Heym then traveled to Mexico to catch up with his wife who had gone there on a trip, likely as part of some sort of matter of party networking.[2] In surprising candor, Heym admitted meeting Paul Merker, the top KPD official in Mexico. Merker, like Katz, Kisch, Abusch, and many other leftist exiles, waited until 1946 to return to the ruins of Europe.[3] In Cuernavaca, Heym met Alvah Bessie, the screenwriter who later became one of the Hollywood Ten [a group of ten Hollywood producers, and screenwriters who refused to answer questions about their political activities before HUAC in 1947].[4]

Cuernavaca had a burgeoning celebrity scene in the late 1940s and 1950s. As noted earlier, the Dodds were building a home there, and several Hollywood starlets and the O'Dwyers had their divorces decided there. Burt Lancaster and Gary Cooper were in Cuernavaca for the shooting of *Vera Cruz* (1954). The area was already popular with the German communist exiles during the war. Some sort of continuity may be evident from the meeting between Heym and Bessie. Whatever was going on, it has been overlooked by the fourth estate and cultural historians, as though the topic itself has been blacklisted.[5]

Heym may or may not have truthfully omitted a meeting with the Kisches and Katzes if their paths crossed on Heym's voyage to Mexico and if Heym's return to New York was not in time for the sailing of the *Queen Elizabeth*. If no meeting occurred, it was likely scheduled. The meeting with Paul Merker cited above is described in *Nachruf* as though Heym had little time for him, perhaps insultingly to Merker's memory who, as a non-Jew, suffered persecution for being overly friendly with Zionists such as Katz/Simone. Merker was almost certainly the sender of missives from the KPD-Paris to the KPD-New York, which were signed "PM." In the Weimar era [1918–1933], Merker had actually been in the U.S. for three years on a Comintern mission during which he also held blue collar jobs.[6]

Upon return to the U.S., Heym began writing his army novel, *The Crusaders*, and toured the country with his wife Gertrude Gelbin as banquet speakers for the United Jewish Appeal (UJA).[7] *Nachruf* reports that Gertrude, under her pseudonym Valerie Stone, represented herself as having worked for the United Nations during its early stages when it was housed in Flushing, New York on the grounds of the 1939 World's Fair. No definite time period was mentioned for her employment in the U.N. photograph department.[8]

It is very likely that Gertrude Gelbin was hired at the United Nations by Alger Hiss or an appointee of his. Hiss assumed broad powers at the State Department in August 1945. He drafted his own office charter with the title "Director of State Department's Office of

Special Political Affairs."[9] Included under his authority was control over 13,000 employees of wartime agencies and American personnel at the United Nations.[10] It is known that the Hiss office sent the U.N. Secretary General lists of qualified applicants in March and April 1946, and that the U.N. complained that an overabundance of communists had been recommended.[11] No thorough investigation was ever done however, making it impossible to determine the degree of Hiss' responsibility.

The Tydings Subcommittee once promised Senator Joseph McCarthy's committee to discover who had hired communist Gustavo Durán at the U.N., but never reported back.[12] The State Department took more than two years to report to the U.N. on the questionable hirings, and CPUSA operatives were kept on for months beyond receipt of negative assessments.[13] Therefore, despite accusations of anti-communist hysteria in the U.S., no one has examined Hiss' hiring record for the period when he held broad powers at the U.S. State Department. Also, Joseph McCarthy's alleged claim of 200 communists at the State Department was likely accurate, if not an underestimate, during 1945 and 1946.

Nachruf reports that Gertrude Gelbin used her position at the U.N. to take up the cause of Greek revolutionary Markos Vafiadis. She wrote an article on Markos, as he was referred to, which she intended to illustrate with her inventory from the U.N. photo office. The article was not published, and Heym describes the episode as though he can't fathom the rejection of communist hero worship. The intended title of Gelbin/Stone's piece was to be "Mission to Markos," an obvious allusion to Paramount's film, *Mission to Moscow* (1943).[14]

In addition to writing *The Crusaders* and working for the UJA, Heym became a public political activist in the postwar era. A leftist gathering at the Henry Hudson Hotel to denounce the Case Bill made page three of the *New York Times* in 1946. Heym and former *Volksecho* columnist Johannes Steele were among the featured speakers.[15] In October, Heym led an "action committee" to attempt to wrest control of the writers' guild on behalf of the radicals.[16] It was reported that

Heym's group succeeded in a legal proceeding to force the entrenched interests to open its minutes from the previous year, but then Heym's involvement seems to have discontinued.[17]

Howard Rushmore, then of the *New York Journal American*, devoted a column to denouncing Stefan Heym and called his committee an attempt to communize literature in America.[18] The attack by Rushmore seems to have been the most vehement criticism Heym suffered in the English language press during his years in the United States.

Heym's friend Alfred Stern gained a few days of news coverage early in the following year with his march or train ride to the New York State capital in Albany.[19] An emergency detachment of state troopers surrounded the legislature to provide security while Stern attended the session of representatives. Stern was suddenly depicted as one who could bring state affairs to a halt, but then disappeared from news coverage just as quickly.

The various [Congressional] committees investigating communism never focused on Heym, except for their records that showed his leftist affiliations. His name did not come up in any of the era's trials or hearings while he was in the U.S. His war novel, *The Crusaders,* was able to become a bestseller as his name was not seriously besmirched. It can be claimed that it was the third most popular war novel of the late 1940s, behind Norman Mailer's *The Naked and the Dead* and Irwin Shaw's *The Young Lions.*[20] Therefore, Stefan Heym, who beyond the 1960s was much more well known in Germany than in the United States, actually enjoyed extraordinary success in a country experiencing an unprecedented economic boom following an unprecedented victory in warfare.

There is a telling historical reference in *The Crusaders* that may have escaped the casual reader. The character named "Dondolo," even as noted in *Nachruf*, is certainly due to Doge Dondolo of Venice who led the Fourth Crusade. In 1204, Dondolo and his entourage invaded Constantinople rather than combat Muslims. The crusade, though a disaster for Greece and the Eastern Roman Empire, was a success for Dondolo of Venice. The name was used in European pop songs including the top hit in Italy in the early 1960s, "Guarda como Dondolo."[21] A direct connection to Heym's novel is, of course, impossible to determine.

From what is available in FBI records, Heym did not appear in public in 1948. Only one slight mention notes that his name appeared in the *Daily Worker* among 102 signatories to a protest petition against the arrest of communist writer Pablo Neruda.[22] Ironically, Neruda is only mentioned once in a later section of Heym's memoir in a deprecating manner, as Heym expressed suspicion Neruda wanted to steal his new Swiss typewriter.

In 1951, Heym's name was volunteered to Hoover's agency by Louis Budenz, who had earlier been an effective prosecution witness. Budenz stated that he knew Heym was a member of the Communist Party in 1943. Budenz had been editor of the *Daily Worker* until he quit the CPUSA in 1945.[23] Budenz claimed that the CPUSA's leading cultural commissars, V.J. Jerome and Alexander Trachtenberg — a pair Stephen Koch referred to as "Gibarti's men" in *Double Lives*— told Budenz that Heym was a communist on several occasions in discussions from 1943 to 1945.[24] As editor of the party's newspaper, Budenz had to be informed on such matters. It is worth noting that by 1951, Heym had already emigrated from the U.S. and Budenz' only book on his experiences as a former communist was published a year earlier. Time has shown Budenz to have been a truthful informant. His testimony helped convict Jerome and Trachtenberg in a sedition trial, which was sometimes a front page story in the following year.[25] Interestingly, the documents on which Budenz is mentioned in Heym's file are stamped "unclassified" as of 1982. Hypothetically, any researcher could have revealed that Budenz informed on Heym since then. As stated in *Nachruf*, Heym requested and received his FBI file, but Budenz is not mentioned in the memoir. Heym did claim to have come to the McCarthy committee's attention, which is supposed to have ruined the chance of a film adaptation of *The Crusaders* by MGM.[26] The assertion is not verified by the information declassified by the FBI, which, to be clear, is not the entirety of the information collected by the government.

The Heyms' voyage to Europe in 1948 to 1949 attracted the curiosity of the Federal police who investigated passport and ship records when they learned of the couple's departure. The prosaic facts discovered were that Heym and Gelbin departed on the *S.S. Veendam* in November 1948 and returned on a French liner, the *S.S. De Grasse*, in April 1949.[27]

The reasons for the journey were connected to the important events of 1948: the coup in Czechoslovakia, the establishment of a Zionist state in Palestine, and possibly also to the increasing scrutiny of the communist movement in the U.S. The Hiss-Chambers conflict began with Chambers' August 1948 testimony before Richard Nixon and the House Un-American Activities Committee. Upon disembarking in Holland, the Heyms boarded a train for Prague via Nuremberg. Behind the Iron Curtain, Heym met with Czech officials including Otto Katz, no longer calling himself "Rudolf Breda" but now "André Simone," the foreign editor for the country's leading newspaper.[28]

According to the memoir narrative, Heym and Katz/Simone didn't know each other. Even the connections already admitted between the two — the friendship with Egon Kisch and the telegram sent upon the debut of the *Deutsches Volksecho* — are not mentioned. One is supposed to accept, it seems, that Heym traveled from America to Prague for appointments with people he didn't know. Egon Kisch had become deceased in March 1948. Noel Field and thousands of local residents attended the funeral in early April for Kisch, who is described, erroneously, as having been postwar Mayor of Prague in at least three books.[29] Some observers joked that he wasn't really gone but was hiding nearby, observing the entire ceremony.[30] The procession for Kisch occurred between the funerals of Jan Masaryk in March and Eduard Benes in September, perhaps the most notable burials held in Prague during the 20th century.

Following the visit to Katz/Simone, Heym traveled to Palestine via Paris and Marseille. Oddly, Heym noted that he thought he saw Leo

Bauer, his old friend from Zionist studies in Chemnitz, on the docks of Marseille leading a group of interested followers.[31] The book by Brandt *et al*, *Karrieren Eines Aussenseiters,* notes that Bauer was sent in the summer of 1948 to the Tatra Mountains to further recover from a car accident, but does not note an additional trip to Prague or Marseille.[32] Wolfgang Kiessling's book, *Partner in "Narrenparadies"*, noted Bauer made a trip to Prague in September 1948 and met with Otto Katz/ André Simone, Gisela Kisch, and Noel Field, but does not mention a journey to Marseille.[33]

A stop in Marseille evokes the activities of Noel Field who made many trips there, partly to help fleeing communists during the early years of the war. Marseille was also claimed to have been an early secret base for Zionist agents, according to one source.[34] The coincidences of meetings with Katz/Simone and crossing paths in Marseille suggest that Heym, Bauer, and Otto Katz collaborated on some sort of covert operation that has not been revealed publicly. Incidentally, when Bauer's wife gave birth to a son in May 1950, he was named André for André Simone.[35]

From Marseille, Heym sailed to Palestine for a stay and then returned to Prague. In Prague, he reported again to Otto Katz, who is disingenuously chided in the narrative for being overly sentimental about the idea of a Jewish state.[36] Heym's trip to the Levant was made as if it had a connection to the Zionist activities begun by Katz and Kisch in Mexico during the war. The Czechoslovakian government had been crucial in supplying Israel with its early makeshift Air Force. Vladimir Clementis, a Jewish cabinet minister who was a friend of Katz' before the war, is claimed to have been instrumental in providing air support.[37] One source also states that Czechoslovakia bought planes from Mexico during the early postwar period.[38] The Czechoslovakian communists with the closest ties to prominent Mexicans were Otto Katz and Egon Kisch.[39] Likely, Heym's voyage from the U.S. to Prague to Marseille to Palestine to Prague was intertwined with Katz' role in the momentous events of 1948.

In 1952, during the Noel Field purges, Otto Katz was hanged for charges that included having been a Zionist spy.[40] Heym noted his arrest and execution rather coolly in his autobiography.[41] Heym remained safe from accusation despite having known Katz. "S.H" had never met Noel Field, not even when Field traveled to Mexico to say hello to the Kisches following World War II.[42] As stated earlier, Gisela Kisch knew all the controversial figures and was never arrested.[43]

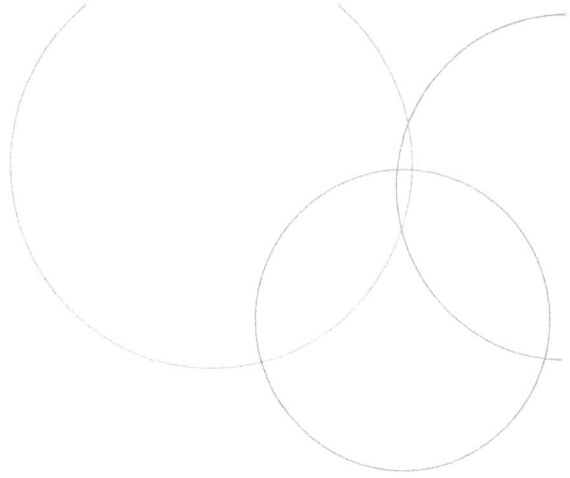

POLITICAL ACTIVITY IN NEW YORK 1949 AND DEPARTURE 1950, A MENDACIOUS DESCRIPTION

Stefan Heym and Gertrude Gelbin missed the Scientific and Cultural Conference for World Peace arranged by the National Council of the Arts, Sciences and Professions, held at the Waldorf-Astoria Hotel in New York City on March 25, 26 and 27, 1949.[1] The couple arrived a day later than the publication of the HUAC report on the conference.[2] The report consists mostly of lists of Soviet-front committees to which sponsors of the event were affiliated. Stefan Heym was among the 288 names of communists and fellow travelers listed, together with Lester Cole, Martha Dodd, Alfred Stern, and Johannes Steele.[3] Alexander Fadayev, the General Secretary of the Union of Soviet Writers was a featured speaker.[4] Among the organizations of which Heym was listed as a member were the "American League for

Peace and Democracy," and "Supporters of Communist Bookshops;" and the publications *New Masses*, *Mainstream*, and a publication of former servicemen called *Salute*.[5] HUAC's pamphlet missed or omitted Heym's participation in earlier May Day parades.[6]

In August 1948, Louis Budenz testified before HUAC, which included Representative Richard M. Nixon, that the National Council of Arts, Sciences and Professions grew out of the Independent Citizens Committee of the Arts, Sciences and Professions, which had been formulated at Budenz' own office at the *Daily Worker*.[7] The name of the group was changed in 1946 when its chairman Harold Ickes, a familiar face at the Roosevelt White House, resigned, belatedly admitting it was a communist front.[8]

Stefan Heym's 1946 opposition to the Case Bill was expressed through a New York committee of the same organization. Heym spoke at a February 1950 meeting of the National Committee of the Arts, Sciences and Professions, held at Carnegie Hall.[9] The gathering was billed as a "rally against the H-Bomb." Heym is reported as having posed the question whether "we," "should follow a 'bomb policy' or a 'peace policy.'"[10] In April 1950, Stefan Heym was named Chairman of the Arts, and hence, one of the organization's top three executives.[11] The FBI was informed later in the year that Heym was listed as one of the chairmen on the committee's letterhead.[12]

The Conference for World Peace [1949] was one of the major events of its type and received press coverage around the world.[13] Heym's appointment to chairman indicates his power and prestige within the Communist Party. His appointment also maintained an indirect continuity to the Muenzenberg conferences of the 1920s and 1930s because of Heym's association with Louis Gibarti, not to mention Leo Flieg. Other celebrity artists and intellectuals who HUAC listed as being affiliated with the Independent Citizens Committee of the Arts, Sciences and Professions were Leonard Bernstein, Aaron Copland, Albert Einstein, Howard Fast, Lillian Hellman, John Howard Lawson, Ring Lardner, Langston Hughes, Thomas Mann, Donald Ogden Stewart, Paul Robeson, Linus Pauling, Max Weber, Artie Shaw, and Dalton Trumbo.[14] *Nachruf* acknowledged Heym's having been voted into the executive of the organization, but didn't explain how prominent the National Committee of the Arts, Sciences and Professions was at the time.[15]

The FBI noted that Heym signed an appeal for attendance at a Continental Congress for Peace, which was held in Mexico City in September, 1949.[16] Heym describes himself as participating in conferences for scholastic and artistic freedom as well as a conference against censorship following his return from Prague.[17] Heym recalled being on a stage in Philadelphia with writer Cliff Odets at a forum to discuss culture.[18] Odets was first husband of *Hostages'* star Luise Rainer, while her second husband, Robert Knittel, helped prepare *The Crusaders* for publication.[19]

The FBI also recorded that Heym signed an appeal in support of a "Bill of Rights conference" printed in *Worker*, the Sunday edition of the *Daily Worker*, in July 1949.[20] According to the FBI's information, Heym signed a petition in support of Hollywood Ten defendants John Howard Lawson and Dalton Trumbo. This may be the instance described in *Nachruf* where Heym protested that his name was used without his permission, implicating the supporters of Lawson and Trumbo with a novel twist.[21] The FBI also has Heym as a member of the Citizens Against the Feinberg Law Committee.[22] The Feinberg Law was a legislative attempt to bar communists from teaching in New York schools.

The FBI obtained an interesting non-public detail written in a report of 1952. Heym and Gertrude Gelbin were registered with the American Labor Party in 1949.[23] Therefore, Stefan Heym was not as careful in maintaining an independent status as he often claimed. Support of the American Labor Party is still entirely consistent with being a communist. Vito Marcantonio, the openly communist congressman, was elected solely on the American Labor Party ticket in 1948. In New York, the CPUSA was known to publicly throw its support to the American Labor Party just before election day.[24]

Heym's notoriety was amplified when the now-overlooked New York City daily, *The Daily Compass*, went into print during May 1949[25]

The emergence of *The Daily Compass* followed the demise of the daily *PM*, in publication from June 1940 to June 1948, and the *New York Star*, which existed from July 1948 to January 1949. All three newspapers — *PM, New York Star,* and *The Daily Compass* —were printed daily, except Saturday.[26] A veteran leftist muckraker, I.F. Stone, was editor of *The Daily Compass* and had been on the staff of *PM*.[27] The slogan of *The Daily Compass* was "a crusader for the truth." The newspaper's first issue included the first installment of the serialization of Stefan Heym's *The Crusaders*. *The Daily Compass* lasted only a few years, but its inception seemed to identify itself with Heym's novel, a rather unique distinction.[28] Heym had already left the United States when *The Daily Compass* discontinued publication in November 1952.

The October 1949 issue of the anti-communist periodical *Counterattack* criticized Gimbel's department store for featuring Heym's *The Crusaders* in a large ad.[29] In June 1949, the State Department had notified the U.S. Embassy in London that Heym was a suspected Comintern agent.[30] The timing is odd, as Heym had returned from his trip to Prague and Palestine in April 1949. There is no record that Heym had been to England previously, with the possible exception of a brief stay before the invasion of Normandy.

Heym attended a June 1950 going-away party for Lawson and Trumbo and included the event in his memoir.[31] The celebration may have secretly been for Heym as well. He and Gertrude Gelbin flew to Europe in late July or early August 1950. FBI records show that his passport, due to expire in late August, was renewed at the embassy in Paris on August 3, 1950.[32] Hoover's men discovered that Heym ordered his furniture from his Manhattan apartment be placed in storage in September 1950.[33] Heym and Gelbin whiled for a time, which in the narrative seems like months, in Paris and Bern, Switzerland, ostensibly waiting for permission from the Soviet Embassy to travel beyond the Iron Curtain.[34]

In Chapter 23 of *Nachruf*, the Heyms were in Warsaw; their first stop in the East Bloc. Heym attended and delivered a speech at the Second World Conference for Peace. The CPUSA's delegate to the meeting was George Lohr, the first person to whom Heym reported when he arrived in New York to accept his position at the *Deutsches Volksecho.* Heym presents his reunion with Lohr as mere happenstance.[35]

In Chapter 21 of *Nachruf,* Heym cited reviews of his novel *The Eyes of Reason* that appeared in Providence, Rhode Island, Richmond, Virginia, and a particularly critical appraisal by a Charles Brady in an unnamed Catholic periodical. Heym scoffs at the insinuation of being a crypto-Stalinist and cites the reviews as one of the causes for his anxiety as he falls asleep in his wife's arms, their view overlooking the East River, in the last paragraph of Chapter 22. The couple's voyage to Europe begins on the following page.

Yet as Heym noted back on page 465 of Chapter 21, corroborated by newspaper reviews and the novel's overleaf, *The Eyes of Reason* wasn't published until 1951. Heym was in Europe without returning to the U.S. from August 1950. The Second World Peace Conference in Warsaw was held in November 1950.[36] One doesn't even need the FBI files to see Heym fabricated events described in Chapter 22.

The Eyes of Reason was an open betrayal of the purported ideals of a small nation's right to sovereignty expressed in *Hostages* less than a decade earlier. The support of the communist takeover in Prague exposes that the earlier anti-fascist cause was merely a guise of convenience, an opportunity for communists to lead the propaganda in democratic Allied countries as well as the Soviet Union. Heym's utter deceit proves Brady's criticism all the more accurate. If a critic can't call someone who is an open defector to the opposition an opponent, how can a malicious and conspirative enemy be resisted?

Heym's change of sides on the question of Czechoslovakia's sovereignty combined with his open and brazen misrepresentation of having been victimized by reviews of *The Eyes of Reason* leaves one wondering how wrong must a communist be before being subject to criticism by liberal intellectuals. It is also difficult to believe that not a single reviewer of *Nachruf* knew that the Second World Peace Conference in Warsaw was held in 1950, despite the date and year being omitted from the narrative.

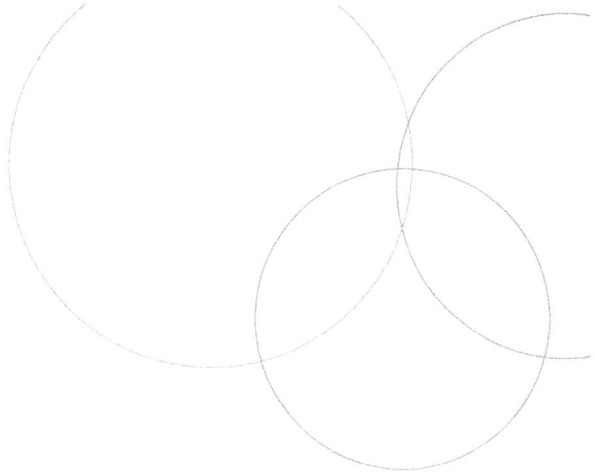

CHAPTER 19

1951, 1952, THE PUBLIC DEFECTION 1953 AND DDR ANECDOTES

Although *Nachruf* stated *The Eyes of Reason* was published in February 1951 and harsh reviews were alleged to have caused Heym to leave the United States, he was actually already in Prague in February 1951 and wrote an article for the newspaper *Lidovy Noviny*. The newspaper noted it was to be the first of a series of articles.[1]

Stefan Heym was, thus, an employee of the Czechoslovakian government contemporaneously with the period he claimed anti-communists were causing him anxiety in the U.S. Very inapt is his expression of disappointment in *Nachruf*, page 469, that he did not receive support from Prague, meaning from Otto Katz, and was forced to struggle on his own. He was in Prague, cheerily in power with the other Stalinists, though, as ever, he portrayed himself as the independent whose courageous effort went unnoticed.[2]

Heym's attendance at a Czechoslovakian state function in August 1951 was considered important enough that the U.S. Embassy in Prague reported it to the chief of the State Department's Security Division, named D. L. Nicholson, who informed FBI Director J. Edgar Hoover.[3] The Americans also noticed Heym's attendance at the National Theater was reported by the official news agency, called CETEKA. The name, of course, sounds similar to the early Bolshevik secret police, the "Cheka." There is no information whatsoever on Heym for the year 1952, at least not from what the FBI has made available. The interested reader will have to wait for an analysis of the East Bloc's archives and Heym's personal papers at Cambridge, England for information that goes beyond his memoir.

Heym's defection was not described as such in the American press until April 1953. Heym wrote an open letter to President Eisenhower expressing his rejection and disapproval of the United States of America. The letter was announced by the East German news service, A.D.N. [*Allgemeiner Deutscher Nachrichtendienst*, General German New Service] and reported by major newspapers in the U.S. on April 16, 1953.[4] A copy of the letter, released just after Stefan Heym's fortieth birthday, was published in *Beitraege zur eine Biographie*, a volume published in honor of Heym's sixtieth birthday.[5]

Heym's message was a parody of the announcement sent by Ignace Reiss to Stalin, during the Great Terror [a brutal campaign of political repression in U.S.S.R, 1936–1938], renouncing his ties to the Soviet Union in a similarly deprecating manner. Heym's correspondence returned his service medals, just as Reiss had done approximately fifteen years earlier.[6] The subsequent assassination of Reiss caused Walter Krivitsky to defect to France and then to the U.S. The form of Heym's letter attempted to inflict on the American executive branch what Reiss had inflicted, at least putatively, on Stalin, while behaving as though the violent death of Reiss was irrelevant.[7] The press did not take notice of the parallels in the two situations. Stalin's shadow hangs over Heym's defection, as the Soviet dictator only became deceased in March 1953, which likely affected the timing of Heym's letter. In addition to returning his medals, Heym also resigned his commission as a lieutenant in the U. S. Army.

Internal FBI records take issue with the resignation, and an inquiry to Army record keepers revealed that Heym's commission expired on April 1, 1953, two weeks before his announcement.[8] More mysterious to the FBI was whether Stefan Heym remained an American citizen. As a naturalized citizen, Heym could be expatriated for disloyalty or showing allegiance to another country. Military service can also be a factor in such cases. Despite the public denunciation of President Eisenhower and acceptance of East German citizenship, no proceedings were brought against Heym. The government was still concerned about his status in 1966 when the State Department sent a letter to its Berlin Mission inquiring whether Heym had already expatriated himself and whether a formal signed renunciation was necessary.[9]

The subject of Stefan Heym was not mentioned in HUAC or McCarthy committee hearings until a month following his public defection in April 1953. He was publicly named by a Julius Epstein, who was born in Austria, lived in New York, and was called a correspondent for a journal in Dusseldorf.[10] Epstein had worked in the Office of War Information and seems to have had a role in the immediate postwar-era occupation press in Germany.[11] The timing suggests the committee felt it had made a glaring omission in not having yet named the popular novelist who had a Hollywood screen credit. Heym's public attack on America and open residence in East Germany also made it impossible and impolitic for communism's U.S. supporters to contest his exposure. In May and June 1953, FBI Director Hoover responded to inquiries of the U.S. legal attaché in London, who apparently had no information at all regarding Heym.[12]

Soon after his open defection, Heym became a newspaper columnist in the DDR. He applauded Soviet tank personnel for their suppression of the uprising of June 17, 1953 when East Germans, disappointed by the lack of economic progress and perhaps emboldened by the vacuum in Soviet leadership, took to the streets in defiance of the Soviet occupation. According to Heym, the Red Army had prevented war from breaking out.[13] In comparison to the revolts in Prague and Budapest, this rebellion is little known outside of Germany. Heym also wrote a novel about the event, though it was disapproved of by the party leadership and remained unpublished for many years. However, since he was such a firm supporter of the regime, one wonders whether his so-called disagreements with the leadership weren't contrived to make a fanatical supporter seem a credible dissident.

Heym didn't start to become a dissident [against communism] until the mid–1960s. During the 1950s, he was still an unbearable sycophant for Moscow. His column "Offen Gesagt" [To Be Frank] ran in the East German version of the *Berliner Zeitung*. Upon the birthday of the recently departed Stalin, Heym called him the most loved man in history. In *Nachruf*, he criticized opponents who remind him of that quote and counters that he also called Stalin the most hated man in history. However, he omits that the actual column stated that only gaudy capitalists and enemies of communism hated Stalin.[14] He is also quoted as enthusiastically supporting the Soviet concentration camp system, the Gulag, claiming they proved that idealistic Soviets believed in helping even criminals perform productive labor.[15]

In 1954, he traveled to the Soviet Union and wrote a book on his tour. The volume, titled *Keine Angst von Russlands Baeren* [*Don't Be Afraid of Russia's Bears*], is an abject paean, with pictures of clean coal miners, modern department stores and explanations such as "red also means beautiful in Russian."[16] It was practically without literary merit and was closer in style and content to an official government pamphlet rather than the travelogue of a talented writer. No liberal assessment of Heym as an alleged dissident will give much attention to this work. It clearly refutes his claim to being independent. In 1955, the West Berlin press called him the official voice of the Central Committee of the DDR, and it seems accurate, judging from his output of that time.[17]

In 1953 and 1959, Heym received the National Prize in East Germany, which meant an improvement in status and a relatively small financial award.[18] In 1959, he and Gertrude were given charge of a new publishing house, Seven Seas Verlag, which printed editions in English for the East Bloc market, its sympathizers, and libraries. They didn't sell a large number of copies, but such status gives one extra clout. Heym and Gelbin will always have the niche of having run the English language publishing house in the DDR.

The FBI files note a couple of obscure cites of Heym's that have likely been forgotten. He wrote an article called "These Are Lands of Anxiety," for the May Day issue of the London edition of the *Daily Worker* in 1958. In 1961, Reuters reported that the East German movie studio DEFA announced that Heym was to write a screenplay based on the incident of the sinking of the "Texas Four."[19] This was not a ship but a radar tower moored off the coast of New Jersey. Twenty-eight men were killed in the accident. The radar tower evoked Heym's own plan with his friends Stern and Schroeter for a floating short wave station. The film was not made however. A bit curious also is that Heym doesn't seem to have any film credits at all for his years in the DDR.

During the 1970s, he wrote an autobiographical novel, *Collin*, about an aging DDR writer whose truthfulness was challenged by the project of writing a memoir. In the end, he decided it was impossible to be completely honest with the public. An English version was released in the U.S. by a small firm.[20] It is also possible that there is an element of autobiography in Heym's 1995 novel *Radek*. Towards the end of the very lengthy tome, notable also for its very loud red binding, Heym, in describing Radek, breaks from the third-person narrative into the first-person. The prose begins, "Only I can say, I who knew him better than most."[21]

It is possible Heym did meet Karl Radek sometime before leaving Prague for Chicago, perhaps while he was still Helmut Flieg. Leo Flieg is not mentioned in *Radek* although Leo Jogiches is a character in an early section. Radek himself was the author of *Rosa Luxemburg Karl Liebknecht Leo Jogiches*, published by Verlag der Kommunistsche Internationale (1921). Radek was very active in Germany following World

War I and maintained close contact with Willi Muenzenberg once he was in Moscow. Radek must have known Leo Flieg, and likely knew him very well. Heym was a member of Germany's Bundestag during the year the book was released. His own many associations with Soviet agents have eluded detection as though Heym was a commissar, even in the West, who simply outranked anyone who might expose him, even following the apparent disintegration of communism.

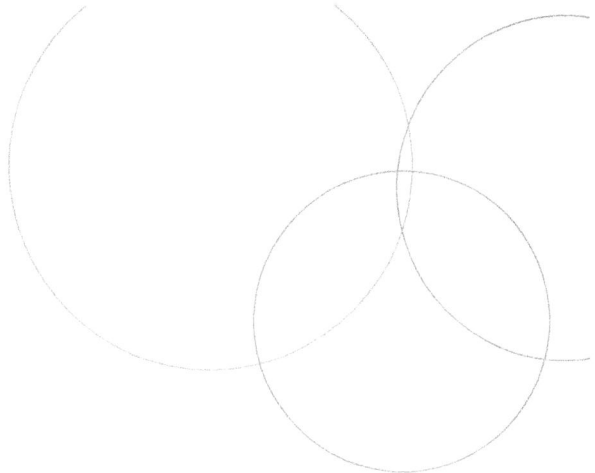

CHAPTER 20

HERBERT WEHNER

Among those Herbert Wehner (1906–1990) spoke critically of to Soviet interrogators during the Great Terror were Hermann Jakobs, Curt Loewe, Johannes Schroeter, and Schroeter's wife, Dr. Reni Begun. These are names that anyone researching the KPD views only infrequently. Still, each of these associates of the *Volksecho* were known to Herbert Wehner. The leader of the postwar SPD was also the main accuser against Leo Flieg who could not disprove allegations of having converted party funds.[1]

Somewhat astonishingly, there may have been a connection between Heym and Wehner during the latter part of the Weimar Republic. Herbert Wehner, born in Dresden, held a party post in Flieg's hometown of Chemnitz, also part of Saxony, during 1928 to 1929.[2] This is adequate grounds for surmising that their paths crossed at gatherings for young socialists. In fact, Heym mentioned Wehner once under Wehner's party alias, "Kurt Funk," in the *Deutsches Volksecho*.[3] Wehner, like Heym, was a friend of Egon Kisch and went along on adventures with the "Raging Reporter." Like Heym, Wehner is even said to have met Kisch's mother in the distinctive family mansion in the old section of Prague. Kisch also once bailed Wehner's wife from jail in Prague, early on in the exile period.[4]

Wehner was also an operative of the secret apparat in Berlin and possibly assumed responsibilities of Leo Flieg's. Wehner stayed underground in Berlin for several months following the Reichstag fire.[5] Several of the communists who worked with Wehner, including KPD leader Ernst Thaelmann, were caught by the Nazi authorities. Wehner's narrow escapes, while his associates were arrested, led to suspicion that he was part of an even deeper conspiracy between Moscow and Berlin.[6] It is clear that his role in Berlin in 1933 reveals he was a leading figure in the secret apparat of which Leo Flieg had long been leader if not founder.

In exile, Wehner is said to have worked with Honnecker in Saarbrücken and with Ulbricht in Prague. Hubert von Lowenstein, of the Hollywood Anti-Nazi League and American Guild of Cultural Freedom, noted Wehner in Spain during the civil war.[7] Heym's classmate from Chemnitz, Leo Bauer, knew Wehner in Paris in the mid 1930s, according to Bauer's biographers. Both worked in administrating KPD exile policies. Bauer and Wehner were very influential in the SPD during the period Willy Brandt was Chancellor of West Germany, and Wehner spoke a eulogy upon Bauer's passing in 1972.[8]

It is curious that several New York coworkers of Heym's, as well as Leo Flieg, merited Wehner's attention, but not Heym himself. Heym's name is also omitted from Guenther Reinhardt's *Crime Without Punishment*. Reinhardt investigated Louis Gibarti during the period Gibarti frequented the *Volksecho* office, yet doesn't mention Heym or the *Deutsches Volksecho*. Reinhardt also wrote critically of Kurt Rosenfeld, in itself rare. In *That Good Old Fool Uncle Sam*, Rudolf Brandl, former editor of the weekly *Aufbau*, wrote about Hermann Jakobs/ Martin Hall, William Dodd Jr., and Oskar Maria Graf during the period they were involved in the *Volksecho*, yet also omits mention of Stefan Heym. *Text und Kritik* published a special issue on Oskar

Maria Graf that included testimony of German exiles who cooperated with the FBI, including Gerhart Seger, but excluded mention of the *Volksecho*. It is as though Heym had some special status that made him immune from certain levels of scrutiny. The posthumous continuation of such a status becomes an absurdity in a democracy with freedom of access to public records and freedom of speech.

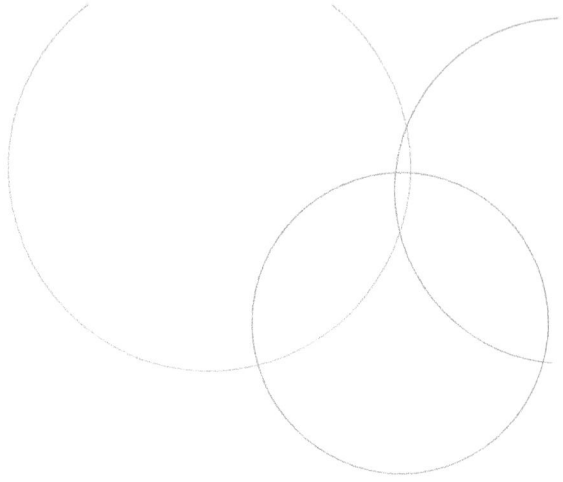

CHAPTER 21

THE REICHSTAG FIRE AND COMMUNIST EXPLOITATION OF THE PRESUMPTION OF INNOCENCE

I t is time to reexamine the presumption that the communists were not involved in setting the Reichstag fire. The KPD's immunity served the victorious Allied powers because communist guilt would undermine justification for the war. The Allied bombing and occupation seems much darker if there was also complicity in establishing that such extreme measures were taken against the Nazi regime, as well as having Allied forces thus being partly culpable of the same crimes the Nazis were accused and sometimes convicted of. Soviet and communist history has many examples of outrages as extreme as those on the Nazis wartime record, including horrors committed during peacetime before World War II. Therefore, there is no objective basis for simply presuming the communists had nothing to do with the Reichstag fire and the establishment of the Nazi regime, except the postwar world seems morally tidier.

Communists were responsible for the terrorist bombing during a state funeral of Svetl Kral Cathedral in Sofia, Bulgaria in 1925. The funeral was for a general assassinated by communists, and over one hundred mourners were killed.[1] Leftist rioters destroyed the Justice Palace in Vienna in 1927.[2] The plethora of assassins of the late 19th and early 20th centuries were overwhelmingly leftists.[3]

The KPD cooperated with the Nazis in strikes and Reichstag voting from 1931 to 1933.[4] There was also an election during the late Weimar era when communists were instructed not to vote for communist candidates. The KPD had a committee prepare for a transition to illegality in 1932.[5] In Austria in 1934, Nazis and communists collaborated in uprisings to topple the regime. If the Nazis did burn the Reichstag without communist help, it would actually be an exception to the pattern of events and shouldn't simply be presumed.

The apparatchik in charge of preparing for exile was Willi Budich, whose ties to Leo Flieg went back to the period when both were assistants to Leo Jogiches. Budich was a veteran of the KPD's secret operations.[6] The preparation for illegality included hundreds of false passports for top functionaries, an obvious indication that Leo Flieg was involved.[7] Shortly before the Reichstag fire, Margaret Buber-Neumann recalled seeing Louis Gibarti in new office space for one of the Soviet front organizations, where he said, "I don't think we will have these offices for very long."[8] Stefan Heym remembered a MASCH meeting with Egon Kisch present. The subject of what should be done in case the Nazis declared martial law was raised. Kisch answered, "I'll be going to Prague in a few days," in what Heym called an *a propos*. A few days later, the Reichstag caught fire, Kisch was arrested, the Czechoslovakian Embassy protested the detention of one of its nationals, and Kisch was delivered to Prague just as he said, though probably not as one would have understood.[9]

Kurt Rosenfeld, attorney for Ernst Torgler, walked his client into the police station, putatively to only refute rumors that Torgler was involved.[10] The ploy seemed to backfire, as Torgler was arrested and held for trial. Rosenfeld, unperturbed, continued his activities as part of the Katz/ Muenzenberg counter trials and as a leftist gadfly in New York.[11] Torgler was later acquitted. Three of his four co-defendants were also cleared and sent to Moscow, consistent with a *quid pro quo* arrangement.[12] Marinus Van der Lubbe, apprehended at the scene, was executed. Following the war, Torgler wrote in *Die Zeit* that one of his first cellmates was Egon Kisch.[13]

One admittedly obscure source states that Harry Schulze-Wilde and Theodor Plivier, reporters with the Muenzenberg concern, were with Rudolf Diels on the evening of the fire.[14] Diels was one of the regime's chief interrogators during the investigation. Strangely, Diels is also said to have had an affair with Martha Dodd and accompanied her to the courtroom in Leipzig.[15] Further, Schulze-Wilde later wrote that Plivier actually met Van der Lubbe three or four days before the arson.[16] This should be considered startling as Van der Lubbe also set three fires in public buildings in Berlin, two to three days before setting fire to the Reichstag.[17]

In exile, Plivier lived near Egon Kisch in Versailles and worked with him on *The Brown Book of the Hitler Terror and the Burning of the Reichstag* published by Editions du Carrefour.[18] Schulze-Wilde also wrote a book on Van der Lubbe, which seems to have vanished from the record but is mentioned in his biography of Plivier.[19] Otto Katz was noted to have written an angry letter to Schulze-Wilde because of a version of events at variance with what Katz had written. Uniformity was important to Katz even if accuracy wasn't. Schulze-Wilde's biography of Marinus van der Lubbe, published in 1967, was co-written with a Jef Last, a Dutch national who too had been a Muenzenberg reporter.[20]

Marinus van der Lubbe, who most agree set the fire, was himself a member of the Dutch Communist Party. He was an organizer who one source said led countless marches in Holland. He was a functionary of rank who held and addressed party meetings in the university town of Leyden. Van der Lubbe is also claimed to have penned leaflets and pamphlets, which would have required standing in the party.[21] However, the propaganda led by Muenzenberg and Katz has successfully created the impression that Van der Lubbe was never anything other than merely a disturbed loner. One presumes he couldn't have been an open party member because that fact makes communist culpability simply too obvious, and yet it is so. The Katz and Kisch "investigation" into his background in Holland was a deception that caused people to believe that Van der Lubbe's background was obscure. They only had to call the party leadership to ask for his files. Of course, the public wasn't told that.

Furthermore, there is evidence that the communists wanted Hitler in power, at least temporarily. Important communists are quoted as saying so several times. The leader of Germany's SPD, Friedrich Stampfer, wrote that Soviet embassy attaché, Boris Vinogradov, declared to Stampfer in January 1933 that negotiations between the SPD and the Communist Party would be useless, that Moscow was convinced Hitler had to come to power before communism could be victorious.[22] Wilhelm Pieck is quoted as saying that the KPD was not afraid of Hitler but was ordered to surrender.[23] Karl Radek is noted as saying Germans would have to bear Hitler in power for two years.[24] A KPD Reichstag deputy once exclaimed exultantly that a Nazi takeover was desired.[25] Comintern executive Dimitri Manuilski is reported to have said at a Comintern meeting in December 1931 that, with Hitler's help, the communists would destroy the SPD as well as what Manuilski termed the Bruning state apparatus. Manuilski also said that in the current situation, Hitler was undoubtedly a comrade.[26]

Two of the judges in the Reichstag fire trial, Froehlich and Warnecke, who had celebrated the verdict in 1934, died following the war while under arrest by the Soviets.[27] Police Lieutenant Heisig, who interrogated Van der Lubbe and thought that the arsonist had been a communist longer than believed, also later died in an accident, as did Rudolf Diels in the 1950s.[28] Given the conjunction of episodes, the communist record of intrigues, assassinations, and coups as well as cooperation with Hitler before and after the fire, the prevailing belief that the Nazis were solely responsible for the Reichstag fire is merely a convenient presumption for Allied victors. The latter are the ones who control the mass media as well as the world's military might, so this is not based on an objective analysis.

The above facts regarding Kisch, Rosenfeld, Dodd, and Gibarti are consistent with Stefan Heym having been part of an elite clique of Soviet agents who were informed of Stalin's plan to have Hitler come to power first. Heym's secreted relationship with Leo Flieg makes the hypothesis seem even more apt. The indications can be termed circumstantial, but all were members of the same conspiracy devoted to violent revolution. Nazi-Soviet cooperation, within their overall rivalry and accounting for each side's propaganda campaigns that targeted the other, continued through the 1930s and culminated in the Molotov-von Ribbentrop Pact of 1939. The agreement led to Stalin's internationally unopposed conquest of eastern Poland, Lithuania, Latvia, Estonia, Karelia, and Bessarabia. Russia's partners in World War I, Britain and France, then declared war on Germany, but not against the Soviet Union.

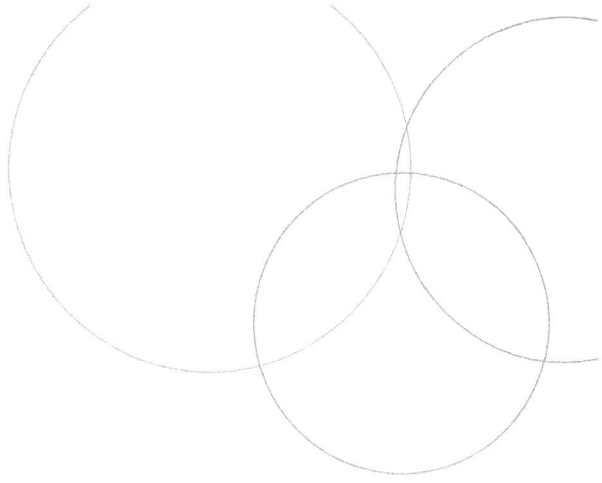

CHAPTER 22

DISCOURSE ON UNSOLVED MURDERS AND FORGOTTEN ENDS

A nother subject that has been little addressed by scholars, though libraries are filled with books by and about Europeans who were exiles during the Hitler period, is the involvement of Egon Kisch and Otto Katz in fatal incidents. Geza von Cziffra was a film director who was acquainted with Kisch during the Weimar era and who also wrote a book on the Hanussen affair. He had the distinction of directing motion pictures in Germany in 1944, 1945, 1946 and 1947.[1] Von Cziffra alleged that following a visit by Kisch and Muenzenberg from Paris to novelist Joseph Roth's residence in Oostende, Belgium, Roth fell ill. Believing Kisch poisoned him, he took the following train to Paris where he died a few days later.[2] There is no other corroboration or refutation of this version of events in print.

A CPUSA correspondent named Alfred Miller apparently drank himself to death by acute alcohol poisoning in Kisch's presence a few years later in Mexico.[3] A marital indiscretion involving Miller is said to have strained relations among the exile crowd. In 1942, famed author

Anna Seghers received a letter critical of her writing from Egon Kisch that included the approximate phrase, "You don't know what we want from you." She was struck by or thrown from a car in 1943. The letter and accident, though eight months apart, are mentioned in juxtaposition in her memoir without explicitly saying that she suspected Kisch or the KPD.[4]

A post-communist biography of Kisch revealed that the prominent resident of Prague, who upon victorious return could have had nearly any available domicile he wished, moved into the house that Adolf Eichmann had resided in during the war. Kisch told an interviewer that the curtains and furnishings were the same ones Eichmann had used.[5] This rather bizarre anecdote in combination with all the other coincidences in his career going back to the Redl tragedy, seems to show Kisch as one Nesta Webster might have called "a light bearer of darkness" or a figure from the dark side of this world who also had a public career.

Radical writer Ernst Toller died an unnatural death in the same week Joseph Roth died.[6] Toller died on May 22, 1939 and Roth on May 27, the day of Toller's funeral. Toller was found in the Mayflower Hotel on the west side of Manhattan with his bathrobe belt tied around his neck. The hook he had apparently hung himself on had given way and his body was slumped against the door.[7] Oddly, Willi Muenzenberg was found with a rope around his neck and was also found lying on the ground as the branch on which he seemingly was hung had snapped. Muenzenberg's death occurred in June 1940; however, his body wasn't found for a few months.[8]

Toller was not destitute or in immediate danger of falling into fascist hands as a likely suicide might be. Toller had been received at the White House earlier in the same month.[9] He had a steamer ticket for a return to England and was overheard by his secretary arguing with his agent over half a percent on the day of his death.[10] Mysteriously, his traveling partner, named Landshof, had fallen ill of food poisoning a day earlier.[11] Toller's death was ruled a suicide; he was presumed to have hung himself while his secretary had left on her lunch break.

The *Paris-Soir* correspondent Curt Riess stopped by the hotel to visit while the secretary was gone. He called the hotel personnel to open the door when Toller didn't answer, leading to the recognition that a death had taken place.[12] Only Riess' memoir notes his discovery of the corpse. His presence is not mentioned by Toller's biographers or mentioned in the *Deutsches Volksecho* that carried Riess' column. The *Volksecho* did print a strange poem by Johannes Becher which seemed closer to mockery than tribute.[13] Recall that Riess was close enough to Otto Katz to have been a witting attendee to his "Breda" playacting in Hollywood.

Otto Katz, close to Egon Kisch in Paris, Spain, New York, Mexico, and Prague, has been the subject of allegations of homicide. Informers claimed to U.S. authorities that as the leading communist press agent for the Spanish Republic during the civil war, Katz had selected for execution men who were considered unreliable.[14]

Research into the career of Whittaker Chambers has also left testimony that Otto Katz was in New York City in the late 1930s to murder Chambers for attempting to break away from his service to the party. Chambers received a tip from his literary agent, Maxim Lieber, and successfully evaded Katz, who was called "Ulrich" during this weird episode.[15] The alias "Ulrich" is one which Katz is not on the record as having used aside from this single incidence. It might be worth noting Heym's *Nazis in USA* mentions a mysterious agent presenting himself as a Nazi reporter named "Ulrich."[16] The name appears with and without quotation marks in different editions of *Nazis in USA*.

In February 1942, *The Nation*, usually quite conciliatory to Stalinists, identified Katz as leader of a smear campaign against five non-Stalinist leftists in Mexico. The smears included a fabricated report purported to be from Washington and authored under a fictitious name. Katz was accused of organizing "vigilante committees" to stop the renegades whom he called Nazi agents.[17] Kisch was also involved in the affair as a signatory to the exiles' reply letter to *The Nation* as having attacked one of the dissidents in an article and in having instructed F.C. Weiskopf on how the same dissident should be attacked.[18] At the instigation of Katz, a communist member of Mexico's parliament attempted to pass a special law to deport the five: Victor Serge, Gustav Regler, Grandisio Muniz, Julian Gorkin, and Marceau Pivert. Julian Gorkin was stabbed in Mexico City in May 1943 but recovered.[19] Victor Serge died mysteriously in a taxi in Mexico in 1947, though most of the communist exiles had left during 1946.

Katz is also recorded as having spoken glibly of having to pay an outrageous sum to the Mafia to have another leftist radical, Carlo Tresca, shot dead in January 1943 on East 15th Street in Manhattan.[20] A known mafioso on parole named Galante was found in possession of the car from which the shots were fired but couldn't be tied more closely to the crime scene.[21] Recall that 1943 was the year Katz was heralded as a heroic resistance fighter in Hollywood propaganda. Others believed him responsible for the death of Muenzenberg in 1940 and the defenestration of Jan Masaryk in 1948, according to Stephen Koch in *Double Lives*, though Koch is dismissive of the claims. Katz was no longer in France by June 1940 when his former boss perished in attempted flight to Switzerland. In the case of Masaryk, the communists immediately labeled the fall a suicide. Jan Papanek, the Czechoslovakian Ambassador to the U.N. with whom Stefan Heym had appeared on "U.N. Day" in 1943, accused the communists of murdering Masaryk and was discharged.[22]

Notorious Comintern assassin, Vittorio Vidali (1900–1983), was also exiled in Mexico City during the war. The veteran international agent was deported from the U.S. in the 1920s despite having been represented by Clarence Darrow. He was expelled from France in 1934, the year following his mission to Berlin and his meeting with Leo Flieg.[23] Though an Italian from Triest, he was called Carlos Contreras in Spain and Mexico. He was known as an executioner during the Spanish Civil War. Ernest Hemingway once remarked on Vidali's hand being sore from a particularly busy day executing "traitors."[24] To be fair, he was also known as a competent field commander.[25]

In Mexico, he was believed to have been responsible for the killing of Cuban communist Luis Mella while Mella was in the company of the noted photographer Tina Modotti.[26] Modotti, later Vidali's mistress, died of a heart attack while seated next to Vidali in a taxi. This strange occurrence took place in Mexico during the war soon after a social event at which many of the KPD exiles were present. He did not attend the funeral.[27] Vidali/Contreras organized the first attack on Trotsky's compound. Trotsky survived this attempt but an American aide named Robert Sheldon Harte was killed. Artist David Alfaro Siqueros, Vidali's adjutant in Spain, led the charge.[28]

Carlo Tresca noted having seen Vidali a few days before his own murder and told writer Ralph de Toledano, "death was in the air."[29] Vidali was reported to have been seen in New Jersey shortly after the slaying.[30] Mafiosi in New York also publicly blamed Vidali for the killing.[31] Vidali always seemed to slip through the fingers of the long arm of the law. J. Edgar Hoover tried to get agents to keep track of him in Mexico but would only receive faulty information after delays in answering.[32] Once, while in jail in Mexico, Vidali was visited by President Cardenas and the charges against him were soon dropped.[33]

Upon return to Triest, Otto Katz, whom Vidali knew well in Spain and Mexico, helped secure financing for resumption of the Communist Party there.[34] He was also involved in the purges of Yugoslavs from the Triest zone. Hundreds of thousands were forced to flee their homes on both sides of the Italy-Yugoslavia border. In the long run, there may have been benefits to diminishing the size of problematic minorities, especially in consideration that the country of allegiance was only a short distance away. However, there has been almost no scholarship in an academic climate that pretends to be very concerned about such issues to determine the numbers killed and displaced. Vidali was pictured in *Time* in 1948 with the caption, "a hunting license."[35] A Triest newspaper accused him of a string of murders in 1954.[36]

The allegations of a violent past weren't much of a hindrance to Vidali's postwar career. He became a member of Italy's parliament and authored several books including a day-by-day history of World War II.[37] Also, like Louis Gibarti, he became an executive in the World Federation of Trade Unions, which had millions of members in North

America and Europe and tens of millions enlisted in the East Bloc.[38] Vidali was also claimed to have been an advisor to Cuban communists in the years before their coup in 1959.[39] There is no documented direct tie from Stefan Heym to Vidali such as exists from Vidali to Egon Kisch, Otto Katz, and Leo Flieg.

One of the reasons the Soviets were anxious to be rid of Carlo Tresca was that he was investigating the 1937 murder of CPUSA operative Juliet Poyntz. She was a Barnard graduate who was involved in organizing and promoting labor unions and was associated with Muenzenberg's International Workers Aid in the 1920s.[40] Poyntz was abducted, possibly on 57th Street, in June 1937. The story eventually received press coverage in December.[41] A commission was formed to investigate and Tresca's testimony also received media attention. The disappearance was forgotten but revived again when Tresca was shot.[42] It has been claimed that Tresca was close to solving the Poyntz mystery when he himself was shot.[43] The unsolved Poyntz, Tresca, and Krivitsky deaths are fairly well known among even casual observers of communist activities in the U.S. during the 20th century. Yet rarely are different versions analyzed for flaws, and it is rarely noted that there may have been a connection between the Poyntz and Tresca cases.

Gary Kern, in his book *A Death in Washington: Walter G. Krivitsky and the Soviet Terror,* noted that at approximately the same time Krivitsky was killed or driven to suicide by Soviet cutthroats, another communist in "disgrace" vanished. Clarence Hathaway, a former editor at the *Daily Worker,* had not been seen for several months. Hathaway had also been a congressional candidate, had authored several pamphlets, and was one of the leading American-born communists in New York City until his expulsion.[44] His secretary and three other functionaries, not named by Kern or anyone else apparently, also disappeared.[45] Hathaway, who may have been engaged in a deception, resurfaced in time to begin a prison term in 1942 and later returned to a high position in the CPUSA.

In the same month of Krivitsky's death and discovery of Hathaway's disappearance, February 1941, a former Russian officer Colonel

Mikhail Borislavsky was found shot to death beside a convent in Manhattan.[46] Kern noted Borislavsky had written critically of Stalin. He was, incidentally, a U.S. citizen at the time of his death, and his murder was never solved by police. In May 1941, former *Frankfurter Zeitung* editor Heinrich Simon, considered an anti-Nazi but not a communist, was bludgeoned to death in Washington, D.C. The attack occurred while he was out on an evening walk. The story seems to have received only one day of press coverage and was soon forgotten.[47] Morton E. Kent, a former employee of the War Department and State Department, was found with his throat cut, floating in the Potomac River in June 1949. His name was mentioned during the Judith Coplon espionage trial. He was ruled to have committed the act himself while on a weekend outing with his wife.[48]

It has also been concealed from the public for several decades that there was a murder of a witness in the Alger Hiss case. Whittaker Chambers successfully evaded potential executioners, but another man deposed during the HUAC stage of the investigation was either driven to suicide or brutally murdered. Walter Marvin Smith, age 53, an attorney at the U.S. Justice Department testified that he acted as a notary public for the sale of a car by Hiss. Shortly after his testimony, he was found dead at the base of the steps of the Justice Department.[49] One of the few newspaper accounts of the incident said he fell five stories to his death.[50]

Smith's death occurred on October 20, 1948. It is incredible and inexplicable that his murder is never mentioned in all the debate and analysis of the Alger Hiss case that has taken place over the past half century. Smith's very suspicious fall happened only two months before Lawrence Duggan fell from an upper floor office window in Manhattan.[51] Duggan was one of the communists in the Roosevelt administration identified by Chambers. One of his shoes was found in his office, a clear sign he was thrown from a window following a struggle.[52]

For many years, the issue of Whittaker Chambers' credibility was a key issue in deciding whether Alger Hiss was guilty, which usually correlated to one's opinion on the larger issue of communist infiltration in the government. Everyone fails to point out that if Chambers, an admitted former Soviet agent, was lying about Alger Hiss, a plenipotentiary at the State Department and first Secretary General of the United Nations, then it is still a case of a Soviet spy trying to defame an important and loyal government official that still called for extra scrutiny of communist activities. Hiss' defenders always ridiculed and obstructed investigations into communism because communism was precisely what they supported.

In 1949, the former Secretary of the Navy and the first person to have the title Secretary of Defense, James Vincent Forrestal, was discharged by President Truman and checked into the Naval hospital for psychiatric care. Forrestal either leapt or was pushed from the sixteenth floor window of his room and, as one account said, "a cord from a bathrobe was found knotted tightly about the neck."[53] Forrestal, known by his middle name Vincent as a youth, had tied one end of the bathrobe belt around the radiator and the other around his neck, if the ruling of suicide is truthful. The knot, or the belt itself, gave way and Forrestal fell to his death on May 22, 1949, exactly ten years to the day of Ernst Toller's apparent suicide.[54]

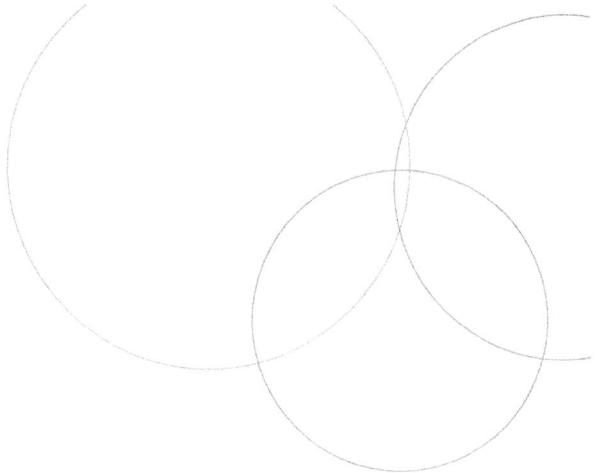

2008 POST-SCRIPT

It was stated earlier that Stefan Heym's announcement of his defection in April 1953 was likely connected to the fact that Josef Stalin died in March 1953. The announcement also coincided with the infamous factfinding junket to Europe made by Roy Cohn and David Schine. Heym publicized the spurning of his status as a U.S. citizen just as Cohn and Schine had finished in Vienna with the German and Austrian segment of their tour inspecting libraries funded by the U.S. government. Cohn and Schine were between inspections in Vienna and Belgrade at the time of Heym's declaration. The American press did not note a connection between Heym's announcement and the Cohn/Schine investigation.

Hansjorg Gehring, in *Amerikanische Literaturpolitik in Deutschland,* cites a quote by Cohn pertaining to Heym as a defector in the May 6, 1953 issue of *The New York Times* on page 5.[1] This quote is not in the archives available on the internet or on a microfilm copy of an issue of the same date that was viewed in a public library. The only remaining possibility is that the cite was from a different edition on the same date. In Roy Cohn's book, *McCarthy*, Cohn discussed the trip on page 85 and the fact that Heym was a communist while editing a newspaper owned by the U.S. government on page 86, but he did not mention the timing of Heym's announcement.[2] Cohn claimed that most expenses were paid by the investigators themselves and that taxpayers were not additionally burdened for the costs of traveling to Europe. The American media has for decades made the voyage a topic of derision.

When Stefan Heym sailed to Holland on the *S.S. Veendam* in 1948, he was met by a cousin named Hans Namm whom he had known in Berlin in 1933.[3] The cognomen Namm is another coincidence. From the late 1800s until 1957, there was a New York City department store called Namm's (two other Namm's stores on Long Island continued for several more years). The company's founder, named Adolph Namm (1856–1920), was born in Posen. His son Benjamin Namm began managing the retail emporium in 1910. Namm was considered an important Republican in Brooklyn and New York State and was mentioned in *The New York Times* as a running mate for mayoral candidates and for Governor Dewey in 1942, though he was never actually listed on a ballot. Benjamin Namm was also President of the National Dry Goods Retailing Association during the war years and, though a Republican, worked for the government on war bond promotions, trade discussions with Brazil, and retailing matters. He was also usually found on lists of the country's most highly paid executives.

Namm was one of two members of the U.S. Chamber of Commerce to be sent to the first postwar U.N. Conference in San Francisco. In 1946, Governor Dewey appointed Namm as one of the seven founding trustees of the New York State Institute of Applied Arts and Sciences. Note that Stefan Heym was one of the three leading members of a Soviet-front organization with a similar name a few years later. Also coincidentally, in 1954 *The New York Times* printed a photograph of Benjamin Namm on board a liner to the Netherlands.

The report of Stefan Heym having been trained in Gettysburg, Pennsylvania, mentioned in Chapter XIII, footnote 24, is perhaps corroborated by Hans Habe in *Our Love Affair with Germany,* where the author states, "I was then directed to establish a 'hush-hush' camp near Gettysburg, Pennsylvania to train a number of American officers and soldiers of German and American descent to take over the German press as soon as important cities were occupied."[4] In April, 1942, Habe married Eleanor Post Hutton, the step-daughter of Joseph Davies, the U.S. Ambassador to the U.S.S.R. Eleanor Post Hutton was the daughter of Mrs. Davies by a previous marriage. The marriage with Habe did not endure the book or a related note in Walter Winchell's column.

Like Leo Flieg, Stefan Heym was acquainted with the Marxist writer Georg Lukacs, according to the posthumously released *Offene Worte in Eigener Sache 1989–2001,* by Wilhelm Goldmann.

M. Stanton Evans in *Blacklisted by History* states that Prompt Press was "the Communist Party print shop."

Stefan Heym, in *Nachruf* on page 424, claims it was Senator McCarthy who quashed his potential deal with MGM for the film rights to *The Crusaders.* There has been much study of Joseph McCarthy and there is no evidence that he interfered in matters involving the entertainment industry. The Hollywood Ten and alleged blacklisting of communists in the movie industry occurred because of a HUAC investigation, not a *Senatausschusses* [Senate committee] as claimed. McCarthy was a senator and therefore could not have been part of the HUAC. The claim in *Nachruf* is unfortunately another of Heym's fabrications. Also, the conference of Hollywood moguls at the Waldorf Astoria in Manhattan noted in connection with the alleged demise of the movie deal for *The Crusaders* occurred in 1947, well before 1950 when Joseph McCarthy began to lead Senate committee investigations into security risks in the U.S. government. Furthermore, the Waldorf Conference occurred well before the mid–1948 publication of *The Crusaders.*

Louis Gibarti was mentioned in HUAC hearings on October 24, 1939 in the testimony of Francis Henson. Henson remembered Gibarti as an administrator of the North American Committee to Aid Spanish Democracy and the Medical Bureau to Aid Spanish Refugees.

The author restates that he does not vouch for the career, or even the identity, of Roy Cohn.

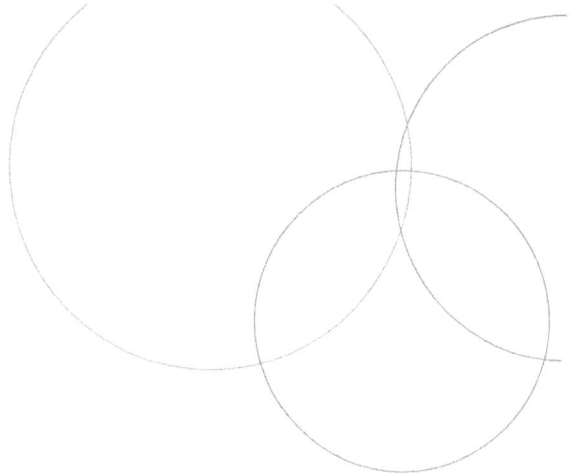

FRAGMENTS ON CHEMNITZ
AND THE KPD

Alexander Helphand, an early financier of the Bolsheviks, once worked at the *Chemnitzer Volksstimme* newspaper.

As stated earlier, Leo Bauer, Hans Teubner (1901–1992), and Walter Trautzsch were from Chemnitz and exiled in Switzerland. Trautzsch was a secret KPD messenger to Ernst Thaelmann during the early years of his imprisonment. Teubner became an editor in Berlin and wrote the official DDR version of exile in Switzerland. He had already authored pamphlets such as "Wer kommandiert die NSDAP" [Who Commands the NSDAP, which stood for *Nationalsozialistische Deutsche Arbeiterpartei*, the National Socialist German Workers' Party, aka, the Nazi Party] during the Weimar Republic. Teubner was a leader of the Chemnitz Jugendverband, was trained at the Lenin school in the 1920s, and worked on Gerhart Eisler's shortwave station in Spain. Bauer's connection to Erica Wallach of the Noel Field case was mentioned in U.S. newspapers in the early 1950s.

The first proposals that the name Chemnitz be changed to Karl Marx Stadt were noted in American newspapers on April 23, 1953 or only eight days following the story of Heym's official defection.

Fritz Heckert (1884–1936), who was on the Executive Commission of the Comintern at the time of his death, was born in Chemnitz. He corresponded with Leo Jogiches and knew Wilhelm Pieck previous to World War I. He was photographed with Stalin at Clara Zetkin's funeral and appeared on the dais at the Amsterdam Peace Conference with Romain Rolland, Albert Einstein, and Heinrich Mann. Karl Frank worked for *Der Kaempfer* newspaper in Chemnitz for a short time.

Rudolf Lindau (1888–1977) was editor of *Der Kaempfer* in Chemnitz in 1930–1931. He worked with Herbert Wehner when the KPD became illegal in 1933. He also escaped both the Nazis and the Stalinist purges.

Writers Kurt Barthels and Walter Janka were also from Chemnitz and of Heym's approximate age. Janka, exiled in Mexico during the war, was sent to prison during the Noel Field purges. Chemnitz was the scene of the KPD party conference in 1923.

Ernst Grube (1890–1945) became Politburo Secretary of Hamburg following the Wittorf affair of 1927. He was from a Saxony group called the "Chemnitzer Linke." He held the post in Hamburg until 1930.

There are a few known purge victims from Chemnitz. Alfred Winkler (b. 1911), Paul Heuschel (b. 1911), and Kurt Bruch (b. 1909) were arrested in the Soviet Union during 1937 and never seen again. Kurt Schumann was expelled from the KPD in 1937, arrested and sent to Nazi Germany in 1938 in one of the deals that led to the Hitler-Stalin Pact. He survived the war and died in Dresden in 1963.

Chemnitz was bombed a few days following the firestorm in Dresden. Dresden was teeming with refugees, mainly from Silesia. Many of the survivors of the Dresden bombing were sent to Chemnitz and had to experience the same horror again.

Luzie Bauer (b. 1914) in Chemnitz, aka Hanna Koenig, attended school in Moscow in 1934. She was arrested in the U.S.S.R. in 1937 and not heard from again. Is it possible she was a sister of Leo Bauer though she is not mentioned in his biography.

Arthur Gross (b. 1903) the first husband of Babette Gross, was also born in Chemnitz.

John Kluge (b. 1914), American media tycoon, was born in Chemnitz. He was in the U.S. from 1922 and served in the U.S. military during the war. Olympic figure skating champion Katarina Witt (b. 1965) was born in Karl Marx Stadt.

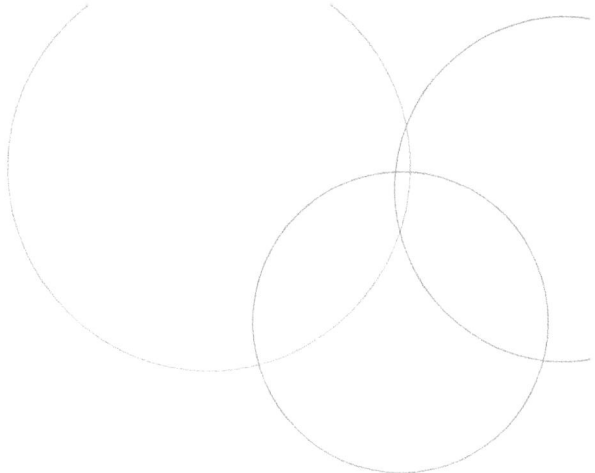

ADDENDA

Le Coup d'Etat de Markus Wolf by Pierre de Villemarest depicts Heym as a servant of the DDR regime. He also notes incriminating information concerning Chancellor Willy Brandt available abroad was ignored by the West German press.

In addition to Stefan Heym, the second President of the United States, John Adams, wrote his memoir in the third person. There aren't many others, however.

In exile, former SAP member Hans Seigewasser was secretary to KPD Politburo member Franz Dahlem. The information that Stalin's regime was responsible for atrocities, a figure of 9.5 million victims killed by 1934, was stated by Grigorii Maksimov in *The Guillotine at Work*, published in 1940.

CBS and NBC destroyed documents of their foreign language departments when they shut down in the late 1940s.

A periodical called *The Barnes Review* took issue with the Venona intercepts. It is claimed the Nazis "Nachtigall" intercepts contain the complete versions of the messages which are truncated in Venona.

Also, many of the missing sections contain names of important members of the Roosevelt administration. It is suggested the omissions are a deliberate attempt to conceal the extent that the FDR administration was a communist regime. See www.tbrnews.org/archives/a073.htm.

There was a Reichstag deputy named Guido Heym (1882–1945). He was shot by the S.S. toward the end of the war.

Flieg-Heym sounds alliterative to the legal name of New York City gangster Dutch Schultz, Arthur Fliegenheimer.

The KPD files in the Archives Nationales in Paris do not seem to be the entirety of the KPD's paperwork. Luckily, it does include communiqués with its members in New York.

The files of Willi Muenzenberg's "Die Zukunft," in the Archives Nationales in Paris, contain a manuscript by Bernard Rosler, a German who was in an NKVD prison in Spain during the Civil War. Rosler's *'Moskau' in Spanien* contains reminiscences of André Marty, Sasha Kinderman, and Alfredo Herz. The latter name was an alias for the vile George Mink. It is alleged Republican soldiers were commonly shot in the back of the head by their own side during battle. André Marty is depicted as killing 200 prisoners shortly before fleeing Spain and stealing the money of 1,500 International Brigadists who were promised tickets to Mexico. Upon Marty's return to France, he became an outspoken critic of concentration camps and held a seat in parliament.

J. Edgar Hoover accurately predicted that Wilhelm Pieck would become leader of East Germany; from Stephan, *Im Visier des FBI* .

As if in prelude to the purges, KPD Germans returned from work on December 1, 1936 to the Hotel Lux to find the lobby being used for the wake of the wife of Wilhelm Pieck. It was about at this time that late night knocks on the door led to disappearances. Even a German cook at the Hotel Lux, Gustav Baumann, was arrested and never seen again. Many prominent functionaries who survived lost relatives, however.

From Franz Dahlem's memoir, Volume one, Pieck arrives in Paris in September, 1938. They hug each other and talk about how the comrades in Moscow are doing.

Peter Blachstein, a member of the SAP who was in exile in Spain and Scandinavia with Willy Brandt, later became West Germany's Ambassador to Yugoslavia.

A picture of Brandt with future Chancellor of Austria, Bruno Kreisky, while in exile in Scandinavia, was printed in *Erinnerung eines linken Sozialisten* by Josef Hindels.

SAP co-founder Max Seydewitz wrote that he made a trip to Oslo to see Brandt but was told Brandt was in the United States. Brandt's *Criminals and other Germans* was written during his Scandinavian exile period. The concept of German collective guilt was being developed at the same time by those connected with Otto Katz' *Freies Deutschland*. It is as though Brandt was imbibing from the same ideological trough.

According to *Commonweal*, March 1944, Gerhart Eisler advocated executing Gerhart Seger. His brother Hannes Eisler once called for the hanging of writer Hans Fallada in a song that is still widely available. Herschel Johnson of the American legation in Stockholm predicted a successful future for Willy Brandt in 1944.

An actor named Michael Mellinger appeared in *Man on a String* (1960), then played a character named "Kisch" in *Goldfinger* (1964) and later appeared as General Weygand in another production.

The Venona intercepts show Pierre Cot to be cooperative with the Soviets during the war, while Cot was in New York. The Nazis considered him a Soviet agent in the 1930s. He was perhaps the reason why Johannes Becher was in possession of the air defense plans for Paris in 1939.

The former German Democratic Republic had dissolved. However, its official newspaper *Neues Deutschland* continues. The February 20, 1997 issue admitted the party once sent Gerhart Eisler to Shanghai and that he worked in the United States under the name "Edwards."

Das Wort was once the title of the official publication of German illuminati as well as a publication of the most hardline German Stalinists. The lack of any commentary drawing this connection shows the incompleteness of scholarship in the two fields.

Between the end of World War II and January 1951, both Stefan Heym and Noel Field were in Switzerland, Paris, Berlin, Mexico City, Warsaw, and Prague. Both knew Paul Merker, Leo Bauer, and Egon Kisch. Their paths could have crossed in Mexico City in early 1946 and in Paris during April 1949. *Nachruf* notes Gertrude Gelbin was in Mexico before Heym traveled there from New York, which means she was socializing with the same group of exiles at the same time the Fields were. Flora Lewis' *Red Pawn* omits mention of the Fields' voyage to Mexico in 1945–1946 and makes no mention of the Kisches at all. Another question is whether the connections Field made in Mexico were used in prosecuting those who met him.

Alfred Stern is father to heirs of the Sears Corporation. *Chicago Syndicate* (1955) was directed by Fred Sears.

In *Advise and Consent* (1962), based on a bestseller by Allen Drury, there were parallels to the Hiss-Chambers-Nixon hearings. Since the characters played by Henry Fonda and Paul McGrath were former professors at the University of Chicago, the Dodds were echoed as well.

Note spoonerisms of European-born actresses Luise Rainer and Lilli Palmer. Leo Flieg's mother's surname was Pill and Gisela Kisch's given surname was Lyner. Some sources say Lilli Palmer was born in Posen.

An actor named Carlos Romero depicted a character named "Carlos Contreras" in *The Gun Runners* (1956), a film about extralegal arms sales to revolutionaries in Cuba. Ricardo Montalban called himself "Vittorio Vidali" in *Sweet Charity* (1969).

Wasn't Arte Johnson's "Ver-r-r-ry Interesting" on the NBC TV series *Laugh-In* (1968–1973) drawn from the character called "the Fly"/"der Flieg" in Bertolt Brecht's *Happy End*?

There was a depiction of Gerhart Eisler in the film *I Was a Communist for the FBI* (1951).

Did Norman Lear form his name from the Liga Escritores y Artistas Revolucionario formed by communist exiles in Mexico City during World War II?

The father of Bernard Mannes Baruch, who ran the U.S. economy during both world wars, was born in Posen, from Margaret Coit, *Mr. Baruch*, Houghton-Mifflin, 1957. As it has developed that Whittaker Chambers, Elizabeth Bentley, and Louis Budenz have been proved truthful, isn't it time anti-anti-communists prove accusers of communists false in even a handful of instances. Exclude Roy Cohn and Matusow. Prove something Joe McCarthy said or wrote was false rather than "outrageous." For example, in his book denouncing George Marshall, McCarthy claimed James Forrestal originally conceived what became known as the Marshall Plan, but that he wanted to include funds for Spain and Greece, which was intolerable to the leftists.

The files of *Die Zukunft* in the Archives Nationales, Paris show Kurt Grossman worked with Louis Gibarti. Grossman does not mention Gibarti in his book on emigration.

Freies Deutschland, August, 1942, p. 26, carried the specious claim that former boxing champion Max Schmeling was a commandant in Auschwitz.

Ho Chi Minh was a collaborator with Communist Youth International executives Lazar Schatzkin and Robert Schueller during Ho's years in France. Leo Flieg was close to Schatzkin and Schueller and a cofounder of the Youth International.

For the record, Trotsky once wrote that the POUM were treacherous. However, he didn't consider them Trotskyites.

During the 1930s, the leader of the Swedish Communist Party was named Niels Flyg. Following the Hitler-Stalin Pact, he became leader of Sweden's Nazi Party. He died in neutral Sweden during the war.

Jane Foster's *Unamerican Lady* claims that the Stern ring did not really commit any serious crimes but was merely a faction on which blame could be dumped. If so, it still makes them an important group of operatives. Jane Foster Zlatovski and her husband were also able to evade prosecution by fleeing abroad.

According to Thierry Wolton's *Le KGB en France,* Otto Katz was involved in the 1944 invasion of Spain by communists based in newly liberated France. It seems impossible since he isn't noted to have left the western hemisphere until 1946. This generally ignored episode was noted in Paul Johnson, *Modern Times,* Ch. 17, p. 608. 150

The communists wanted to test the theory that Franco's regime was unstable and would collapse under the slightest pressure.

Hedda Hopper once wrote, "There were some mighty angry citizens who saw a new paper-bound novel, *Goldsboro,* by Stefan Heym, in their favorite Beverly Hills bookstore." The item appeared in the *Los*

Angeles Times, July 8, 1954, p. A8 and was captioned "Lest We Forget."

There are several hypotheses as to how Karl Radek, born Sobelsohn, chose the name by which he was known to the public. Is it possible he took the name from Karl von Rade (b. 1768), a German theologian and writer. Incidentally, there was a French clergyman and writer named André Simon and a historian named Ernst Rheinhardt; the latter was a pseudonym used by Alexander Abusch.

George Murphy, the U.S. embassy official whom Louis Gibarti attempted to cultivate, played a key role in North Africa during the Vichy period. Though officially posted in Petain's capital, he spent his time establishing contacts with French generals in Maghreb. The Murphy-Weygand Accord allowed the U.S. to send non-military supplies to the possessions isolated by the war. He also coordinated the appointment of extra U.S. vice consuls to French colonies. This caused the Germans to pressure Marshal Petain to recall General Weygand. Murphy's intelligence gathering formed much of the basis for America's landing in Morocco in 1942. General Eisenhower awarded him the Distinguished Service Medal in Algiers in 1943. Murphy's efforts were a turning point in North African history. Moroccans and Algerians live in Europe by the millions and carry not only French but British, Belgian, Dutch, German and even Swedish passports. European governments fanatically support their immigration and the building of mosques throughout Europe. Critics of this policy are sent to jail, guilty of banned hate speech.

Helene Roussel's *Deutsche Exilpress in Frankreich* is one of the few works which has used the KPD files in Paris as a source.

Howard Rushmore, who wrote one newspaper column devoted to criticizing Stefan Heym in 1946, was a former communist who became an outspoken anti-communist. His career took another turn when he became editor of magazines called *Uncensored* and *Confidential,* devoted mostly to celebrity gossip. *Uncensored* was also the name of a pro-isolationist publication banned by the Roosevelt regime in December 1941. Rushmore was frequently embroiled in legal controversies. He shot his wife and himself in a taxi in Manhattan in 1958. It's difficult to determine which is stranger; the fact that his death evokes Modotti's and Serge's, or that no one has said so in print. Leo Flieg was part of an entity called the "International Revisionskommission" according to "Rote Aufbau," July 1929. Exiled writer Odon von Horvath was killed when a tree fell on him in 1937 on the Champs Elysees.

Nachruf, p. 495, cites the Sterns as grounds for asking for asylum in Czechoslovakia in 1950, though the Sterns didn't emigrate to the East Bloc until 1957. This critique presumes, however, that Heym and the leaders in Prague didn't know in 1950 that the Sterns would be later granted asylum in Czechoslovakia.

Leo Lania was born as Lazar Herrmann in Kharkov in 1896, but grew up in Vienna and attended school with Karl Frank and the Eislers. He became a dedicated communist and worked on the *Rote Fahne* newspaper. Lenin is claimed to have publicly praised his work and offered him leadership of the journal. Lania snubbed him and quit the party. Despite his rejection of Lenin, Lania was welcome in the U.S.S.R. in 1936. He worked in the Office for War Information, created by Executive Order of Franklin Delano Roosevelt, from its inception to beyond the end of the war. He also dabbled as a screenwriter and novelist. A film he wrote released in 1932 featured Hedy Lamarr and Peter Lorre, well before they became internationally famous. His postwar novel *The Foreign Minister* is based around two characters; one purportedly based on Otto Katz and the other on Eduard Benes. Recall that Leo Flieg was called the head of the "Leo Lania Committee" and all other illegal operations.

Several FBI informants were convinced there was a connection between Claud Cockburn's *The Week* and Heym's periodicals, the

Deutsches Volksecho and *Underground News*, but gave no grounds for their assertion.

The British Public Record Office, file numbers HW 17 14 and HW 17 15 show that at least for 1936, Willi Muenzenberg was included in the Soviet Union's public relations strategies in regard to the Spanish Civil War. Muenzenberg is called "Herfurt," his code name, in Moscow to Paris messages of August and December 1936. Muenzenberg was officially rehabilitated in 1990, according to *Neues Deutschland*, June 25, 1990, p. 1-2. Fritz Raddatz, *Erfolg oder Wirkung,* claims Muenzenberg was the illegitimate son of Freiherr von Seekendorf and that he shot his mother's husband at age eleven. The Nazis had a spy at Muenzenberg's Paris "Freedom Party" meetings according to file MA 644 in the Institut fuer Zeitgeschichte in Munich.

ACKNOWLEDGMENTS

The author's family would like to recognize the following for their professional expertise and guidance in the publication of this book.

Vicki Lagoudis for guiding us to the Jenkins Group publishing firm, which then connected us with Allan Graubard whose editorial and design expertise we are thankful for.

Susan Shankin and Rick Benzel from Precocity Press for their many hours of manuscript review, layout, and helpful suggestions.

To a dear friend of the author and his family, James Beck. Many thanks are extended for your time and dedication.

Appreciation is extended to Hubert's cousin, Dirk Veneman, for assisting Bert on his journey in June of 2019 to visit the ancient colosseum in Trieste.

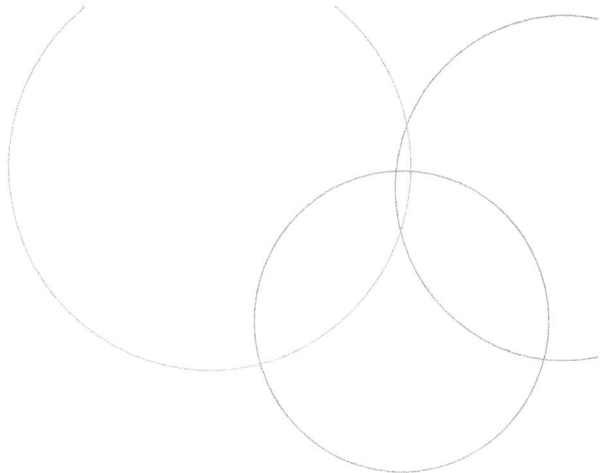

BIBLIOGRAPHY

Alexander Abusch, *Der Deckname*, Dietz, Berlin, 1981

Alexander Abusch, *Mit offenen Visier*, Dietz, Berlin, 1986

Sara Alpern, *Freda Kirchwey a Woman of the Nation*, Harvard University, Cambridge (Massachusetts), 1987

Christopher Andrew, Oleg Gordievsky, *KGB The Inside Story*, Harper, New York City, 1991

Werner Angress, *Die Kampfzeit der KPD 1921-1923*, Droste, Dusseldorf, 1973

Werner Angress, *Stillborn Revolution*, Princeton University, Princeton, 1963

Joerg Armer, *Die Wiener Weltbuehne, Wien, 1932-1933 Die Neue Weltbuehne, Prag/Paris 1933-1939*, K.G. Saur, Munich, 1992

Robert Asprey, *The Panther's Feast*, Putnam, New York City, 1959

Gloria Barron, *Leadership in Crisis: FDR and the Path to Intervention*, Kennikat, London, 1973

Karel Bartosek, *Les Aveux des Archives*, Seuil, Paris, 1996

Leland Bell, *In Hitler's Shadow*, Kennikat, Port Washington (New York), 1973

Gyorgy Borsanyi, *The Life of a Communist Revolutionary*, Columbia University, New York City, 1993

Alain Boureau, *Histoire d'un Historien Kantorowicz*, Galimard, Paris, 1990

Rudolf Brandl, "That Good Old Fool Uncle Sam," New York City, 1940

Peter Brandt, Joerg Schumacher, Goetz Schwarzrock, Klaus Suehl, *Karrieren eines Aussenseiters*, Verlag J.H.W. Dietz Nachf., Berlin, 1983

Bertholt Brecht, *Letters 1913-1956*, Routledge, New York City, 1990

Willi Bredel, *Spanienkrieg*, Aufbau, Berlin, 1977

Max Brod, *Der Prager Kreis*, Kohlhammer, Stuttgart, 1966

Alain Brossat, *Agents de Moscou: Le Stalinisme et son Ombre*, Galimard, Paris, 1988

Pierre Broue, *Rivoluzione in Germania*, Einaudi, Turin, 1977

Shareen Brysac, *Resisting Hitler*, Oxford University Press, New York City, 2001

Margaret Buber-Neumann, *Von Potsdam nach Moskau*, Deutsche Verlags-Anstalt, Stuttgart, 1971

William F. Buckley, L. Brent Bozell, *McCarthy and his Enemies*, H. Regnery , Chicago, 1954

Louis Budenz, *Men Without Faces*, Harper, New York City, 1950

Alfred Burmeister, *Dissolution and Aftermath of the Comintern*, New York City, 1955

Pino Cacucci, *Tina*, Interno Giallo, Milan, 1997

David Caute, *The Fellow -Travellers: A Postscript to the Enlightenment*, Weidenfeld and Nicolson, London, 1973

Robert Cazden, *German Exile Literature in America*, American Library Association, Chicago, 1970

Whittaker Chambers, *Witness*, Random House, New York City, 1952

Claud Cockburn, *Crossing the Line*, MacGibbon and Kee, London, 1959

Gary Cohen, *The Prague Germans 1861-1914*, Dissertation, Princeton, 1975

Roy Cohn, *McCarthy*, The New American Library, New York City, 1968

Committee on Un-American Activities, *Review of the Scientific and Cultural Conference for World Peace*, U.S. Government Printing Office, Washington, 1949

Hans Coppi, *Die Rote Kapelle in Widerstand gegen Nationalsozialismus*, Edition Hentrich, Berlin, 1994

Hans Habe, *Our Love Affair with Germany*, G.P. Putnam's Sons, New York City, 1953

Karl Corino, *Aussen Marmor innen Gips*, ECON, Dusseldorf, 1996

Karl Corino, *Robert Musil*, Rowohlt, Reinbek bei Hamburg, 1988

George Crocker, *Roosevelt's Road to Russia*, H. Regnery, Chicago, 1959

Herbert Crueger, *Verschwiegene Zeiten*, Linksdruck Verlag, Berlin, 1990

Geza von Cziffra, *Kauf dir einem bunten Luftballon*, F. A. Herbig, Munich, 1975

Geza von Cziffra, *Im Wartesaal des Ruhms*, Luebbe, Bergische-Gladbach, 1985

Franz Dahlem, *Am Vorabend des Zweiten Weltkriegs*, Dietz, Berlin, 1977

Robert Dallek, *Democrat and Diplomat*, Oxford University Press, New York City, 1968

David Dallin, *Soviet Espionage*, Yale University, New Haven, 1955

Jane De Gras, Editor, *The Communist International 1919-1943*, Frank Cass, London, 1971

Richard Deacon, *A History of the Russian Secret Servuce*, Muller, London, 1972

Richard Deacon, *The Israeli Secret Service*, Sphere, London, 1979

Peter Demetz, *After the Fires*, Harcourt, Brace, Jovanovich, San Diego, 1986

Isaac Deutscher, *The Prophet Outcast: Trotsky 1929-1940*, Oxford University Press, New York City, 1963

Bernard Dick, *Hellman in Hollywood*, Fairleigh Dickinson University, Rutherford (New Jersey), 1982

Richard Dove, *He Was a German*, Libris, London, 1990

Werner Eberlein, *Geboren am 9. November*, Das Neue Berlin, Berlin, 2002

Axel Eggebrecht, *Der halbe Weg*, Rowohlt, Reinbek bei Hamburg, 1975

Adolf Ehrt, *Communism in Germany*, Eckart Verlag, Berlin, 1933

Wolfgang Elfe *et al*, Editors, *The Fortunes of German Writers in America*, University of South Carolina, Columbia (South Carolina), 1992

M. Stanton Evans, *Blacklisted by History*, Crown Forum, New York City, 2007

Roger Faligot, Remi Kauffer, *Histoire Mondial du Renseignement*, R. Laffont, Paris, 1993

Lion Feuchtwanger, *Briefwechsel mit Freunden: 1933-1958*, Aufbau, Berlin, 1991

Louis Fischer, *Men and Politics*, Duell, Sloan and Pearce, New York City, 1941

Ruth Fischer, Arkady Maslow, *Abtruennig wider Willen*, R. Oldenbourg, Munich, 1990

Ruth Fischer, *Stalin and German Communism*, Harvard University, Cambridge (Massachusetts), 1948

Franklin Fo;som, *Days of Anger Days of Hope*, University of Colorado, Niwot (Colorado), 1994

Fondation Jules Humbert-Droz, *Centenaire Jules Humbert-Droz*, Fondation Jules Humbert-Droz, La Chaux de Fonds, 1992Jane Foster, *Unamerican Lady*, Sidgwick and Jackson, London, 1980

Ben Fowkes, *Communism in Germany under the Weimar Republic*, MacMillan, London, 1984

Emil Franzel, *Gegen den Wind der Zeit*, Aufstieg-Verlag, Munich, 1983

Bruno Frei, *Hanussen, ein bericht, mit einem Vorwort von Egon Erwin Kisch*, S. Brant-Verlag, Strassburg, 1934

Bruno Frei, *Die Papiersaebel*, S. Fischer, Frankfurt am Main, 1972

A. Freudenhammer, K. Vater, *Herbert Wehner*, Bertelsmann, Munich, 1978

Gerhard Frey, Publisher, *Prominente ohne Maske*, FZ-Verlag, Munich, 2001

Bella Fromm, *Blood and Banquets*, Harper, New York City, 1942

Arthur Frontenac, *Gisel contre Gilda Deux Armes Secretes en Lutte pour la Prochaine Guerre*, Editions Internationales, Paris, 1948

Wolfgang Fruehwald, John Spalek, Editors, *Der Fall Toller*, Hanser, Munich, 1979

John Fuegi, *Brecht and Company*, Grove Press, New York City, 1994

Dorothy Gallagher, *All the Right Enemies*, Rutgers University, New Brunswick (New Jersey), 1988

Helga Gallas, *Marxistische Literaturtheorie*, Luchterhand, Neuwied, 1971

Hansjorg Gehring, *Amerikanische Literaturpolitik in Deutschland*, Deutsche Verlags-Anstalt, Stuttgart, 1976

David Gelernter, *1939 The Lost World of the Fair*, The Free Press, New York City, 1995

Israel Getzler, *Martov*, Cambridge University Press, London, 1967

Heinz Gittig, *Illegale antifaschistische Tarnschriften 1933 bis 1945*, Roederberg Verlag, Frankfurt am Main, 1972

Erich W. Gniffke, *Jahre mit Ulbricht*, Verlag Wissenschaft und Politik, Cologne, 1966

Wilhelm Goldmann, *Offene Worte in Eigener Sache 1989-2001*, Muenchen, 2003

Alfons Goldschmidt, *Moskau 1920*, Berlin, 1920

Julian Gorkin, *El Revolucionario Profesional*, Ayma, Barcelona, 1975

Ruth Greuner, *Gegenspieler*, Buchverlag der Morgen, Berlin, 1969

Babette Gross, *Willi Muenzenberg eine politische Biographie*, Deutsche Verlags-Anstalt, Stuttgart, 1967

Babette Gross, *Willi Muenzenberg a Political Biography*, Michigan State University, East Lansing (Michigan), 1974

Michael Groth, *The Road to New York*, Minerva Publikation, Munich, 1984

Rolf Harder, Editor, *Briefe an Johannes Becher*, Aufbau, Berlin, 1993

Hanno Hardt *et al*, *Presse in Exil*, K. G. Saur, Munich, 1979

Samuel Harper, *The Russia I Believe in*, University of Chicago, Chicago, 1945

Klaus Haupt, Harald Wessel, *Kisch war Hier*, Verlag der Nation, Berlin, 1985

Hans Hautmann, *Geschichte der Raetebewegung in Oesterreich*, Europaverlag, Vienna, 1987

Arthur Garfield Hays, *City Lawyer*, Simon and Schuster, New York City, 1942

Ben Hecht, *A Child of the Century*, Simon and Schuster, New York City, 1954

Georg Heintz, *Index des "Freien/Neuen Deutschland" (Mexiko) 1941-1946*, G. Heintz, Worms, 1975

Stefan Heym, *Collin*, L. Stuart, Secaucus (New Jersey), 1980

Stefan Heym, *The Eyes of Reason*, Little Brown, Boston, 1951

Stefan Heym, *Hostages*, G. P. Putnam's Sons, New York City, 1942

Stefan Heym, *Immer sind die Weiber weg*, M. von Schroeder, Dusseldorf, 1997

Stefan Heym, *Keine Angst vor Russlands Baeren*, Brucken Verlag, Dusseldorf, 1955

Stefan Heym, *Beitraege zu einer Biographie*, Kindler, Munich, 1973

Stefan Heym, *Nachruf*, Buchverlag der Morgen, Berlin, 1990

Stefan Heym, "Nazis in USA," The American Committee for Anti-Nazi Literature, New York City, 1938

Stefan Heym, *Offengesagt*, Verlag Volk und Welt, Berlin, 1957

Stefan Heym, *Radek*, C. Bertelsmann, Munich, 1995 Josef Hindels, *Erinnerungen eines linken Sozialisten*, Das Archiv, Vienna, 1996Historische Kommission bei der Bayerischen Akademie der Wissenschaften, *Neue Deutsche Biographie*, Duncker und Humblot, Berlin, 1953-

Ludwig Hoffmann *et al*, *Exil in der Tschechoslowakei*, Roederberg Verlag, Frankfurt am Main, 1981

Karl Hofmaier, *Memoiren eines schweizer Kommunisten*, Rotpunkt Verlag, Zurich, 1978

Erich Honnecker, *From My Life*, Pergamon, New York City, 1981

Gustav Horn, Editor, *Judische Jugend in Uebergang*, Bitaon, Tel Aviv, 1980

Guenther Hortzschansky *et al*, *Ernst Thaelmann eine Biographie*, Verlag Marxistische Blaetter, Frankfurt am Main, 1979

Peter Huber, *Stalins Schatten in die Schweiz*, Chronos, Zurich, 1994

Angela Huss-Michel, *Literarische und politische Zeitschriften des Exils 1933-1945*, J. B. Metzler, Stuttgart, 1987

Peter Hutchinson, *Stefan Heym the Perpetual Dissident*, Cambridge University Press, Cambridge, 1992

Institut fuer Geschichte der Arbeiterbewegung, *In den Faengen des NKWD*, Dietz, Berlin, 1991

Karl-Heinz Jahnke, *Geschichte des deutschen Arbeiterjugendbewegung*, Weltkreis, Dortmund, 1995

Paul Johnson, *Modern Times*, Harper, New York City, 1992

Claere Jung, *Paradiesvogel*, Nautilus, Hamburg, 1987

Karel Kaplan, *Report on the Murder of the General Secretary*, Ohio University, Columbus, 1990

Otto Katz (as Franz Spielhagen), *Spione und Verschworer in Spanien*, Editions du Carrefour, Paris, 1936

Bernd Kaufmann, *Der Nachrichtendienst der KPD: 1919-1937*, Dietz, Berlin, 1993

Diethart Kerbs, Walter Uka, *Willi Muenzenberg*, Edition Echolot, Berlin, 1988

Gary Kern, *A Death in Washington*, Enigma Books, New York City, 2003

Lauren Kessler, *Clever Girl*, Harper Collins, New York City, 2003

Wolfgang Kiessling, *Brucken Nach Mexiko*, Dietz, Berlin, 1989

Wolfgang Kiessling, *Exil in Lateinamerika*, Reclam, Leipzig, 1980

Wolfgang Kiessling, *Leistner ist Mielke: Schatten einer gefaelschten Biographie*, Aufbau, Berlin, 1998

Wolfgang Kiessling, *Partner im "Narrenparadies,"* Dietz, Berlin, 1994

Kim Kyong-Kun, *Die Neue Zeitung*, Dissertation, 1974

Egon Kisch, *Briefe an den Bruder Paul und an die Mutter 1905-1936*, Aufbau, Berlin, 1978

Guido Kisch, *Der Lebensweg eines Rechtshistorikers*, Thorbecke, Sigmaringen, 1975

Harvey Klehr, John Haynes, Fridrikh Igorevich Firsov, *The Secret World of American Communism*, Yale University, New Haven, 1995

Harvey Klehr, John Haynes, *Venona: Decoding Soviet Espionage in America*, Yale University, New Haven, 1999

Peter Kleist, *Wer ist Willy Brandt?*, National Verlag, Hamburg, 1970

Stephen Koch, *The Breaking Point*, Counterpoint, New York City, 2005

Stephen Koch, *Double Lives*, The Free Press, New York City, 1994

Stephen Koch, *Double Lives*, Enigma Books, New York City, 2004

Arthur Koestler, *The Invisible Writing*, Beacon Press, Boston, 1955

Wolfgang Kramer, Editor, *Der Gegen-Angriff (Prag/Paris 1933-1936)*, G. Heintz, Worms, 1982

Egbert Krispyn, *Anti-Nazi Writers in Exile*, University of Georgia, Athens (Georgia), 1978

Jurgen Kuczynski, *Ein hofnungsloser Fall von Optimismus*, Aufbau, Berlin, 1994

Erik von Kuehnelt-Leddihn, *Leftism*, Arlington House, New Rochelle, 1974

Alfred Kurella, *Grundung und Aufbau der Kommunistischen Jugendinterna-tionale*, Verlag der Jugendinternationale, Berlin, 1929

Ursula Langkau-Alex, *Volksfront fuer Deutschland?*, Syndikat, Frankfurt am Main, 1977

Leo Lania, *The Foreign Minister*, P. Davies, 1957

Leo Lania, *Today We are Brothers*, Houghton Mifflin, Boston, 1942

Branko Lazich, *Biographical dictionary of the Comintern*, Hoover Institution Press, Palo Alto, 1973

V. Leers, *Das Judentum in der Rechtswissenschaft*, Band 3, Berlin, 1936

Wolfgang Leonhard, *Voelker Hoert die Signale*, Bertelsmann, Munich, 1981

Flora Lewis, *Red Pawn*, Doubleday, Garden City (New York), 1965

Boris Lewytzky, *Die rote Inquisition*, Societaets Verlag, Frankfurt am Main, 1967

Hubertus von Loewenstein, *Botschafter ohne Auftrag*, Droste, Dusseldorf, 1972

Hubertus von Loewenstein, *Towards the Further Shore*, Gollancz, London, 1968

Hubertus von Loewenstein, *Was war die deutsche Widerstandsbewegung*, Grafes, Bad Godesberg, 1965

John Loftus, Mark Aarons, *The Secret War Against the Jews*, St. Martin's Press, New York City, 1994

Heinz Lorenz, *Die Universum Buecherei 1926-1939*, Antiquariat und Verlag E. Tasbach, Berlin, 1996

Katharina Luebbe *et al*, *Die Reichstagabgeordeneter der Weimarer Republik in der Zeit des Nationalsozialismus*, Droste, Dusseldorf, 1991

James Lyon, *Bertholt Brecht in America*, Princeton University, Princeton, 1980

Eugene Lyons, *Assignment in Utopia*, Harcourt, Brace, Jovanovich, New York City, 1937

Ursula Madrasch-Groschopp, *Die Weltbuehne*, Athenaeum, Konigstein, 1983
Grigorii Maksimov, *The Guillotine at Work*, Chicago Section of the Alex-ander Berkman Fund, Chicago, 1940

Maurice Malkin, *Return to my Father's House*, Arlington House, New Rochelle, 1972

Klaus Mammach, Editor, *Die Brusseler Konferenz der KPD*, Dietz, Berlin, 1975

Klaus Mann, *Tagebuecher*, Spangenberg, Munich, 1989

Klaus Mann, Erika Mann, *Escape to Life*, Houghton Mifflin, Boston, 1939

Joseph McCarthy, *America's Retreat from Victory*, Devin-Adair, New York City, 1952

Maxwell McCartney, *Five Years of European Chaos*, Chapman and Hall, London, 1923

David McCullough, *Truman*, Simon and Schuster, New York City, 1992

Sean McMeekin, *The Red Millionaire*, Yale University, New Haven, 2003

Marion Meade, *Dorothy Parker What Fresh Hell is This?*, Villard Books, New York City, 1988

Franz N. Mehling, Publisher, *Knaurs Lexikon A-Z*, Droemer Knaur, Munich, 1987

Joan Mellen, *Hellman and Hammett*, Harper Collins, New York City, 1996

Karl Mewis, *Im Auftrag der Partei*, Dietz, Berlin, !971

Eike Middel *et al*, *Exil in den USA*, Roederberg Verlag, Frankfurt am Main, 1980

William H. Miller, *Transatlantic Liners at War*, David & Charles, Newton Abbot, 1985

Horst Moeller, *Parlementarismus in Preussen 1919-1932*, Droste, Dusseldorf, 1985

David Morgan, *The Socialist Left and the German Revolution*, Cornell University, Ithaca (New York), 1975

Boris Morros, *My Ten Years as a Counterspy*, Viking Press, New York City, 1959

Horst Mueller, *Kurt Hiller*, Christians, Hamburg, 1969

Reinhard Mueller, Editor, *Die Akte Wehners*, Rowohlt, Berlin, 1993

Reinhard Mueller, Editor, *Die Saeuberung*, Reinbek bei Hamburg, 1991

Robert Murphy, *Diplomat Among Warriors*, Doubleday, Garden City (New York), 1964

Arthur Murray, *At Close Quarter*, John Murray, London, 1946

Alma Neumann, *Always Straight Ahead*, Louisiana State University, Baton Rouge, 1993

Guenther Nollau, *Die Internationale*, Verlag fuer Politik und Wissenschaft, 1959

Albert Norden, *Ereignisse und Erlebtes*, Dietz, Berlin, 1981

William O'Dwyer, *Beyond the Golden Door*, St. John's University, Jamaica (New York), 1987

Henry Pachter, *Weimar Etudes*, Columbia University, New York City, 1982

Karl Otto Paetel, *Don Quichote en Miniatur*, Druckhaus Nuernberg, Nuremberg, 1971

Mario Passi, *Vittorio Vidali*, Edizioni Studio Tesi, Triest, 1991

Werner Pastor, *Willy Budich*, Kommittee zur Erforschung der Geschichte d. ortl. Arbeiterbewegung bei d. Bezirksleitung d. SED, Cottbus, 1988

Marcus Patka, *Egon Erwin Kisch: Stationen im Leben eines streitbaren Autors*, Boehlau, Vienna, 1997

Marcus Patka, *Der Rasende Reporter Egon Erwin Kisch*, Aufbau, Berlin, 1998

Walter Peterson, *The Berlin Liberal Press in Exile*, Tubingen, M. Niemeyer, 1987

Helmut Pfanner, *Exile in New York*, Wayne State University, Detroit, 1983

Osip Piatnitski, *Souvenirs d'un Bolshevik*, Bureau d'Editions, Paris, 1931

David Pike, *German Writers in Soviet Exile*, University of North Carolina, Chapel Hill, 1982

David Pike, *Lukacs and Brecht*, University of North Carolina, Chapel Hill, 1985 David Pike, *Prolegomena to the Study of German Writers in Soviet Exile*, Dissertation, 1978

David Pike, *The Politics of Culture in Soviet-Occupied Germany*, Stanford University, Stanford (California), 1992

Fritz Pohle, *Das mexikanische Exil*, Metzler, Stuttgart, 1986

Elisabeth Poretsky, *Our own People*, Oxford University Press, London, 1969

Otto Preminger, *Preminger an Autobiography*, Doubleday, Garden City (New York), 1977

Indalecio Prieto, *Epistolario Prieto-Negrin*, Planeta, Barcelona, 1990

R. John Pritchard, *Reichstag Fire Ashes of Democracy*, Ballantine Books, New York City, 1972

Erdmute Prokosch, *Egon Erwin Kisch*, Keil, Bonn, 1985

Fritz Raddatz, *Erfolg oder Wirkung*, C. Hanser, Munich, 1972

Fritz Raddatz, Editor, *Georg Lukacs in Selbstzeugnissen und Bilddokumenten*, Rowohlt, Reinbek bei Hamburg, 1972

Karl Radek, *Rosa Luxemburg, Karl Liebknecht, Leo Jogiches*, Verlag der Kommunistische Internationale, Hamburg, 1921

Joachim Radkau, *Die deutsche Emigration in den USA*, Bertelsmann, Dusseldorf, 1971

Eudocio Ravines, *The Yenan Way*, Scribner, New York City, 1951

Gustav Regler, *Das Ohr des Malchus*, Kiepenhauer & Witsch, Cologne, 1958

Gustav Regler, *Gustav Regler Dokumente und Analysen*, Saarbrucker Druckerei, Saarbrücken , 1985 Marcel Reich-Ranicki, *Der doppelte Boden*, Ammann, Zurich, 1992

Gunther Reinhardt, *Crime Without Punishment*, Hermitage House, New York City, 1952

Werner Roeder *et al*, *Biographisches Handbuch der deutschsprachigen Emigration nach 1933*, K. G. Saur, Munich, 1983

Werner Roeder, *Die deutsche sozialistischen Exilgruppen in Grossbritannien*, Verlag Neue Gesellschaft, Bonn, 1968

Romain Rolland, *Gandhi et Romain Rolland*, A. Michel, Paris, 1969

Herbert Romerstein, "Heroic Victims," The Council for the Defense of Freedom, Washington, 1994

Herbert Romerstein, Stanislav Levchenko, *The KGB Against the "Main Enemy,"* Lexington Books, Lexington (Massachusetts), 1989

Eleanor Roosevelt, *This I Remember*, Harper, New York City, 1949

Thomas Ruprecht, *Felix Boenheim*, Olms, Hildesheim, 1992

Eli Sacharov, *Out of the Limelight*, Gefen, Hewlett (New York), 2004

Will Schaber, *Profile der Zeit*, Edition Isele, Eggingen, 1992

Max Scheer, *Ein unruhiges Leben*, Verlag der Nation, Berlin, 1975

Joseph Schildkraut, as told to Leo Lania, *My Father and I*, Viking Press, New York City, 1959

Tania Schlie, Sylvie Roche, *Willi Muenzenberg (1889-1940)*, Peter Lang, Frankfurt am Main, 1995

Tania Schlie *et al*, *Willi Muenzenberg un Homme Contre*, La Bibliotheque, Aix en Provence, 1983

Karl Schmidt, *Henry Wallace Quixotic Crusade*, Syracuse University, Syracuse (New York), 1960

Martin Schouten, *Rinus van der Lubbe*, Bezige Bij, Amsterdam, 1986

Nancy Lynn Schwartz, *Hollywood Writers' Wars*, Knopf, New York City, 1982

Anna Seghers, Wieland Herzfelde, *Gewoehnliches und gefaehrliches Leben*, Luchterhand, Darmstadt, 1986

Max Seydewitz, *Es hat sich gelohnt zu leben*, Dietz, Berlin, 1978

Leonard Slater, *The Pledge*, Pocket Books, New York City, 1971

Hartmut Soell, *Der junge Wehner*, Deutsche Verlags-Anstalt, Stuttgart, 1991

Heinz Sommer, *In Zeichen der Solidaritaet*, Institut fuer Marxismus-Leninismus, Berlin, 1986

John Spalek, *Guide to the Archival Materials of the German-Speaking Emigration to the United States After 1933*, University of Virginia, Charlottesville (Virginia), 1978

Hilde Spiel, *Die hellen und die finsteren Zeiten*, List, Muenich, 1989

George Spiro (as George Marlen), *Earl Browder Communist or Tool of Wall Street*, Van Rees Press, New York City, 1937

Donald Spoto, *Lenya a Life*, Little Brown, Boston, 1989

Friedrich Stampfer, *Erfahrungen und Erkenntnisse*, Verlag fuer Politik und Wirtschaft, Cologne, 1957

Joachim Steffen, *Auf zum letzten Verhoer*, Bertelsmann, Munich, 1977

Nathan Steinberger, *Berlin Moskau Kolyma und Zuruck*, ID-Archiv, Berlin, 1996

Alexander Stephan, *Im Visier des FBI*, Metzler, Stuttgart, 1995

Hartmut Stern, *"Judische Kriegserklaerungen an Deutschland,"* FZ-Verlag, Munich, 2000

Charles Tansill, *Back Door to War*, H. Regnery, Chicago, 1952

Hugh Thomas, *The Spanish Civil War*, Harper, New York City, 1961

Wayne C. Thompson, *The Political Odyssey of Herbert Wehner*, Westview Press, Boulder (Colorado), 1993

Fritz Tobias, *The Reichstag Fire*, Putnam, New York City, 1964

Ralph de Toledano, *Lament for a Generation*, Farrar, Straus and Cudahy, New York City, 1960

Nikolai Tolstoy, *Stalin's Secret War*, J. Cape, London, 1981

Leopold Trepper, *The Great Game*, McGraw-Hill, New York City, 1977

Bodo Uhse, F.C. Weiskopf, *Briefwechsel 1942-1948*, Aufbau, Berlin, 1990

Bodo Uhse, *Gesammelte Werke in Einzelausgaben*, Aufbau, Berlin

Bodo Uhse, *Reise und Tagebuecher*, Aufbau, Berlin, 1981

Klaus Vater, *Herbert Wehner*, Bertelsmann, Munich, 1978

Salka Viertel, *The Kindness of Strangers*, Holt, Rinehart and Winston, New York City, 1969

Vittorio Vidali, *Missione a Berlino*, Vangelista, Milan, 1978

Pierre de Villemarest, *Le Coup d'Etat de Markus Wolf*, Stock, Paris, 1991

John Walker, Editor, *Halliwell's Filmgoers Companion*, Twelfth Edition, Harper, New York City, 1997

George Walsh, *Public Enemies the Mayor the Mob and the Crime that Was*, Norton, New York City, 1980

Hans-Albert Walter, *Der Reporter der Keiner war*, Metzler, Stuttgart, 1988

Dorothy Waring, *American Defender*, R. Speller, New York City, 1935

Hermann Weber, *Der Generallinie*, Droste, Dusseldorf, 1981

Hermann Weber, *Terror: stalinistische Parteisaeuberung 1936-1953*, F. Schoeningh, Paderborn, 1998

Hermann Weber, *"Weisse Flecken" in der Geschichte*, ISP-Verlag, Frankfurt am Main, 1990

Hermann Weber, *Die Wandlung des deutschen Kommunismus*, Europaeische Verlagsanstalt, Frankfurt am Main, 1969

James Wechsler, *The Age of Suspicion*, Random House, New York City, 1953

Herbert Wehner, *Zeugnis*, Kiepenhauer & Witsch, Cologne, 1982

Allen Weinstein, *Perjury: the Hiss-Chambers Case*, Knopf, New York City, 1978

Allen Weinstein, *The Haunted Wood*, Random House, New York City, 1999

F. C. Weiskopf, *Unter fremden Himmeln*, Aufbau, Berlin, 1981

Harald Wessel, *Muenzenberg's Ende*, Dietz, Berlin, 1991

G. Edward White, *Alger Hiss's Looking Glass Wars*, Oxford University Press, New York City, 2004

Harry Wilde, *Theodor Plievier Nullpunkt der Freiheit*, Kurt Desch, Munich, 1965

Robert Williams, *Klaus Fuchs Atom Spy*, Harvard University, Cambridge (Massachusetts), 1987

Charles Willoughby, *Shanghai Conspiracy*, Dutton, New York City, 1952

Christian Windecke, *Der rote Zar*, Quelle und Meyer, Leipzig, 1932

Ella Winter, *And not to Yield*, Harcourt, Brace and Jovanovich, New York City, 1963

Markus Wolf, *Die Troika*, Claasen, Dusseldorf, 1989

Thierry Wolton, *Le KGB en France*, Bernard Grasset, Paris, 1986

Peter Wyden, *Stella*, Simon and Schuster, New York City, 1992

Ypsilon, *Pattern for World Revolution*, Ziff-Davis, Chicago, 1947

Kurt Zielenziger, *Juden in der deutsche Wirtschaft*, Heine Bund, Berlin, 1930

Hedda Zinner, *Auf den roten Teppich*, Buchverlag der Morgen, Berlin, 1978

Patrik von zur Muehlen, *Spanien war ihre Hoffnung*, Verlag Neue Gesellschaft, Bonn, 1983

Encyclopedia Brittanica, William Benton, London, 1957

"Film Daily Yearbook," New York City

"Jahrbuch fuer Historische Kommunismusforschung," Akademie Verlag, Berlin

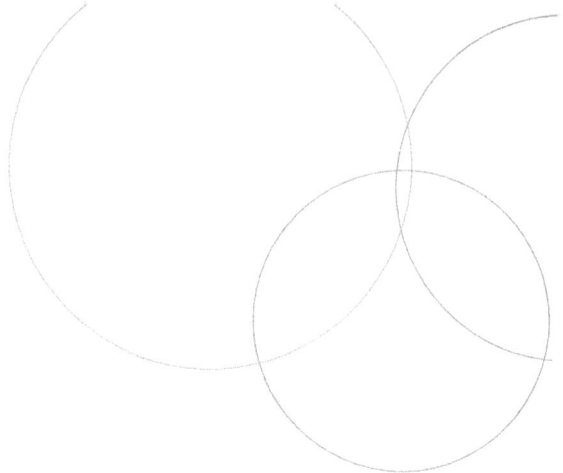

GLOSSARY OF ACRONYMS

A.D.N. – *Allgemeiner Deutscher Nachrichtendienst*, East German news service

ARPLAN – *Arbeitsgemeinschaft zum Stadium der Sowjetrussichen Planwirtschaft*, the Society for the Study of the Soviet Russian Planned Economy; an organization established in Germany and the US by the Soviets to educate Germans on the mechanisms of Soviet economy

BRD – *Bundesrepublik Deutschland*, Federal Republic of Germany, i.e., West Germany

CETEKA – Czechoslovakian official news agency

Comintern – Communist International, a.k.a. Third International (1919–1943), an international organization that advocated for world communism

CPUSA – Communist Party USA

DEFA – East German movie studio

DDR – *Deutsche Demokratische Republik*, the Democratic Republic of Germany, the former East Germany from 1949 to 1990

GPU – *Gosudarstvennoe Politicheskoe Upravlenie*, Soviet military intelligence service in the early 1920s

HUAC – U.S. House Un-American Activities Committee, investigated communist threats in the U.S. in the 1950s

KPD – *Kommunistische Partei Deutschlands*, Communist Party of Germany, a major political party during the Weimar Republic (1918-1933) and an underground resistance organization during the Nazi period

L.A.W. – League of American Writers

MASCH – *Marxistische Arbeiterschule*, Marxist Workers School

NSDSAP – *Nationalsozialistische Deutsche Arbeiterpartei*, the National Socialist German Workers' Party, aka, the Nazi Party, 1920 to 1945

NKVD – *Naródnyy Komissariát Vnútrennikh Del*, Soviet Interior Ministry, which was also a secret police organization

OMS – Secret service of the Comintern

OSS – Office of Strategic Services, the wartime U.S. intelligence agency

P.O.U.M. – *Partido Obrero de Unificación Marxista*, The Workers' Party of Marxist Unification, a Spanish communist political party

SAP or SADP – *Sozialdemokratische Arbeiterpartei Deutschlands* or *Sozial Arbeiter Partei*, the Social Democratic Workers' Party of Germany, a centrist Marxist party that split off from the SPD in Gremany in 1931

SPD – *Sozialdemokratische Partei Deutschlands*, Social Democrats Party (SPD), one of the major political parties of Germany since 1890

TASS – Russian news agency

U.J.A. — United Jewish Appeal

USPD – *Unabhängige Sozialdemokratische Partei Deutschlands*, The Independent Social Democratic Party, a far left wing group that merged into the SPD party

U.S.S.R – Union of Soviet Socialist Republics, comprising a confederation of Russia, Belorussia, Ukraine, and the Transcaucasian Federation

Vopo – *Volkspolizei*, East Germany's Police

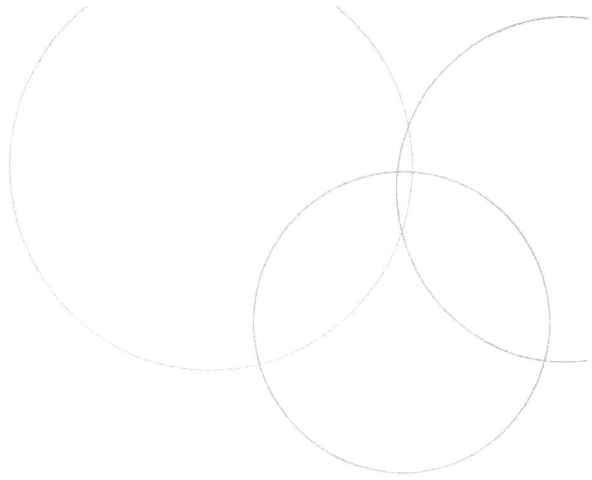

END NOTES

Chapter 1

1. In 1996, the author hired a researcher in Berlin to find Leo Flieg's birth records. The records show he was born in the Tempelhof district of Berlin. His father, Heymann Flieg, had a clothing business on Berlinerstrasse in Tempelhof. Leo Flieg had two siblings; an older half-brother whose mother was presumably Heymann Flieg's first wife, and a sister. His father died in 1926 at age 81. His mother died in Berlin in 1938 at age 73. Heymann Flieg is shown to have been born in Schrimm in 1845. Heym's father's birthplace is mentioned on the very first page of text in his autobiography *Nachruf,* Buchverlag der Morgen, Berlin, 1990, p. 5

2. *Encyclopedia Brittanica,* William Benton, London, 1957, vol. 18, p. 396 entry under "Poznan" gives the Jewish population there as 0.1% in 1931 while it had been many times higher before the annexation by Prussia. See also Alain Boureau, *Histoires d'un Historien Kantorowicz,* Galimard, Paris, 1990

3. Heym, *Nachruf,* p. 7-10 mentions Daniel Flieg's vocation in the textile trade. See also above note 1

4. Heym, *Nachruf,* p. 54-55

5. Ibid, p. 45-52

6. Peter Brandt, Joerg Schumacher, Goetz Schwarzrock, Klaus Suehl, *Karrieren eines Aussenseiters,* Verlag J.H.W. Dietz Nachf., Berlin, 1983, p. 37 notes Bauer in Berlin; Leo Bauer's early acquaintance with Helmut Flieg/Stefan Heym noted in *Nachruf,* p. 33

7. Chemnitz' founding by Benedictines noted in *Lexikon des Mittel Alters*, J. B. Metzler, Stuttgart, 1999, vol. II, p. 1791; Chemnitz as "Little Manchester" in Brandt et al, *Karrieren eines Aussenseiters*, p. 19 and *Encyclopedia Brittanica*, vol.5, p. 409 entry for "Chemnitz" where it is referred to as "Saxon Manchester."

8. Brandt et al, *Karrieren eines Aussenseiters,* p. 17

9. Heym, *Nachruf,* p. 33; Helmut Flieg/Stefan Heym is not mentioned at all in Brandt et al, *Karrieren eines Aussenseiters.*

10. See Karl Corino, *Aussen Marmor Innen Gips*, ECON, Duesseldorf, 1996

11. See Brandt et al, *Karrieren eines Aussenseiters*, p. 36-42; Heym, *Nachruf,* p. 57-59; also Will Schaber, *Profile der Zeit*, Edition Isele, Essingen, 1992

12. See Werner Roeder, *Die deutsche sozialistischen Exilgruppen in Grossbritanien 1940–1945,* Verlag Neue Geselschaft, Bonn, 1968. Kurt Rosenfeld, SAP founder, joined the KPD in 1937. Co-founder Max Seydewitz became president of Saxony in the DDR.

13. See Peter Kleist, *Wer ist Willy Brandt,* National Verlag, Hannover, 1970 and Peter Brandt et al, *Karrieren eines Aussenseiters,* p. 255-256

14. Brandt et al, *Karrieren eines Aussenseiters,* p. 36-50

15. Bernd Kaufmann, *Der Nachrichtendienst der KPD:1919–1937,* Dietz, Berlin, 1993; "Der Spiegel," Heft 12, 1993, p. 208; Sean McMeekin, *The Red Millionaire,* Yale University Press, New Haven, 2003; Mask Intercepts, British Public Record Office, Kew, Richmond, Document File HW 17 13, communique of October 16, 1934; "Permanente Revolution" Heft 12, June, 1932 quoted in Hermann Weber, *Die Wandlung des deutschen Kommunismus,* Europaeische Verlagsanstalt, Frankfurt am Main, 1969; vol. I, p. 407; Hermann Weber, *Der Generallinie*, Droste, Dusseldorf, 1981, p. lxxxviii; Werner Roeder et al, *Biographisches Handbuch der deutschsprachigen Emigration nach 1933*, K.G. Saur, Munich, 1983; Margaret Buber-Neumann, *Von Potsdam nach Moskau*, Deutsche Verlags-Anstalt, Stuttgart, 1971, p. 191, 212, 328; Guenther Nollau, *Die Internationale*, Verlag fuer Politik und Wissenschaft, Koln, 1959, p. 109, 113; David Dallin, *Soviet Espionage*, Yale University Press, New Haven, p. 88, 94 for a general idea of Leo Flieg's party duties.

16. See Bernd Kaufmann, *Der Nachrichtendienst*

17. Brandt et al, *Karrieren eines Aussenseiters*, p. 43; on Kippenberger see ibid; Institut fuer Geschichte der Arbeiterbewegung, *In den Faengen des NKWD*, Dietz, Berlin, 1991, p. 113; Dallin, *Soviet Espionage*, p. 88; Dallin calls Flieg an "aide" to Kippenberger which seems to be a minority view. Doubtlessly, though, they worked together frequently.

18. Dallin, *Soviet Espionage*, p. 92-94; Buber-Neumann, *Von Potsdam nach Moskau*, p. 361, 383; Wolfgang Leonhard, *Volker Hoert die Signale*, Bertelsmann,

Munich, 1981, p. 293; Katharina Luebbe et al, *Die Reichstagabgeordeneter der Weimarer Republik in der Zeit des Nationalsozialismus*, Droste, Dusseldorf, 1991, entry for Thielen, Nikolaus; Institut fuer Zeitgeschichte, Munich, file number Dc 15.02, p. 58; "Der Spiegel," Heft 12, 1993, p. 208

19. Brandt et al, *Karrieren eines Aussenseiters*, p. 49

20. Ibid, p. 54-63; also Exilarchiv, Deutsche Bibliothek, Frankfurt am Main, Nachlass W. Sternfeld, EB/75/177, a letter by Babette Gross of June, 1964, notes that Bauer brought material that was from Nazi files to Muenzenberg's publishing concern in Paris for the propaganda book *Das Braune Netz* that was published in 1935. A letter written by Bauer of August, 1964, admits work on the same book.

21. Ibid

22. Brandt et al, *Karrieren eines Aussenseiters*, p. 67

23. Horst Mueller, *Kurt Hiller*, Christians, Hamburg, 1969, p. 319

24. Brandt et al, *Karrieren eines Aussenseiters*, p. 36

25. Ibid, p. 68-76, Mueller, *Kurt Hiller*, p. 319

26. Brandt et al, *Karrieren eines Aussenseiters*, p. 57 citing Bauer's unpublished memoir.

27. Ibid, p. 68-76

28. Ibid, p. 318

29. Ibid, p. 95-99 citing the German translation of *Red Pawn* by Flora Lewis.

30. See George Hodos, *Show Trials*, Praeger, New York City, 1987 and Stepen Koch, *Double Lives*, The Free Press, New York City, 1994

31. Brandt et al, *Karrieren eines Aussenseiters*, p. 103-108

32. Ibid, p. 108-129 The "Free Germany" movement was promoted by communists in all the German exile centers including Mexico, U.S.A., and U.S.S.R.

33. That Bauer worked with Teubner in Switzerland from Ibid, p. 118; Teubner's and Trautzsch's origins in Chemnitz mentioned in Franz Dahlem, *Am Vorabend des Zweiten Weltkrieges*, Dietz, Berlin, 1977, vol. I, p. 430-436 and vol. II, p. 60; Trautzsch is portrayed as an operative in the vicinity of Bauer in Wolfgang Kiessling, *Partner in "Narrenparadies,"* Dietz, Berlin, 1994, p. 59

34. Pierre de Villemarest, *Le Coup d'Etat de Markus Wolf*, Stock, Paris, 1991, p. 143; Herbert Crueger, *Verschweigene Zeiten*, Linksdruck Verlag, Berlin, 1990, p. 129

35. Brandt et al, *Karrieren eines Aussenseiters*, p. 123

36. Ibid, p. 157, 167-168

37. Ibid, p. 172-173; Wolfgang Kiessling, *"Leistner ist Mielke": Schatten einer gefaelschte Biographie*, Aufbau, Berlin, 1998, p. 142

38. Brandt et al, *Karrieren eines Aussenseiters*, p. 256

39. Buber-Neumann, *Von Potsdam nach Moskau*, p. 190ff, 212f, 328f

40. "Frankfurter Allgemeine Magazin," Heft 538, June, 1990, p. 21

41. Karl-Heinz Jahnke, *Geschichte der deutschen Arbeiterjugendbewegung*, Weltkreis, Dortmund, 1995, p. 109, 251, 259; see also Roeder et al, *Biographisches Handbuch der deutschsprachigen Emigration nach 1933*; Reinhard Mueller, editor, *Die Akte Wehners: Moskau 1937 bis 1941*, Rowohlt, Berlin, 1993, p. 256

42. Ibid; for Jogiches' death see Jochen Steffen, *Auf zum letzten Verhoer*, Bertelsmann, Munich, 1977, p. 42

43. Buber-Neumann, *Von Potsdam nach Moskau*, p. 190f, 212f, 328f

44. Ibid

45. Ibid; Roeder et al, *Biographisches Handbuch der deutschsprachigen Emigration nach 1933*; "Der Spiegel," Heft 12, 1993, p. 208; Archives Nationales, Paris, F 7 12900; Pierre Broue, *Rivoluzione in Germania*, Einaudi, Turin, 1977; Peter Huber, *Stalins Schatten in die Schweiz*, Chronos, Zurich, 1994, p. 147, 241; Dallin, *Soviet Espionage*, p. 87-88

46. Buber- Neumann, *Von Potsdam nach Moskau*, p. 190f, 212f, 328f

47. The biographical outlines available indicate Flieg's status at the Comintern was unchanged by the party demotion. Roeder et al, *Biographisches Handbuch der deutschsprachigen Emigration*, Branko Lazich, Milorad Drachkovitch, *Biographical Dictionary of the Comintern*, Hoover Institution Press, Palo Alto, 1973

48. Ibid and Institut fuer Geschichte der Arbeiterbewegung, *In den Faengen des NKWD*, p. 71-72; Babette Gross, *Willi Muenzenberg eine politische Biographie*, Deutsche Verlags-Anstalt, Stuttgart, 1967; also mentioned in David Pike, *German Writers in Soviet Exile*, University of North Carolina Press, Chapel Hill, 1982; Werner Eberlein, *Geboren am 9. November*, Das Neue Berlin, Berlin, 2002, p. 29, 85

49. Buber-Neumann, *Von Potsdam nach Moskau*, p. 328

50. "Exil," Nr. 1, 1991, p. 46-69

51. Ibid and Buber-Neumann, *Von Potsdam nach Moskau*, p. 212

52. See, Stefan Heym, *Immer sind die Weiber weg*, M. von Schroeder, Dusseldorf, 1997

53. See, Kurt Zielenziger, *Juden in der deutschen Wirtschaft*, Heine Bund, Berlin, 1930, p. 210; Gustav Horn, editor, *Judische Jugend in Uebergang Ludwig Tietz 1897-1933*, Bitaon, Tel Aviv, 1980, p. 31; Records of the Birnbaum secondary school available in the Oesterreichische National Bibliothek show a teacher named Tietz listed in the late 1800s.

54. Heym, *Nachruf*, p. 22

55. Karl-Heinz Jahnke, *Geschichte der deutschen Arbeiterjugendbewegung*, p. 109

56. Buber-Neumann, *Von Potsdam nach Moskau*, p. 190f

57. FBI Freedom of Information Act file on Walter Krivitsky which is available on the internet.

58. Roeder et al, *Biographisches Handbuch der deutschsprachigen Emigration nach 1933*

59. Flieg's involvement in the socialist youth group in 1908 noted in Broue, *Rivoluzione in Germania.*

60. Julian Marchlewski, born 1866 in Wloclawek or Leslau, Prussia but was a founder of the Polish Socialist Party in 1893. Rosa Luxemburg, born 1870 in Zamosc, Poland. Leo Jogiches, born 1867 in Vilnius, presently in Lithuania. Karl Radek born in Lemberg, today Lvov, Ukraine.

61. Toller, born in 1893 in Samotschin, near Bromberg, in Posen. For a lampooning of his regime in Bavaria by an eye witness, see Ben Hecht, *A Child of the Century*, Simon and Schuster, New York City, 1954, p. 299-316

62. See, Alfred Kurella, *Grundung und Aufbau der Kommunistischen Jugend Internationale*, Verlag der Jugendinternationale, Berlin, 1929 and Jahnke, *Geschichte der deutschen Arbeiterjugendbewegung*, p. 251, 259; "Beitraege zur Geschichte der deutschen Arbeiterbewegung," J.12, Nr. 1, 1970, p. 4; a rare picture of Flieg with Muenzenberg at a youth international meeting appears in Diethard Kerbs, Walter Uka, *Willi Muenzenberg, Zeitgenossen I*, Edition Echelot, Berlin, 1988

63. McMeekin, *The Red Millionaire*, p. 213 and Gross, *Willi Muenzenberg eine politische Biographie*

64. Leo Flieg, Willi Muenzenberg, *Die Jugend der Revolution*, Berlin, 1920; the university library in Frankfurt is one of the few places where it is available.

65. Kurella, *Grundung und Aufbau der Kommunistischen Jugendinternationale*, p. 80, 95, 124, 157

66. The term conciliator, or "Versoehnler," is found over and over in transcripts of hearings during the Great Terror. See Reinhard Mueller, editor, *Die Saeuberung*, Rowohlt Taschenbuch Verlag, Reinbek bei Hamburg, 1991 in which actual transcripts of party discussions and cross-examinations are published.

67. Flieg's time as a representative in the Prussian Diet is only mentioned in biographical outlines. Roeder et al, *Biographisches Handbuch der deutschsprachigen Emigration* and Institut fuer Geschichte der Arbeiterbewegung, *In den Faengen der NKWD*, p. 72

68. Dallin, *Soviet Espionage*, p. 88; Buber-Neumann, *Von Potsdam nach Moskau*, p. 191; Nollau, *Die Internationale*, p. 109; Archives Nationales, Paris, F 7 12900 the Deuxième Bureau was aware "Fliege" was liaison with the International by 1925.

69. "Der Spiegel" Heft 44, 1995; see also Werner Angress, *Stillborn Revolution*, Princeton University Press, Princeton, 1963

70. See note 18

71. "Der Spiegel," Heft 12, 1993, p. 208 and Dallin, *Soviet Espionage*, p. 92

72. Dallin, *Soviet Espionage*, p. 100

73. Ibid, p. 101

74. Ibid

75. Ibid, p. 99

76. Leonhard, *Volker Hoert die Signale*, p. 293

77. Luebbe, *Die Reichstagabgeordneten der Weimarer Republik in der Zeit der Nationalsozialismus*, entry for Thielen. A Nazi work, *Das Judentum in der Rechtswissenschaft*, Nr.3, Berlin, 1936, p. 47; article by V. Leers notes an old problem with forged passports from Posen but does not mention Flieg's Passzentrale.

78. For Buber-Neumann, see Buber-Neumann, *Von Potsdam nach Moskau*, p. 383; for Mewis, see Karl Mewis, *Im Auftrag der Partei*, Dietz, Berlin, 1971; for Von Ranke see Alain Brossat, *Agents du Moscou:Le Stalinisme et Son Ombre*, Galimard, Paris, 1988, p. 101; for Raichmann see Leopold Trepper, *The Great Game*, McGraw-Hill, New York City, 1977, p. 105–106

79. "Internationale wissenschaftliche Korrespondenz der deutschen Arbeiterbewegung," Nr. 4, 1981, p. 526ff

80. Institut fuer Geschichte der Arbeiterbewegung, *In den Faengen des NKWD*, p. 72

81. Ibid, p. 63, 72; Lazich, Drachovitch, *The Biographical Dictionary of the Comintern*, ; Gross, *Willi Muenzenberg eine poltische Biographie*, p. 316; Eberlein, *Geboren am 9. November*, p. 29

82. Eberlein, *Geboren am 9. November*, p. 18-19, 28-29 Eberlein also notes a third Harms sister was married to Polish communist Gutek Rwal.

83. Ibid, p. 85

84. Ibid, p. 45,49, 65

85. Fritz Raddatz, editor, *Georg Lukacs in Selbstzeugnissen und Bilddokumenten*, Rowohlt, Reinbek bei Hamburg, 1972, p. 76; Flieg is also involved in literary matters in Helga Gallas, *Marxistische Literaturtheorie*, Luchterhand, Neuwied, 1971, p. 60, 191; one of the 20th century's leading Marxist intellectuals, Georg Lukacs, is quoted by Gallas as opining that Flieg had significant influence on cultural questions; also Pike, *German Writers in Soviet Exile*, p. 41

86. Guenther Hortschansky et al, *Ernst Thaelmann eine Biographie*, Verlag Marxistische Blatter, Frankfurt am Main, 1979 describes many encounters between Flieg and Ernst Thaelmann who was the KPD's candidate for Chancellor in the last years of the Weimar Republic.

87. Ibid, p. 465, 508

88. Ibid, p. 508

89. Ibid, p. 544

90. The KPD set up a committee for transition to illegality in 1932 headed by another former assistant to Leo Jogiches. Leo Flieg must certainly have been well apprised of this. See David Dallin, *Soviet Espionage*, p.93; Werner Pastor, *Willy Budich: eine biographische Skizze*, Kommittee zur Erforschung der Geschichte d. ortl. Arbeiterbewegung bei d. Bezirksleitung d. SED, Cottbus, 1988, p. 45

91. Guenther Nollau claimed that Pieck preceded Flieg as party liaison to the OMS. Nollau, *Die Internationale*, p. 113

92. Institut fuer Zeitgeschichte, Munich, MA 643, frame 2797323 also notes Flieg away in Russia.

93. Weber, *Die Generallinie*, p. lxxxviii cites "Permanente Revolution," Nr. 12, June, 1932

94. Vittorio Vidali, *Missione a Berlino*, Vangelista, Milan, 1978

95. See Pastor, *Willi Budich*, p. 18, 49 the description on page 53 may be the incident recounted by Vidali. Budich is called boss of the M-Apparat in Kaufmann, *Der Nachrichtendienst*, p. 33

96. Wilhelm Bahnik is called an underground supervisor active just after the Reichstag fire in Dallin, *Soviet Espionage*, p. 84 and is noted to have been in the BB-Apparat and having been born in Posen in Roeder et al, *Biographisches Handbuch der deutschsprachigen Emigration*; Willi Bredel was a politically active writer who was in the military during the Spanish Civil War.

97. The "Eighth International Sports Base" is noted in Gross, *Willi Muenzenberg eine politische Biographie* and Koch, *Double Lives*, 1994 ed., p. 98-99; for Mirov-Abramov in connection with Pleyel, see Tanja Schlie, *Willi Muenzenberg un Homme contre*, La Bibliotheque, Aix-en-Provence, 1983, p. 50 and Dahlem, *Am Vorabend des Zweiten Weltkrieges*, p. 50 or 550

98. Ibid and Koch, *Double Lives*, 1994 ed., p. 38-39, 64 Note Koch mentions Louis Gibarti as a leading figure in the conference's organization.

99. Koch, *Double Lives*, 1994 ed., p. 99; Dallin, *Soviet Espionage*, p. 103; Lazich, Drachkovitch, *Biographical Dictionary of the Comintern*; not widely known previous to the opening of Soviet archives to western scholars is that Mirov-Abramov worked for the GPU, see Hermann Weber, editor, *Jahrbuch fuer historische Kommunismusforschung 1993*, Akademie Verlag, Berlin, 1993, p. 273 article "Berta Zimmerman" by Peter Huber; Mirov-Abramov is also mentioned in Elisabeth Poretsky, *Our Own People*, Oxford University Press, London, 1969 , Ypsilon, *Pattern for World Revolution*, Ziff-Davis, Chicago, 1947, Roger Faligot, *As-Tu Vu Cremet?*, "Exil," Heft 1, 1991 Lebenslauf of Margaret Buber-Neumann, Mask Intercepts, British Public Records Office, Kew, Richmond including file HW 17 16

100. Institut fuer Zeitgeschichte, Munich, BA R58/1249 and MA 643 frame 2798177

101.Muenzenberg also traveled personally to Saarbrücken, from Alexander Abusch, *Der Deckname*, Dietz, Berlin, 1981, p. 327; Moscow advised Muenzenberg on "Sarre" strategy in a communiqué, Mask Intercepts, British Public Record Office, Kew, Richmond, HW 17 13; Flieg's presence in Saarbrücken is noted in Institut fuer Zeitgeschichte, Munich, Dc 15.02 "Erfassung fuehrender Maenner der Systemzeit," p. 58 and could be deduced from Dallin, *Soviet Espionage*, p. 101-102; also Eberlein, *Geboren am 9. November*, p. 85

102. The passport forgery operation's move to Saarbrücken from Dallin, *Soviet Espionage*, p. 101-102

103. See Erich Honnecker, *From My Life*, Pergamon, New York City, 1981

104. Franz N. Mehling, publisher, *Knaurs Lexikon A-Z*, Droemer Knaur, Munich, 1987, p. 807

105. *The New York Times*, September 9, 1939, p. 1. Many other papers carried the news of Moroccan participation in the encirclement of Saarbrücken including the *Mansfield News Journal* of Mansfield, Ohio and the *Nevada State Journal* on the same date.

106. Mask Intercepts, British Public Record Office, Kew, Richmond, HW 17 13 message of October 16, 1934. Knorin in Moscow asks Flieg and Runge to take an on the spot inquiry regarding Langrock and Ernst. The matter is likely in connection with Flieg's duties as member of the Comintern's Control Commission. Wilhelm Knorin was on the Executive Committee of the Comintern.

107. Klaus Mammach, *Die Brusseler Konferenz der KPD (3-15 Oktober 1935)*, Dietz, Berlin, 1975, p. 21, 28, the so-called Brussels Conference was actually held in a suburb of Moscow.

108. See Kaufmann, *Der Nachrichtendeinst der KPD*

109. Mammach, *Die Brusseler Konferenz*, p. 21 makes quasi-official Flieg's use of "Alfons" as an alias. It is also mentioned in several biographical outlines in works that mention Flieg.; Mask Intercepts, British Public Record Office, Kew, Richmond, HW 17 6, Moscow to and from Prague from August, 1935 to June 1936.

110. Mask Intercepts, British Public Record Office, HW 17 6 and HW 17 8

111. Sass and Martini currency swindle is in first section FBI FOIA file on Walter Krivitsky

112. Eberlein, *Geboren am 9. November*, p. 85

113. *Der Spiegel*, Heft 12, 1993, p. 208 and Mueller, *Die Akte Wehner;* incidentally one finds the expression "fliegende Abstimmung" several times e.g., p. 130; also, "Berliner Kurier," August 27, 2004, p. 3 "KGB-Akten Enthuellen"

114. Wayne Thompson, *The Political Odyssey of Herbert Wehner*, Westview Press, Boulder, 1993, p. 203 and Herbert Wehner, *Zeugnis*, Kiepenhauer & Witsch, Koln, 1982

115. Institut fuer Geschichte der Arbeiterbewegung, *In den Faengen des NKWD*, p. 63, 71-72; the Great Terror's effect on Germans in the Soviet Union is described extensively in Pike, *German Writers in Soviet Exile* and David Pike, *Prolegomena*, dissertation, 1978, p. 364-504 and Hermann Weber, *Terror: Stalinistische Parteisaeuberung 1936-1953*, F. Schoeningh, Paderborn, 1998

116. Institut fuer Geschichte der Arbeiterbewegung, *In den Faengen des NKWD*, p. 160-161, 183; both were also convicted by the military court.

117. McMeekin, *The Red Millionaire*, p. 278-294

118. Koch, *Double Lives*, 1994 ed., p. 309-320 explains theories on Muenzenberg's death.

119. Broue, *Rivoluzione in Germania*; Buber-Neumann, *Von Potsdam nach Moskau*, p. 190-191; Roger Faligot, Remi Kauffer, *Histoire Mondial du Renseignement*, R. Laffont, Paris, !993, vol. I, p. 309; Boris Lewytzky, *Die rote Inquisition*, Societaets Verlag, Frankfurt am Main, 1967, p. 135-136

120. Alfred Doeblin, "Karl and Rosa" the copy perused by the author was an English translation.

Chapter 2

1. Heym, *Nachruf*, p. 54-76

2. Ibid, p. 54, 74

3. Shareen Brysac, *Resisting Hitler*, Oxford University Press, New York City, 2001, p. 111, 122-123, 145; It is claimed Arvid Harnack had just finished a book on the Soviet Union when the Reichstag fire occurred. The plates set up for printing were destroyed by the publisher to avoid accusations of supporting communism; p. 128 citing an interview.

4. Mildred Harnack was, for a time, president of the American woman's club in Berlin. See Brysac, *Resisting Hitler*, p. 144; on Mildred Harnack's friendship with Martha Dodd, see Brysac, *Resisting Hitler*, p. 140-143; a September 1933 letter of Martha Dodd's notes she once co-wrote a book review column with Mildred Harnack. Martha Dodd seems to have arrived in Berlin a bit too late to have had an acquaintanceship with Stefan Heym during 1933.

5. Brysac, *Resisting Hitler*, p. 107-109

6. Ibid, p. 108; Marxist intellectual Georg Lukacs was also acquainted with the Harnacks and Leo Flieg; see also note 85, Chapter I.

7. Brysac, *Resisting Hitler*, p. 117-118

8. Like Leo Flieg, Piatnitski perished during the Terror.

9. The Red Orchestra is the subject of many books including Chapter 6 of Dallin, *Soviet Espionage,* and works by Hans Coppi, Wilhelm Flicke, V. E. Tarrant, and Manfred Roeder. There are also several works on individual members

of the ring. Their operation is also noted in most books on espionage during World War II, most books on resistance within Germany, and many which deal with Soviet espionage in general.

Chapter 3

1. Heym, *Nachruf*, p. 68-69

2 Ibid, p. 77-83

3. Kisch was long known as *Der Rasende Reporter* or "The Raging Reporter." Even to this day a yearly prize is awarded in his name by "Stern" magazine in Germany. Nobody calls "Stern" a communist publication.

4. Historische Kommission bei der Bayerischen Akademie der Wissenschaften, *Neue Desutsche Biographie*, Duncker und Humblot, Berlin, 1953- , vol. 11, p. 680

5. Ibid

6. Guido Kisch, *Der Lebensweg eines Rechthistorikers*, Thorbecke, Sigmaringen, 1975, p. 208

7. Donald Spoto, *Lenya: A Life*, Little Brown, Boston, 1989, p. 60

8. Leipzig, Schwerin, the Wartenberg district of Berlin, and the Suedvorstadt district of Dresden, Gera and Neustrelitz each have a street named for Egon Erwin Kisch. According to Hans-Albert Walter, *Ein Reporter der Keiner war*, J. B. Metzler, Stuttgart, 1988, p. 6, Egon Kisch's likeness was once featured on a postage stamp.

9. Emil Franzel, *Gegen den Wind der Zeit*, Aufstieg Verlag, Munich, 1983, p. 510

10. Ibid, Harold B. Segel, *The Vienna Coffeehouse Wits 1890-1938*, p. 293ff section on Anton Kuh

11. "Internationale Wissenschaftlich Korrespondenz zur Geschichte der Deutsche Arbeiterbewegung," Heft 1, 1996, p. 56, "Anspiel" by Henryk Skrzypczak; He was called an Associated Press correspondent in Leo Lania, *Today We are Brothers*, Houghton Mifflin, Boston, 1942, p. 183; both might be correct at different times.

12. Geza von Cziffra, *Kauf dir einem bunten Luftbalon*, F.A. Herbig, Munich, 1975, p. 54-58; von Cziffra once directed a motion picture with the same title.

13. Kisch's role in the affair is noted in Robert Asprey, *The Panther's Feast*, Putnam, New York City, 1959. He is not mentioned in several other accounts of the scandal.

14. See Karl Corino, *Robert Musil*, Rowohlt, Reinbek bei Hamburg, 1988

15. Kisch's role as a revolutionary leader in Vienna after World War I is given great attention in Hans Hautmann, *Geschichte der Raetebewegung in Oesterreich 1918-1924*, Europaverlag, Vienna, 1987 and nearly nowhere else.

16. Since the monarchy remained deposed, Kisch became a reputable radical rather than a perfidious one.

17. Gerhart Eisler may have been the most powerful communist in the United States during long periods of the 1930s and 1940s when he resided in New York City. See, for example, Louis Budenz, *Men Without Faces*, Harper, New York City, 1950. Karl Frank led a movement called "Neu Beginnen" following his ostensible departure from the Communist Party. It is likely that he was far from disloyal but was leading an opposition movement exactly because he could be relied upon. He was also a member of the SAP in 1931-1932, which seems to account for his sustained relationship with Willy Brandt.

18. See, Ella Winter, *And not to Yield*, Harcourt, Brace, New York City, 1963

19. See, "Publizistik und Kunst," Nrs. 7,8, p. 57 article by Beatrix Geisel.

20. Christian Windecke, *Der Rote Zar*, Quelle und Meyer, Leipzig, 1932, p. 231

21. Ursula Madrasch-Groschopp, *Die Weltbuehne*, Athenaeum, Konigstein, 1983, p. 312

22. Bodo Uhse, *Gesammelte Werke*, Aufbau Verlag, Berlin, vol. 6, p. 336

23. Alexander Abusch, *Der Deckname*, p. 327

24. See, Stephen Koch, *Double Lives* for information on Otto Katz.

25. Charles Willoughby, *Shanghai Conspiracy*, E.P. Dutton, New York City, 1952, p. 308

26. Harald Wessel, *Muenzenbergs Ende*, Dietz Verlag, Berlin, 1991, p. 76 states Kisch was sent to Australia in autumn 1934; Abusch, *Der Deckname*, p. 385 notes he returned to Prague in March 1935

27. Heym, *Nachruf*, p. 99-101

28. Arthur Koestler, *The Invisible Writing*, Beacon Press, Boston, 1955, p. 232; her given legal name is revealed in Kiessling, *Partner im "Narrenparadies,"* p. 145

29. Klaus Haupt, Harald Wessel, *Kisch war Hier*, Verlag der Nation, Berlin, 1985, p. 177

30. Erdmute Prokosch, *Egon Erwin Kisch*, Keil, Bonn, 1985, p. 230

31. Rosl Jungmann is named in Kiessling, *Partner im "Narrenparadies,"* p. 141; Frau Jungmann's name is recalled otherwise in Julian Gorkin, *El Revolucionario Professional*, Ayma, Barcelona, 1975. However, Kiessling has been a scholar on the subject of Kisch's exile for several decades and Gorkin only knew them as adversaries in Mexico during his asylum there during World War II and seems more likely to have recalled the name erroneously; Erich Jungmann as the youngest member of parliament is noted in Kaufmann, *Der Nachrichtendienst*, p. 309.

32. See Elisabeth Poretsky, *Our own People*; incidentally Kisch is called an agent of Reiss' in Gary Kern, *A Death in Washington*, Enigma Books, New York

City, 2003, p. 85 Hede Massing, later a witness against Alger Hiss, is mentioned in the same sentence as part of Reiss' auxilliary.

33. Referring to Arthur Frontenac, *Gisel Contre Gilda, Deux Armes Secretes en Lutte pour la Prochaine Guerre*, Editions Internationales, Paris, 1948

34. Kiessling, *Partner im "Narrenparadies,"* p. 140

35. Uhse, *Gesammelte Werke*, vol. 5, p. 293 mentions her *in passim* during an event of 1957.

36. Gary Cohen, *The Prague Germans 1861-1914*, dissertation, 1975, University Microfilms, Ann Arbor, p. 47 reprints a statement that Prague was one third German in 1861; p. 573-574 states that Prague was still 4.9 percent German in 1930; the work also notes that nearly fifty percent of those calling themselves German were German-speaking Jews while approximately three quarters of the Jews in Prague called themselves German; p. 182 notes F.C. Weiskopf's 1931 novel *Slawenlied* about a German adolescent in Prague before and after World War I; *Encyclopedia Brittanica*, 1957 edition, Volume 18, p. 415 states that 4.6 percent of the total population of 676,657 persons was German in 1921 and that the population was 848,823 in 1930; Kisch's acquaintanceship with Kafka is implied in Max Brod, *Der Prager Kreis*, Kohlhammer, Stuttgart, 1966 and Egon Kisch, *Briefe an den Bruder Paul und an die Mutter*, Aufbau, Berlin, 1978.

37. Heym, *Nachruf*, p. 92-93

38. Ibid

39. Ibid, p. 92-93; Abusch, *Der Deckname*, p. 413

40. Heym, *Nachruf*, p. 494-500; the ambassador/caricaturist referred to is Adolf Hoffmeister.

41. Alexander Stephan, *Im Visier des FBI*, Metzler, Stuttgart, 1995, p. 351-352 notes Weiskopf as plenipotentiary in 1948. The same pages state he was also emissary to China. Between 1945 and 1948, Weiskopf used being apparently German to his advantage by claiming to the U.S. government he had to remain in the country because Germans were being expelled from Czechoslovakia.; see also F. C. Weiskopf, *Unter Fremden Himmeln*, Aufbau, Berlin, 1981

42. Mask Intercepts, British Public Records Office, Kew, Richmond, File number HW 17 19, message of September 4, 1936

43. Heym, *Nachruf*, p. 92; a "Konrad" noted without a surname as Heym did in Ludwig Hoffmann, *Exil in der Tschechoslowakei*, Roederberg, Frankfurt am Main, 1981

44. "Konrad" matched to Duenow or Dynow in Dallin, *Soviet Espionage*, p. 100-103 Dallin's spelling Dynow may be a problem of transliteration from German to Russian to English.

45. Ibid, p. 103

46. Heym, *Nachruf*, p. 90-91; though Heym claimed the circular was unknown to him, it was compiled by a General Janoschik, which is a name of a character in Heym's first novel *Hostages* which takes place in Prague.

47. Ibid, p. 91

48 Ibid

49. Egbert Krispyn, *Anti-Nazi Writers in Exile*, University of Georgia Press, Athens (Georgia), 1978, p. 32-34; the incident is recorded in less detail in David Caute, *The Fellow Travellers: A Postscript to the Enlightenment*, Weidenfeld and Nicolson, London, 1973; Ruth Fischer, Arkady Maslow, *Abtruennig Wider Willen*, R. Oldenbourg, Munich, 1990, p. 480 notes Budzislawski gave free advertising space to SAP founder and *Deutsche Volksecho* publisher Kurt Rosenfeld; Mask Intercepts, British Public Records Office, Kew, Richmond, HW 17 5, message of February 8, 1935, Prague to Moscow asks for article by Radek for Weltbuehne as soon as possible; see Markus Wolf, *Die Troika*, Claasen, Dusseldorf, 1989, p. 147-149; Abusch, *Der Deckname*, p. 389; Axel Eggebrecht, *Der Halbe Weg*, Rowohlt, Reinbek bei Hamburg, 1975, p. 222; Ruth Greuner, *Gegenspieler*, Buchverlag der Morgen, Berlin, 1969, p. 39, 164; Madrasch-Groschopp, *Die Weltbuehne*, p. 317

50. Pike, *German Writers in Soviet Exile*, p. 163

51. Peter Hutchinson, *Stefan Heym*, Cambridge University, Cambridge, 1992, p. 249-250 provides a list of Heym's contributions, which is extensive but not absolutely complete. It does show Heym contributed poems to *Die Weltbuehne* in 1932-1933 previous to Schlamm's editorship while still in Berlin.

52. A copy of Volksecho stationery appeared in *Deutsches Volksecho*, June 17, 1939

53. Pike, *German Writers in Soviet Exile*, p. 201; Hutchinson, *Stefan Heym*, p. 249-250

Chapter 4

1. Heym, *Nachruf*, p. 112-113
2. Ibid, Chapter 7; see note 12 below
3. Heym, *Nachruf*, p. 144-145
4. Ibid, p. 19, 66-67
5. Ibid, p. 107
6. Rolf Harder, editor, *Briefe an Johannes Becher*, Aufbau, Berlin, 1993, p. 95-97
7. Ibid
8. Heym, *Nachruf*, p. 140-141
9. Ibid

10. Kisch, *Briefe an den Bruder Paul*, p. 152; *Chicago Daily Tribune*, February 24, 1938, p.1 "Seize Ex-Prof and 4 Others in Nazi Clashes" calls von Schroetter a "former professor of languages at the University of Chicago and Northwestern."

11. FBI FOIA File on Stefan Heym, "Summary of File" August 23, 1950, p. 3, Main File No. 100-142236; the article "Though not Marxists" appeared in the September 29, 1936 issue of *New Masses* according to FBI documents. Heym also wrote for the KPD's illegally smuggled propaganda sheets, see Heinz Gittig, *Illegale Antifaschistische Tarnschriften 1933 bis 1945*, Roederberg, Frankfurt am Main, 1972. By coincidence Herbert Wehner also compiled economic statistics such as those used in Heym's article in *The Nation*. The author does not know whether the figures the two compiled match.

12. The summer job at night school was not mentioned in *Nachruf*. The job is mentioned in the Army section of Heym's FOIA file. The report dated June 16, 1943 was filed by the Francis Cody noted in the memoir. It is also mentioned in FBI Report, October 12, 1948, Boston Office, File No. 100-20223.

Chapter 5

1 Heym, *Nachruf*, p. 150-151; for Rosenfeld as Justice Minister see perhaps Horst Moeller, *Parlementarismus in Preussen 1919-1932*, Droste, Dusseldorf, 1985

2. Fischer, Maslow, *Abtruennig Wider Willen*, p. 658; Roeder et al, *Biographisches Handbuch der deutschsprachigen Emigration nach 1933*; David Morgan, *The Socialist Left and the German Revolution*, Cornell University, Ithaca (New York), p. 465; Schaber, *Profile der Zeit* states explicitly that the SAP's newspaper was also founded by Rosenfeld and Seydewitz.

3. Osip Piatnitski, *Souvenirs d'un Bolshevik*, Bureau d'Editions, Paris, 1931, p. 87; Rosenfeld is noted as defending revolutionaries in 1904.

4. Fischer, Maslow, *Abtrunnig Wider Willen*, p. 658; Morgan, *The Socialist Left and the German Revolution*, p.465; there also exists published correspondence between Rosenfeld and Luxemburg.

5. See Morgan, *The Socialist Left and the German Revolution*

6. Israel Getzler, *Martov*, Cambridge University, London, 1967, p. 212; Rosenfeld's motion at a meeting received no support at all showing he was, perhaps, the most extreme leftist in attendance.

7. *Washington Post*, May 27, 1922

8. Ruth Fischer, *Stalin and German Communism*, Harvard University, Cambridge, 1948

9. Booklet titled *Das Reichskommittee der Internationale Arbeiterhilfe*, Berlin, May, 1924, p. 25

10. *Deutsches Volksecho*, May 27, 1939 article by Rosenfeld upon Toller's death; Madrasch-Groschopp, *Die Weltbuehne,* p. 285, 305 notes Rosenfeld as Ossietzky's lawyer; Fritz Tobias, *The Reichstag Fire,* Putnam, New York City, 1964, p. 93; Arthur Garfield Hays, *City Lawyer,* Simon and Schuster, New York City, 1942, p. 342; also articles by Torgler in *Die Zeit,* October 21, 1948 and October 28, 1948 note Rosenfeld had been Torgler's attorney.

11. Gyorgy Borsanyi, *The Life of a Communist Revolutionary,* Columbia University, New York City, 1993, p. 315-316, 342

12. A library catalogue lists the periodical as a *Halbmonatschrift,* a third co-publisher was named Max Adler.

13. Institut fuer Zeitgeschichte, Munich ED 210/24 Hans Jaeger *"Materialen zur deutsche politischen Emigration,"* p. 2

14. "Europaeische Ideen" 1992, Nr. 79, p. 162

15. A. Freudenhammer, K. Vater, *Herbert Wehner,* Bertelsmann, Munich, 1978, p. 364

16. Alfred Burmeister, *Dissolution and Aftermath of the Comintern,* New York City, 1955, p. 31; "Beitraege zur Geschichte," Nr. 4, 1989, p. 489-490 notes Wilhelm Pieck was especially concerned about the Seydewitzes' disappearance; Institut fuer Geschichte der Arbeiterbewegung, *In den Faengen des NKWD,* p. 220

17. *Neues Deutschland*, February 10, 1987, p. 4; *Neues Deutschland,* March 30, 1989, p. 4 The official DDR newpaper also gives Mrs. Seydewitz credit for helping the Red Army help save some of Dresden's treasures.

18. *Reno Evening Gazette*, June 9, 1932, p. 5; *Wisconsin Rapids Daily Tribune*, June 9, 1932; this is likely a wire service article that was printed in dozens if not hundreds of newspapers around the country. The cites are from the internet subscription site, newspaperarchive.com.

19. Ursula Langkau-Alex, *Volksfont fuer Deutschland?,* Syndikat, Frankfurt am Main, 1977; Michael Groth, *The Road to New York*, Minerva Publikation, Munich, 1984, p. 139; Max Scheer, *Ein unruhiges Leben*, Verlag der Nation, Berlin, 1975, p. 175

20. *The New York Times,* June 9, 1934, p. 2; Robert Cazden, *German Exile Literature in America*, American Library Association, Chicago, 1970, p. 46, 53; Luebbe et al, *Die Reichstagabgeordneten der Weimarer Republik*, notes speeches by Rosenfeld before smaller audiences in Denver and Seattle in August 1934.

21. Hays, *City Lawyer*; According to Tobias, *The Reichstag Fire*, p. 93, 202; Wilhelm Pieck wanted Torgler to employ Hays as his trial lawyer; Gross, *Willi Muenzenberg eine politische Biographie*, p. 383 states Louis Gibarti recruited Hays for the counter-trial; *Deutsches Volksecho,* February 20, 1937, p. 14 promotes a speaking engagement for Hays on behalf of the League Against War

and Fascism; "Un-American Activities in California," Fourth Report, 1948 notes Mrs. Arthur Hays and Kurt Rosenfeld as having been on the National Council of American-Soviet Friendship.

22. Statement by Helen Konieczny Dobos on July 2, 1952 in Room 457, Senate Office Building, in the presence of Frank W. Schroeder and Donald D. Connors, Jr. professional staff members the Senate Subcommittee on Internal Security, p. 5, from FOIA file on Louis Gibarti. Mrs. Dobos was married to the Soviet agent who arranged the visa with Representative Dickstein. She had been a typist at the KPD Headquarters in Berlin, the Karl Liebknecht Haus, and also claimed that Kurt Rosenfeld had secretly been a communist for many years; Dorothy Waring, *American Defender*, R. Speller, New York City, 1935 is a biography of Dickstein. It is a paean by one who is seemingly a society lady to an ethnic Soviet agent and is the sort of thing that makes one wonder what is going on in this country. Also, it is rarely pointed out that Dickstein helped found the House Un-American Activities Committee (HUAC) in order to expose and prosecute Nazi activities.

23. Wolfgang Kramer, editor, *Der Gegen Angriff (Prag/Paris 1933-36)*, G. Heintz, Worms, 1982 notes Stefan Heym contributed three articles and Kurt Rosenfeld four; Heym and Rosenfeld also both contributed to *Die Neue Weltbuehne*. See Joerg Armer, *Die Wiener Weltbuehne, Wien, 1932-1933, Die Neue Weltbuehne, Prag/Paris, 1933-1939*, K.G. Saur, Munich, 1992; Hutchinson, *Stefan Heym*, p. 249-250

24. Fischer, Maslow, *Abtruennig Wider Willen*, p. 480; an example of an advertisement for *Die Neue Weltbuehne* is in *Deutsches Volksecho*, October 9, 1937, p. 5

25. "Exil," Nr. 2, 1989, p. 8 article by Frithjof Trapp; The same article notes Rosenfeld's affiliation with the "Deutsche Liga fuer Menschenrecht."

26. There are at least five mentions of Rosenfeld in the KPD files; Archives Nationales, Paris, F 7 15132; One notes a letter from Pieck to Rosenfeld in 1937, two are critical of Rosenfeld's debating performances, and one notes him present at a KPD-New York meeting in 1939.

27. Fischer, Maslow, *Abtruennig Wider Willen*, p. 658 notes Rosenfeld officially joined the KPD in 1938. The same volume on page 502 states Rosenfeld was also the attorney for the Soviet Embassy in Berlin, which is another indication that the communists trusted him.

28. Alfons Goldschmidt, *Moskau 1920*, E. Rowohlt, Berlin, 1920

29. Wolfgang Kiessling, *Brucken nach Mexiko*, Dietz, Berlin, 1989, p. 192; "Das Reichskommitee der Internationale Arbeiterhilfe," Berlin, May, 1924, p. 39 calls Goldschmidt the founder of IAH.

30. See Kiessling, *Brucken nach Mexiko* and Fritz Pohle, *Das mexikanisches Exil*, Metzler, Stuttgart, 1986

31. Archives Nationales, Paris, F 7 12900

32. Whittaker Chambers, *Witness*, Random House, New York City, 1952, p. 352; *Witness* and Allen Weinstein, *Perjury: The Hiss-Chambers Case*, Knopf, New York City, 1978 are considered two of the most important books on Soviet infiltration in the United States and are almost never cited in Germany.

Chapter 6

1. Herb Romerstein, Stanislav Levchenko, *The KGB Against the "Main Enemy*," Lexington Books, Lexington (Massachusetts), 1989, p. 89

2. Chambers, *Witness*, p. 390; the editor's name was Ludwig Lore.

3. Middel et al, *Exil in den USA*; Gerhart Seger, "Reminiscences," Oral History Office, Butler Library, Columbia University, New York City; Angela Huss-Michael, editor, *Literarische und Politische Zeitschriften des Exils 1933-1945*, J.B. Metzler, Stuttgart, 1987; each give slightly different dates for the beginning of Seger's editorship. Incidentally, Seger's "Reminiscenses" is a transcript of an interview during which the Hans Weber incident is not discussed.

4. Heym, *Nachruf*, p. 143-144; Hutchinson, *Stefan Heym*, p. 29

5. Jane DeGras, editor, *The Communist International 1919-1943*, Frank Cass, London, 1971, vol. III, p. 348f shows the Popular Front was official policy of the Comintern; see also Koch, *Double Lives*.

6. Heym, *Nachruf*, p. 144

7 Heym, *Nachruf*; Hutchinson, *Stefan Heym*, p. 29-30

8. Noted in Hartmut Soell, *Der Junge Wehner*, Deutsche Verlags-Anstalt, Stuttgart, 1991, p. 211

9. Noted in Kaufmann, *Der Nachrichtendienst*, p. 141

10. *Deutsches Volksecho,* December 11, 1937, p. 4; note also Heym's editorial "Wo steht der Feind?" of late May or early June 1937 suggested outrage was the appropriate response to those who would propose that Stalin could even be compared to Hitler.

11. Rudolf Katz was co-publisher, *herausgeber*, of the "Neues Volkszeitung" with Gerhart Seger in 1937; see Huss-Michel, *Literarische und Politische Zeitschriften des Exils 1933-1945*.

12. Microfilm copies of the *Deutsches Volksecho* are available at the New York Public Library but, apparently, nowhere else.

13. Heym, *Nachruf*, p. 161

14. Ibid, p. 161-162; printed together vertically are greetings from John Heartfield (Wieland Herzfelde's brother) from Prague, Egon Erwin Kisch from Paris, "Rudolf Breda" from Paris, Georg Bernhard from Paris, and Congressman Vito Marcantonio. Marcantonio was an openly communist politician who had been Fiorello LaGuardia's campaign manager and succeeded him in the House

of Representatives from a district in East Harlem that was then populated by immigrants from southern Italy and Sicily; Kisch also contributed an article to the *Volksecho* in 1938.

15. It is stated explicitly that Katz used the name "Breda" because Van der Lubbe had lived there as a youth in Hubertus von Loewenstein, *Botschafter ohne Auftrag*, Droste, Dusseldorf, 1972, p. 129-130, 132 and Hubertus von Loewenstein, *Towards the Further Shore*, p. 171; Bruno Frei, *Die Papiersaebel*, S. Fischer, Frankfurt am Main, 1972, p. 184 states that Katz actually traveled to Breda in 1933 purportedly to research Van der Lubbe; von Loewenstein claims Van der Lubbe was born in Breda. However, a biography of Van der Lubbe has his birthplace as Leyden while his family did move to Breda in his early childhood; see Martin Schouten, *Rinus van der Lubbe*, Bezige Bij, Amsterdam, 1986

15. Von Loewenstein, who participated with Katz in the fraud during April 1936, describes it blandly in *Botschafter ohne Auftrag*, p. 129-130, 132 and in *Towards the Further Shore*; Stephen Koch, *The Breaking Point*, Counterpoint, New York City, 2005, p. 229-230, 303-304 portrays Katz screening *The Spanish Earth* at celebrities' homes during the summer of 1937; Klaus Mann, *Tagebucher*, Spangenburg, Munich, 1989 diary entry of July 26, 1938 also shows Katz maintaining the "Breda" facade; see also Curt Riess, *Das war ein Leben!*, Ullstein, Frankfurt am Main, 1990,p. 238, 373-374, Nancy Lynn Schwartz, *Hollywood Writers Wars*, Knopf, New York City, 1982, p. 84; Stephen Koch, *Double Lives*; Marion Meade, *Dorothy Parker*, Villard, New York City, 1988

17. As stated before, Katz and Kisch were lifelong friends. Leo Flieg's former roommate Willi Muenzenberg is said to have dispatched Katz/Breda on his mission acording to von Loewenstein, *Towards the Further Shore*.

18. McMeekin, *The Red Millionaire*, p. 283-284

19. Ibid, p. 283-285, 364-365 McMeekin explains the swindle clearly and succinctly. Bernhard was found liable for court expenses and defamation charges. He was also placed under arrest in October 1938; the case is also mentioned in Walter Peterson, *The Berlin Liberal Press in Exile*, M. Niemeyer, Tubingen, 1987

20. Obscure works on intra-red terror in Spain are Herb Romerstein, *Heroic Victims*, The Council for the Defense of Freedom, Washington, 1994 and Bernard Rosler, "Moskau in Spanien" an unpublished manuscript which has languished in the files of "Die Zukunft" in the National Archives of France since 1940.

21. Hutchinson, *Stefan Heym*, p. 29-30

22. Ibid

23. For example Peter Demetz, *After the Fires*, Harcourt Brace Jovanovich, San Diego, 1986, p. 129 calls the paper "an anti-fascist weekly of Popular Front orientation"; Wolfgang Elfe *et al*, editors, *The Fortunes of German Writers in America*, University of South Carolina, Columbia (South Carolina), 1992, p. 137

calls it "the German daily of the Social Democrats in New York"(it was actually a weekly); Hutchinson, *Stefan Heym* also fails to explain direct links to the Communist Party.

24. The New York Public Library's catalogue lists it so, as does "Confidential Intelligence Memorandum" to London of April 30, 1938 from the FOIA file on Louis Gibarti. The same file also contains a statement that the *Volksecho* assumed the physical premises of *Der Arbeiter*; also Heym, *Nachruf* states Curt Loewe who is portrayed as business manager of the *Volksecho* had earlier been editor of *Der Arbeiter* and accepted a demotion to remain employed.

25. Hutchinson, *Stefan Heym*, p. 26

26. Eike Middel et al, *Exil in den USA*, Roederberg Verlag, Frankfurt am Main, 1980, p. 144-145

27. An analysis of Steele's career is beyond the scope of this composition. However, a close examination of his activities from the time he joined the *Volksecho* will likely reveal that he followed the political line of a typical fellow traveler. Steele ran for office in 1946 for the heavily infiltrated American Labor Party; noted in Karl Schmidt, *Henry A. Wallace Quixotic Crusade*, Syracuse University, Syracuse, New York, 1948, p. 68

28. *Deutsches Volksecho*, January 14, 1939, p. 5 an editor's note previous to the article by Riess states that his column, which appeared in eight different languages in Europe, was being reprinted with the author's permission. Riess' column appeared weekly for the next several months; Riess, *Das war ein Leben!*, p. 374 notes Katz/Breda in Hollywood and that he was concerned U.S. security services were interested in his relationship with Katz. It didn't prevent him for working for the OSS in Europe during and after the war.

29. *Deutsches Volksecho*, December 4, 1937, article "Auf Schwarzwaelder Floessen" by Hermann Hesse

30. Heym, *Nachruf*, p. 162, 168, 173 mention interaction with Thomas Mann during the Volksecho period. German scholars have yet to come to terms with the extent of Mann's fellow traveling during the Hitler years.

31. See Georg Heintz, *Index des "Freien/Neuen Deutschland" (Mexiko) 1941-1946*, Heintz, Worms, 1975; Heym, *Nachruf*, p. 168 notes Mann's speech at the opening of the Soviet Pavilion at the World's Fair in Flushing in 1939.

32. *Deutsches Volksecho*, August 26, 1939, "Ein Deutscher Katholik in der Sowjet Union"

33. Archives Nationales, Paris, F 7 15132

34. Ibid; there are also messages signed "PM" and "EJ" who are likely Paul Merker and Erich Jungmann. A letter by Lion Feuchtwanger to F. C. Weiskopf of April 3, 1942, says that Eleanor Roosevelt once intervened on behalf of Jungmann; from Lion Feuchtwanger, *Briefwechsel mit Freunden*, Aufbau, Berlin, 1991

35. Archives Nationales, Paris, F 7 15132 dated July 31, 1937; the report also mentions "Genosse Browder" and mentions Heinrich Mann's article on the Soviet Volga German Republic.

36. Archives Nationales, Paris, F 7 15132

37. Ibid, especially notes dated July 19, 1938 and July 29, 1938; the question perhaps should be whether the *Volksecho* office was also the KPD office for New York City. The Hotel Lutetia was, for practical purposes, the KPD office in Paris.

38. "FBI Summary of File," August 23, 1950, p. 119, Main File No. 100-142236 citing 65-49085-81 referring to a letter from the Office of Censorship to the FBI, from Freedom of Information Act or FOIA file on Stefan Heym.

39 Archives Nationales, Paris, F 7 15132 the letter also notes that Kurt Rosenfeld is being overworked.

40. *The New York Times*, December 18, 2001, p. C15 notes Heym's secret membership in the CPUSA, which he disclosed in a form he filled out in the DDR. The article even notes Heym's claim "that he 'never belonged to a party in my whole life.'" Possibly his membership had something to do with his editing a communist newspaper in the U.S. Once the paper closed, he simply retained his prior undisclosed affiliations.

Chapter 7

1. Archives Nationales, Paris, F 7 15132

2. For example, see Eberlein, *Geboren am 9. November*, p. 69-86; Pike, *German Writers in Soviet Exile* is a good place to become acquainted with the subject; Institut fuer Geschichte der Arbeiterbewegung, *In den Faengen der NKWD* sought to account for the fates of arrested German communists but there were hundreds who disappeared without documentation about to which prison or gulag camp they were sent.

3. *Deutsches Volksecho,* March 6, 1937, "Ueberfall auf Die Weckruf-Redaktion" is the full-breadth of the front page headline; *Deutsches Volksecho,* March 13, 1937, "Bund in Aufruhr Gegen Fritz Kuhn" headline across the width of the front page.

4. Heym, *Nachruf*, p. 134

5. FOIA file on Stefan Heym. Noted are tips from informants and one phone call made to the *Volksecho* office by an agent. It is unclear as to how the agent identified himself.

6. FBI "Summary of File," August 23, 1950, p. 20, Main File No. 100-142235 citing 61-7566-978; Romerstein, Levchenko, *The KGB Against the "Main Enemy"* claims Mother Bloor's son Harold Ware was the leading figure in the communist cells organized in Washington during Franklin Roosevelt's first term. Ware was

killed in a car accident before the end of the decade but his work remains notorious. An interview with "Mother Bloor" appeared in the July 3, 1937 issue of the
Deutsches Volksecho.

7. FBI "Summary of File," August 23, 1950, p. 26 citing the "Daily Worker,"
August 4, 1938. From FOIA File on Stefan Heym

8. FBI "Summary of File," August 23, 1950, p. 28, Main File No. 100-142236
citing 61-7566-1102. From FOIA File on Stefan Heym

9. For example, *Deutsches Volksecho,* February 20, 1937 a "Deutsches Volks-
fest" with Stefan Heym also featuring Dr. Paul Reid "Natl. Sec'y, American League
Against War & Fascism;" *Deutsches Volksecho,* October 23, 1937 and February 3,
1938; there are many others including ads for Heym's radio appearances such as
Deutsches Volksecho, October 9, 1937 promoting Heym's upcoming appearance
on radio station WQXR.

10. *Ironwood Daily Globe,* Ironwood, Michigan, March 6, 1937, p. 7; this was
a wire service story that doubtlessly made many other papers around the U.S.

11. *The New York Times,* January 2, 1939, p. 24

12. *The New York Times,* August 6, 1937, p. 20; the FBI files also note an article
titled "Nazi War on Labor in America Charged by German Editor-Widespread
Spy System Fights Unions, Says Stefan Heym" in the "Philadelphia Record,"
November 19, 1937. This story was also reported by the Associated Press. See,
"Clearfield Progress," Clearfield, Pennsylvania, November, 19, 1937, p. 1 "Editors
Charges Against Germany Draws Attention"

13. FBI "Summary of File," August 23, 1950, p. 124, Main File No. 100-142236.
From FOIA File on Stefan Heym

14. N.Y.P.L. Catalogue; "Underground News," #81, March 31, 1939, #85, April
28, 1939, #89, May 31, 1939

15. See Koch, *Double Lives*

16. Koch, *Double Lives* 1994 edition, p. 282, 343

17. Archives Nationales, Paris, F 7 15131, a list of members and executives
of communist front organizations lists her so; Heinz Lorenz, *Die Universum
Bucherei*, Antiquariat und Verlag E. Tasbach, Berlin, 1996, p. 175 notes her role
in founding another organization.

18. "Statement made by Helen Konieczny Dobos on July 2, 1952 in Room 457,
Senate Office Building, Washington D.C. in the presence of Frank W. Schroeder
and Donald D. Connors, Jr. Professional Staff Members of the Senate Subcommittee on Internal Security" from the FOIA File on Louis Gibarti

19. FBI "Summary of File," August 23, 1950, p. 4, Main File No. 100-142236.
From FOIA File on Stefan Heym

20. "Statement made by Helen Konieczny Dobos"

21. See Koch, *Double Lives,*1994 edition

22. Gyula Alpari, Theodor Mally, Alexander Rado and Sandor Goldberger aka J. Peters were some of the most notable Hungarian agents; who were the Hungarians Helmut Flieg/Stefan Heym knew in Prague?, Heym, *Nachruf*, p. 83; Helen Konieczny mentioned a Yuri Friedman whom she and Gibarti knew in Berlin. Friedman is mentioned as being active in South America in Eudocio Ravines, *The Yenan Way*, Scribner, New York City, 1951, p. 113

23. Department of State, Office of Special Agent in Charge of New York Division, J. Fitch to R. Bannerman, May 2, 1938 from FOIA File on Louis Gibarti

24. Ibid. Gibarti gave this reason in 1921.

25. Koch, *Double Lives*,1994 edition; Department of State, Division of European Affairs, May 4, 1939, "Summary of Information Regarding Ladislas Dobos" from FOIA file on Louis Gibarti

26. McMeekin, *The Red Millionaire*, p. 208

27. Koch, *Double Lives*,1994 edition, p. 32, 38-40, 64 notes Gibarti in his roles in Muenzenberg's committees and as having been active in the Far East. The relationship with Einstein should not be shocking to one who has studied Einstein's political involvements during the Weimar Republic; Department of State, Division of European Affairs, Memorandum, May 25, 1938 notes Gibarti persuaded Einstein to sign a letter of endorsement for a farewell dinner for Ludwig Renn, a German communist writer who was in New York on his way from Spain to Mexico. The dinner would have been sponsored by Heym's *Volksecho* as well; *Deutsches Volksecho,* June 11, 1938, full-breadth of front page headline "Einstein Gegen Faschismus Fuer Kollektive Sicherheit" with coverage of Einstein's speech to graduating class of Swarthmore College; Gross, *Willi Muenzenberg*, German version, p. 281, 297

28. Gross, *Willi Muenzenberg*,English version, p.216 reprints a letter by Rolland of July, 1932 which mentions Gibarti; *Gandhi et Romain Rolland*, Editions AlbinMichael, Paris, 1969, p. 460-461; Fondation Jules Humbert-Droz, *Centenaire Jules Humbert-Droz*, Fondation Jules Humbert-Droz, La Chaux de Fonds, 1992, p. 472; Tania Schlie, *Willi Muenzenberg*, p. 102 states Gibarti lost his post as Barbusse's secretary in 1932; Gross, *Willi Muenzenberg*,German version, p. 369-370 also notes involvement with Barbusse.

29. "Rote Aufbau," October, 1929, p. 259 "Der Fall Gastonia" by Louis Gibarti an article on a strike against the Manville-Jenkins Corporation in North Carolina; see also Heinz Sommer, editor, *"Im Zeichen der Solidaritaet"* and Kramer, *Der Gegen-Angriff (Prag/Paris 1933-1936)* for other articles written by Louis Gibarti.

30. Department of State, Division of European Affairs, Memorandum, May 25, 1938 from the FOIA file on Gibarti

31. Heym, *Nachruf*, p. 174

32. Koch, *Double Lives*,1994 edition, p. 343

33. Ibid, p. 194-195

34. Ibid, p. 121-122; Tobias, *The Reichstag Fire*, p. 106 also notes the *Manchester Guardian* role in the Oberfohren Memorandum forgery.

35. Koch, *Double Lives*,1994 edition, p.350-351, Guenther Reinhardt, *Crime Without Punishment*, Hermitage House, New York City, 1952 describes Gibarti as considering himself with the authority to give orders to Browder; "Statement made by Helen Konieczny Dobos" corroborates Gibarti having had frequent meetings with Browder and visiting CPUSA headquarters on 12th Street often.

36. "Statement made by Helen Konieczny Dobos"; for example Katz, Flieg and Muenzenberg were in Saarbrücken during the plebiscite campaign. For Katz in Saarbrücken, see Gustav Regler, *Das Ohr des Malchus*, Kiepenhauer & Witsch, Koeln, 1958, p. 213

37. Heym, *Nachruf*, p. 140 on first meeting with von Schroetter.

38. "Statement made by Helen Konieczny Dobos" The FBI noted he was at the Volksecho office less frequently beginning in May, 1938.

39. Archives Nationales, Paris, F 7 15132

40. Archives Nationales, Paris, F 7 15131

41. Stefan Heym, "Nazis in USA," The American Committee for Anti-Nazi Literature, New York City, 1938 there were at least three editions of the short volume printed in 1938 and 1939.

42. Whether Saunders is an apparatchik who has escaped scholastic attention or is an alias for a well-known operative is uncertain to this author.

43. William Dodd Jr.'s name appears on the booklet as chairman or president of the committee.

44. McMeekin, *The Red Millionaire*, p. 299-300

45. Gross, *Willi Muenzenberg*,German version, p. 383, 410-411, "Statement made by Helen Konieczny Dobos" states Gibarti arranged Rosenfeld's immigration to the U.S. with Congressman Sam Dickstein who is indicated to have accepted bribes from the Soviets in the Venona intercepts; *The New York Times,* June 9, 1934, p. 2; British Public Records Office, Kew, Richmond, HW 17 12 message from Kun in Moscow to Muenzenberg in Paris of March 16, 1934 states Dimitrov will not be sent to U.S. as part of the Reichstag fire counter-trial tour.

46. The story of Muenzenberg's dispossession is told in Koch, *Double Lives*, McMeekin, *The Red Millionaire,* and Gross, *Willi Muenzenberg*; it also receives attention in the memoir of a Swiss Comintern functionary who was actually involved in the confiscation. See Karl Hofmaier, *Memoiren eines schweizer Kommunisten*, Rotpunkt Verlag, Zurich, 1978; The Mask Intercepts, British Public Records Office, Kew, Richmond, File HW 17 14 Moscow informs "Herfurt"

(Muenzenberg's cover name — "Herr" and "Erfurt," his hometown) in Paris, on August 15, 1936 that Smeral's visa is arranged.

47. McMeekin, *The Red Millionaire*, p. 294, 299; Koch, *Double Lives*

48. Gibarti's involvement with "Die Zukunft" is shown by the periodical's files, which are held at the Archives Nationales, Paris, F 7 15123, F 7 15126, F 7 15127; "Die Zukunft" was formed in conjunction with Muenzenberg's "Freedom Party." Someday its ostensible independence will have to be reconciled with a document in the KPD Archive, Archives Nationales, Paris, F 7 15132, which asks that the Freedom Party in New York take a critical stance on the *Volksecho*.

49. Besides letters of Muenzenberg, Koestler and Wirth, there are also letters from important French officials. A letter from Curt Riess to Muenzenberg asks him not to delay a trip to the U.S. for too long. There are many letters from September 1939 to April 1940 from Germans who were sent to concentration camps in France with the outbreak of the war. Also, there are extant unknown literary efforts by minor figures of the exile, which would be of interest to academics.

50. Gibarti's missives were titled "Letters of the Nine" and were supposedly confidential intelligence assessments on the situation in Germany.

51. Archives Nationales, Paris, F 7 15123, F 7 15126; Ickes also contributed writings to publications of the American Council on Public Affairs which was located at 20 Vesey Street, in the same building which housed the offices of the *Deutsches Volksecho, Underground News*, The American Committee on Anti-Nazi Literature, *The Nation* and *New Republic*. One letter sent to Gardner Jackson expresses hope that Perkins or Hull will cooperate because they had helped the American Council on Public Affairs. The letter is unsigned but seems like other letters written by Gibarti.

52. Archives Nationales, Paris, F 7 15123

53. Ibid

54. One could conjecture that it might be former KPD Comintern agent Yakov Reich who was known as "Comrade Thomas." Of course, one couldn't be introduced to Winston Churchill as "Comrade." Reich became distanced from the KPD, so the fringe communists of Muenzenberg's party would have been a fitting setting for him. "Comrade Thomas" is mentioned in Christopher Andrew, Oleg Gordievsky, *KGB The Inside Story*, Harper, New York City, 1991, p. 67-70 and Claere Jung, *Paradiesvogel*, Nautilus, Hamburg, 1987; another letter in the same file states Alexander Wirth was being sent to meet with Churchill and Eden. Wirth, as an ex-Chancellor, doesn't seem to be one who would meet with important officials under an alias.

55. Tania Schlie et al, *Willi Muenzenberg,*German version, p. 130 notes Gibarti in Italy in 1940 citing a Hungarian source; Fritz Raddatz, *Erfolg oder Wirkung*, C.

Hanser, Munich, 1972; p. 82-83 notes Muenzenberg and Mussolini at the same conference in Milan.

56. David Dallin Papers, New York Public Library; Dallin conducted an interview with Gibarti in July, 1953. The notes available from their meeting are not very revealing except for acknowledging a connection to the WFTU and stating he knew Alexander Rado and Gyula Alpari.

57. Koch, *Double Lives*, p. 350

58. Noted in Schlie et al, *Willi Muenzenberg*,German version, p. 129-130

Chapter 8

1. Advertisements for appearances by Martin Hall in *Deutsches Volksecho,* October 9, 1937, p. 5 and October 16, 1937, p.5, Hall to speak at the "Klub Deutscher Antifaschisten" of 180 East 82nd Street about "Einheitszeitung," which seems a continuation of the efforts against Seger; an article in *Deutsches Volksecho,* September 16, 1939, p. 4 contains the text of a speech Hall gave in Cleveland.

2. Heym, *Nachruf*, p. 154; His actual name noted in Rudolf Brandl, *That Good Old Fool Uncle Sam*, New York City, 1940, p. 13

3. Brandl, *That Good Old Fool Uncle Sam*, p. 13

4. See Roeder et al, *Biographisches Handbuch der deutschsprachigen Emigration*; biographical notes on Jakobs/Hall can be found in Mueller, *Die Akte Wehners* and Weber, *Die Wandlung des Deutschen Kommunismus*; Jakobs was born in 1901.

5. "Internationale Wissenschaftliche Korrespondenz zur Geschichte der Deutschen Arbeiterbewegung," Nr. 4, 1981, p.519, "Der M-Apparat der KPD" by Franz Feuchtwanger; one will be in a quandry to find published evidence that Franz X. Feuchtwanger was related to Lion Feuchtwanger. Both were from Bavaria and shared an obvious facial resemblance in addition to the name which is similar to the name of a Bavarian town. A photo of F. X. Feuchtwanger was printed in Pohle, *Das mexikanische Exil*; In F. Feuchtwanger's article, work with "Konrad" and Kippenberger is noted. He left the KPD when Leo Flieg told him he wasn't permitted to give Feuchtwanger travel documents. He then joined Karl Frank's organization; Mueller, *Die Akte Wehners*, p. 372-375, corroborates that Jakobs had been in Switzerland outside of his KPD role.

6. "Volksfront," September 9, 1939 for example.

7. Archives Nationales, Paris, F 7 15132, letter of September 27, 1938; it is also stated that a Trotskyite paper published Hall's legal name; another letter in same file of November 22, 1937 from "Jonny" in New York mentions that Hall was in Chicago.

8. For a general view of German newpapers in the U.S, see Hanno Hardt, "Jounalism in Exile"

9. Heym, *Nachruf*, p. 154-155, 171, 173

10. Kiessling, *Partner im "Narrenparadies*," p. 251-262

11. Ibid, p. 253 and Heym, *Nachruf*, p. 179 note Schroeter wrote as "Alfred Langer;" an example of an article under that name in *Deutsches Volksecho*, August 26, 1939, p.1, "Was bedeutet ein Nichtangriffspakt Moskau-Berlin?"; Lubbe et al, *Die Reichstagabgeordneten der Weimarer Republik*, shows Schroeter was, as Heym claimed, once a KPD representative in the Reichstag. Schroeter was born in Erfurt, also Muenzenberg's home town, in 1896. Having been a Reichstag deputy makes Heym's claim that he never knew his name even more implausible. Another detail is that, according to Kiessling, Schroeter had been wounded in World War I.

12. See Pierre Broue, *Rivoluzione in Germania*, Einaudi, Turin, 1977; Feuchtwanger, "IWK," Nr. 4, 1981, p. 501-502 claims Kippenberger wasn't "Langer."

13. Excerpted in Adolph Ehrt, *Communism in Germany*, Eckart Verlag, Berlin, 1933; Feuchtwanger, "IWK," Nr. 4, 1981, p. 501 claims the work Alfred Langer, *Der Weg zum Sieg*, 1927 was a "catechism" for a young revolutionary in Berlin.

14. Institut fuer Geschichte der Arbeiterbewegung, *In den Faengen der NKWD*, p. 113

15. Purge victims were always fascist, imperialist, or Trotskyite spies. No one was ever condemned for simply violating usual legal norms.

16. Kiessling, *Partner im "Narrenparadies*," p. 255-256; Begun stated she went to Mexico with Otto and Ilse Katz and Egon and Gisela Kisch. Since she discussed this forty years later, it is perhaps not absolutely certain they all traveled on the same ship or train.

17. Ibid

18. Ibid

19. Ibid. As noted, Muenzenberg and Schroeter were both from Erfurt. Schroeter was six years younger than Muenzenberg. Begun wrote an article on abortion in "Rote Aufbau," July 1931.

20. Stephan, *Im Visier des FBI*; p. 406-407; Heym, *Nachruf*, p. 154

21. Pohle, *Das Mexikanische Exil*, Metzler, Stuttgart,1986, p. 374, 382; Kiessling, *Partner im "Narrenparadies*," p. 269; Kiessling, *Brucken nach Mexiko*, p. 271

22. Kiessling, *Partner im "Narrenparadies*," p. 263-275

Chapter 9

1. Brandl, *That Good Old Fool Uncle Sam*, p. 12-13 describes Dodd's relationship with Hall/Jakobs; "Statement made by Helen Konieczny;" the cover of Heym, *Nazis in USA* shows Dodd as chairman of the American Committee for Anti-Nazi Literature.

2. Ibid

3. Brysac, *Resisting Hitler*, p. 209, 422; Harvey Klehr, John Haynes, *Venona*, Yale University, New Haven, 1999, p. 270

4. Archives Nationales, Paris, F 7 15131; Brysac, *Resisting Hitler*, p. 422; *Newsweek*, August 26, 1957, p. 29

5. Brysac, *Resisting Hitler*, p. 209; the younger Dodd also once accompanied his father on a visit to FDR at Hyde Park in 1937, from David Dallek, *Democrat and Diplomat,* Oxford University Press, New York City, 1968, p. 314

6. Ibid, p. 422

7. Ibid; *The New York Times,* August 3, 1938, p. 1

8. Brysac, *Resisting Hitler,* p. 422, *Newsweek*, August 26, 1957, p. 30 mentions Dodd's government work. Dodd was fired along with several other subversives by an Act of Congress. In 1946, the U.S. Supreme Court found that Congress did not have such jurisdiction over employees in the executive branch. Dodd and his co-complainants were compensated; *The New York Times,* June 25, 1940, p. 12 on Dodd's wedding. Merely having been son of a former diplomat usually doesn't merit coverage in the first section of the *Times.*

9. Brysac, *Resisting Hitler*, p. 422-423; Klehr, Haynes, *Venona*, p. 270

10. Heym, *Nachruf*, p. 183

11. Groth, *The Road to New York*, p. 257 states the American Guild for Cultural Freedom distributed $30,000 from April 1935 to 1940, which seems like a relatively small sum in 2006.

12. Heym wrote a letter to one of the Guild's executives, Erwin Piscator, the theatrical director and producer, on July 27, 1939, asking support for his request for $200.00. See Erwin Piscator Papers, Special Collections/Morris Library, Southern Illinois University, Carbondale; Incidentally, Piscator once employed Otto Katz as business manager of his theater in Berlin.

13. *Deutsches Volksecho,* September 16, 1939, p. 4, "Samuel Ginsburg in 'Weckruf.'"

14. Flieg and Krivitsky were major figures among Soviet agents in Berlin up until 1933 and from 1933 to 1937 in Paris. It is impossible that they weren't well acquainted.

15. See note 13; Kern, *A Death in Washington*, p. 197-198, 441; one should recall Heym's own defiance at having an illegitimate alias exposed. It is easy to see how he would react to inquiries regarding the name Flieg; the last issue of the *Volksecho*, in which Heym criticized Krivitsky for calling the Pact an alliance, came out September 16, 1939 only a day before the Red Army invaded Poland.

Chapter 10

1. Heym, *Nachruf*, p. 184

2. The Martha Dodd acquaintanceship with Mildred Fish-Harnack was first publicized in Bella Fromm, *Blood and Banquets: A Berlin Social Diary*, Harper, New York City, 1942; also Allen Weinstein, Alexander Vassiliev, *The Haunted Wood*, Random House, New York City, 1999, p. 53; Brysac, *Resisting Hitler*, p. 140 notes they likely first became acquainted at the American Women's Club in Berlin in August, 1933. Their friendship included co-writing a column and going on outings with Arvid Harnack.

3. *The New York Times,* August 19, 1957, p. 3, "Novelist in Flight"; *Time*, September 2, 1957, p. 17, "Expatriates;" Obviously Martha Dodd and Helmut Flieg were not present at the University of Chicago at the same time. Dodd was in Berlin from 1933 to 1937, arriving shortly after Heym departed.

4. *Newsweek,* August 26, 1957, p. 29-30, "Ex-Ambassador's Daughter: A Red Spy;" Romerstein, Levchenko, *The KGB Against the 'Main Enemy'*, p. 187

5. A check of the university's website shows a major building named for Rosenwald. Perhaps, see also, *The Julius Rosenwald Centennial Observance at the University of Chicago October 15, 1962*, Chicago, 1963

6. Stefan Heym, *Immer sind die Weiber weg*, M. Von Schroeder, Duesseldorf, 1997

7. The Dodd-Vinogradov relationship has only relatively recently made the printed record. see Weinstein, Vassiliev, *The Haunted Wood*, p. 50-71; Brysac, *Resisting Hitler*, p. 155-160, 209-214

8. Maurice Malkin, *Return to My Father's House*, Arlington House, New Rochelle, 1972, p.116; also Brysac, *Resisting Hitler*, p. 138 citing Dodd's memoir; *Newsweek,* August 26, 1957, p. 29, "Ex-Ambassador's Daughter: A Red Spy"

9. Brysac, *Resisting Hitler*, p. 160 the publicity of the American Ambassador's daughter's visit to Moscow annoyed the Germans.

10. Brysac, *Resisting Hitler*, p. 199-200; Weinstein, Vassiliev, *The Haunted Wood*, p. 54-58; one letter from Ambassador Dodd to President Roosevelt was found in the Comintern's archives; see Harvey Klehr et al, *The Secret World of American Communism*, Yale University, New Haven, 1995, p. 112-118

11. Brysac, *Resisting Hitler*, p. 210-213

12. Weinstein, Vassiliev, *The Haunted Wood*, p. 55; perhaps in connection; see Louis Fischer, *Men and Politics*, p. 450

13. Heym, *Nachruf*, p. 173 the *Volksecho* office was in Room 303. From the depiction, *The Nation* and *New Republic* were located on the fourth floor according to the American standard for floor enumeration.

14. and 15. see Fischer, *Men and Politics*, p. 125, 450, 454; Katz mentioned knowing Fischer in his forced confession before being sentenced to death in Karel Kaplan, *Report on the Murder of the General Secretary*, Ohio University, Columbus, 1990, p. 227; of course, this sort of forced statement shouldn't be considered reliable if not well-corroborated; Indalecio Prieto, *Epistolario Juan Negrin*, Planeta, Barcelona, 1990, p. 126; Markus Wolf, *Die Troika*; Eugene Lyons, *Assignment in Utopia*, Harcourt Brace, New York City, 1937 complained about not being able to enroll his children in an elite school.

16. Eleanor Roosevelt, *This I Remember*, Harper, New York City, 1949, especially p. 244

17. Brysac, *Resisting Hitler*, p. 212

18. Ibid

19. FDR traveled several times to Germany in his youth accompanying his father who took cures in Europe. His attendance at German schools for six months is noted in Gloria Barron, *Leadership in Crisis*, Kennikat, London, 1973, p.12 and Arthur Murray, *At Close Quarter*, John Murray, London, 1946, p. 86 citing a letter from Franklin Roosevelt.

20. Robert Dallek, *Democrat and Diplomat*, p. 15-26 notes Dodd's years in Leipzig; the same work notes several people declined the post before Dodd accepted it. Likely, Roosevelt could have found a hundred people to decline the post but only had to appoint a career diplomat to have satisfactorily resolved the matter. It is odd that the most important diplomatic appointment became subject of such an *ad hoc* procedure. Those who refused the position included FDR's 1920 running mate James Cox, former Secretary of War Newton Baker, Owen Young, and Ed Flynn. Flynn is said to have declined because his children were too young to leave the Bronx; *Newsweek*, August 26, 1957, p. 28; oddly, Jack Soble, later accused of being part of Martha Dodd's spy ring also attended university in Leipzig according to Foster, *Unamerican Lady*, p. 166; the book that Ambassador Dodd edited can be verified at major libraries. Woodrow Wilson was, at that point, obviously among the Americans considered the most antagonistic towards Germany.

21. See Erik von Kuennelt-Leddihn, *Leftism*, Arlington House, New Rochelle, 1974, p. 276; Edward Flynn, *You're the Boss*, Viking Press, New York, 1947; Westbrook Pegler noted the affair periodically in his columns, in 1947, 1954, 1957 and 1960. For example, *Post Standard*, Syracuse, New York, September 24,

STEFAN HEYM

1947; *Dixon Evening Telegraph*, Dixon, Illinois, September 25, 1947; *Post Standard*, Syracuse, New York, September 7, 1954; *Times Recorder*, Zanesville, Ohio, September 8, 1954; *Odessa American*, Odessa, Texas, September 17, 1957, *Lima News*, Lima, Ohio, September 20, 1960.

22. *The Bridgeport Post*, Bridgeport, Connecticut, September 24, 1947, p. 9, "Fair Enough"

23. Ibid

24. Ibid

25. Charles Tansill, *Back Door to War*, H. Regnery, Chicago, 1952, p. 45-46; *The Portsmouth Herald*, Portsmouth, New Hampshire, September 7, 1954, editorial by Westbrook Pegler cites George Viereck and claims further that House was behind FDR's plane flight to the convention in Chicago in 1932.

26. *The New York Times,* September 5, 1938, p. 3, "Martha Dodd Wed in Virginia Home," weddings of former diplomats' offspring rarely make out-of-town papers; Brysac, *Resisting Hitler*, p. 395

27. Weinstein, Vassiliev, *The Haunted Wood*, p. 60; Hans Coppi, *Die Rote Kapelle*, refers to Martha Dodd as saying that Alfred Stern had already helped the German underground.

28. *Newsweek,* August 26, 1957, p. 29-30; Jane Foster, *An Unamerican Lady*, Sidgwick & Jackson, London, 1980, p. 98; Romerstein, Levchenko, *The KGB Against the 'Main Enemy'*, p. 187

29. *Lima News*, Lima, Ohio, September 20, 1960; Pegler was a nationally syndicated columnist so the item appeared in scores of other newspapers also; Howard Rushmore's charges against the University of Chicago noted in the *Edwardsville Intelligencer*, Edwardsville, Illinois, April 29, 1949; another University of Chicago professor wrote an openly pro-communist memoir, see Samuel Harper, *The Russia I Believe in*, University of Chicago, Chicago, 1945.

30. *Newsweek,* August 26, 1957, p. 29-30; Romerstein, Levchenko, *The KGB Against the 'Main Enemy'*, p. 187; Foster, *Unamerican Lady*, p. 98 mentions the important fact that Alfred Stern was father of two Rosenwald heirs.

31. *Time*, September 2, 1957, p. 17; James Wechsler, *The Age of Suspicion*, Random House, New York City, 1953, p. 161

32. Heym, *Nachruf*, p. 184; by coincidence Otto Katz brought $10,000 from New York to the KPD in Paris to fund a shortwave station in 1939, from, Kiessling, *Partner im 'Narrenparadies'*, p. 246

33. Institut fuer Zeitgeschichte, ED 210/24, Hans Jaeger, "Materialen zur deutschen politischen Emigration;" disturbingly one source claims "Neu Beginnen" was known derisively as the "Black Hand," see Henry Pachter, *Weimar Etudes*, Columbia University, New York City, 1982, p. 317; Frank also attended some of Muenzenberg's "Social Unity" meetings in Paris, from, McMeekin, *The*

182

Red Millionaire, p. 300; also Karl Frank corresponded with Eleanor Roosevelt during the war years. At first, Frank wrote to ask for help for refugees. Later, he wrote as someone trying to influence the postwar circumstances in Germany. He once asked Mrs. Roosevelt to intercede to obtain Frank a special visa, in order to travel outside the U.S. with permission to return. Eleanor Roosevelt did indeed ask Sumner Welles to look at the matter, but Welles refused to make an exception for Frank. Mrs. Roosevelt also invited Karl Frank to visit the White House more than once and also offered to arrange a meeting with Harry Hopkins; Karl Frank used the alias "Paul Hagen" while in the United States. It is claimed in Thomas Ruprecht, *Felix Boenheim*, Olms, Hildesheim, 1992 that Frank "borrowed" the name from Charney Vladek, a New York City official, who "owned" it previously; Reinhardt, *Crime Without Punishment*, p. 179 said Frank/Hagen was once convicted of kidnapping; Willi Bredel, *Spanienkrieg*, Aufbau, Berlin, 1977, vol. 2, p. 292 says Frank, not openly a communist, led Bredel's battalion; Archives Nationales, F 7 15132 message of August 1938 states that Stern was to travel to Europe to meet with "Neu Beginnen" members in Prague and Paris. Published accounts of the Sterns do not mention whether they traveled following the wedding in Virginia in September 1938.

34. Heym, *Nachruf*, p. 184-185

35. *Advocate*, Newark, Ohio, April 14, 1939, p. 7, "Ex-Envoy's Daughter Sees German Women Set Back Many Years," by Ruth Millett; on the other hand, one memoirist said Martha Stern had no taste in clothes, Foster, *Unamerican Lady*, p. 97

36. Foster, *Unamerican Lady*; *Newsweek,* August 26, 1957, p. 30 notes their lifestyle in Mexico; Brysac, *Resisting Hitler*, p. 395-396

37. *The New York Times,* September 10, 1957, p. 21, "Sterns Indicted on Spy Charges;" Foster, *Unamerican Lady*, p. 98; Army records in Heym's FOIA file indicate Heym's address was 171 West 73rd Street from 1937 to the summer of 1940.

38. *Look*, November 26, 1957, p. 35-36, "My Ten Years as a Counterspy," by Boris Morros; Foster, *Unamerican Lady*, p. 99; *The New York Times,* August 18, 1957, p. 12; *Newsweek,* August 26, 1957, p. 30; The Venona intercepts corroborate that Stern financed a venture for the amount stated and did so on behalf of the NKVD.

39. Jane Foster, *Unamerican Lady* portrays Morros as a bit obtuse but someone who scored over a hundred films isn't likely to be less than sharp. Morros stated he was general music director of Paramount Pictures during the mid- to late-1930s, from, *Look*, November 26, 1957, p. 34

40. Harvey Klehr, John Haynes, *Venona*, Yale University, New Haven, 1999, p. 270; the intercepts are also available on the internet.

41. *The New York Times,* September, 20, 1957, p. 21; Boris Morros, *My Ten Years as a Counterspy,* Viking Press, New York City, 1959 claims another hit record and that Stern's money was repaid.

42. *The Post Standard,* Syracuse, New York, February 19, 1947, p. 1; *The Post Standard,* Syracuse, New York, February 20, 1947, p. 2; the Sterns noted as supporting Henry Wallace in *Time,* September 2, 1957, p. 17,"Expatriates," Brysac, *Resisting Hitler,* p. 136, 395

43. Martha Stern as a recruiter noted in *Time,* September 2, 1957, p. 17; *Newsweek,* August 26, 1957, p. 29; Brysac, *Resisting Hitler,* p. 396; *Look,* November 26, 1957, p. 36 one imagines that the Sterns' many social gatherings were also for recruiting and extending invitations to more openly communist meetings; Martha Dodd Stern's appraisals of other agents in Brysac, *Resisting Hitler,* p. 199-200 on Mildred Fish-Harnack and *Look,* November 26, 1957, p. 36 on Morros

44. Brysac, *Resisting Hitler,* p. 396; *The New York Times,* September 10, 1957, p. 21; Pohle, *Das mexikanisches Exil,* p. 193 notes Alfred Stern among the KPD exiles in Mexico in 1942

45. *The New York Times,* August 21, 1957, p. 11, "Passports Refused in 1956" cites the State Department as the source.

46. *Newsweek,* August 26, 1957, p. 30, Romerstein, Levchenko, *The KGB Against the 'Main Enemy',* p. 188-189

47. Brysac, *Resisting Hitler,* p. 396; Jane Foster expressed her fear of the death penalty in *Unamerican Lady,* p. 228-232; incidentally Morros in *Look,* December 10, 1957 stated Jane Foster said she knew Martha Dodd during the 1930s while her memoir doesn't have them meeting until 1941. Foster does admit she was in Berlin while Martha Dodd resided there.

48. The association with Soviet Embassy Secretary Zubilin is noted in *Look,* November 26, 1957, p. 35 and *Newsweek,* August 26, 1957, p. 30

49. William O'Dwyer, *Beyond the Golden Door,* St. John's, Jamaica (New York), 1987, p. 425 in epilogue by Paul O'Dwyer who represented the Sterns in court in New York City.

50. Romerstein, Levchenko, *The KGB Against the 'Main Enemy',* p. 190-191; Brysac, *Resisting Hitler,* p. 273-275, 396; Morros also recalled Korotkov in *Look,* November 26, 1957, p. 38-39 and *Look,* December 10, 1957, p. 134, 137; if, however, what Morros wrote was correct, Korotkov had already been executed in the U.S.S.R.

51. Romerstein, Levchenko, *The KGB Against the 'Main Enemy',* p. 188-189

52. *Look,* December 10, 1957 describes Morros' last brushes with the Soviets and learning that prosecutions would begin.

53. O'Dwyer, *Beyond the Golden Door,* p. 425-426; Romerstein, Levchenko, *The KGB Against the 'Main Enemy',* p. 188-189; O'Dwyer is mentioned in connection with the Sterns in *The New York Times,* April 26, 1957, p. 10

54. *The New York Times,* September 10, 1957, p. 21, "Stern Indicted on Spy Charges," *The New York Times,* August 14, 1957, "Pair in Spy Case Foil U.S. on Fine"

55. That the Sterns never returned to the U.S. in Romerstein, Levchenko, *The KGB Against the 'Main Enemy',* p. 192-193, Foster, *Unamerican Lady,* p. 236-237; Bodo Uhse, *Gesammelte Werke in Einzelausgaben,* Aufbau, Berlin, vol. 5, p. 423 notes seeing Martha Stern in the East Bloc in 1959; the Sterns in Cuba mentioned in Brysac, *Resisting Hitler,* p. 396, *The New York Times,* August 29, 1990, p. D22, "Martha Dodd Stern is Dead at 82"; The New York Times which had the Morros-Stern story on the front page for four days in August, 1957 printed a dozen more stories on the Sterns from 1957 to 1960. See, for example, *The New York Times,* October 1, 1957, p. 5, *The New York Times,* October 16, 1957, p. 15, *The New York Times,* January 3, 1958, p. 3, *The New York Times,* March 16, 1958, *The New York Times,* July 22, 1958, p. 14

56. Ernest Borgnine depicted Morros whose name was also changed for the movie. Ed Prentiss and Colleen Dewhurst portrayed the characters based on the Sterns.

57. If Martha Dodd Stern visited Germany again between 1938 and 1957, it hasn't made the printed record. The author did view a VHS tape of the film. The author has not seen the FOIA file on the Sterns. It is strange that few Americans admit anything odd about having the decision to enter a war in Europe influenced by agents of an ideology that is an avowed enemy of Christianity.

58. See William O'Dwyer, *Beyond the Golden Door;* among other things, O'Dwyer's memoir is rare for noting an Allied-Axis conflict in New York City in the 1930s. Heym noted the Bund and its rallies but O'Dwyer portrays the tension as pervasive, p. 149-153

59. Ibid, p. 159-160, 363

60. Ibid, p. 183-192; *The New York Times,* July 18, 1944, p. 4, *The New York Times,* July 23, 1944, p. 10, *The New York Times,* September 5, 1944, p. 3, *The New York Times,* September 7, 1944, p. 7, *The New York Times,* September 9, 1944, p. 4, *The New York Times,* November 3, 1944, p. 11; also see George Walsh, *Public Enemies,* Norton, New York City, 1980, p. 112

61. The Italian leaders were chosen by a meeting of Rome and Naples party leaders once Rome was occupied by the Allies. There was early difficulty as the Allies recognized Mussolini's betrayer Badoglio while the Italian party leaders chose Ivanoe Bonomi. The Allies dropped Badoglio after a few weeks. George Crocker, *Roosevelt's Road to Russia,* H. Regnery, Chicago, 1959 notes FDR sent a special cruiser to the Black Sea to transport Togliatti from the Soviet Union back to Italy as expeditiously as possible. Togliatti had survived a long exile in Room #1 of the Hotel Lux in Moscow from which many disappeared. Besides

Brooklyn D.A. O'Dwyer, FDR sent Bronx party boss Ed Flynn to Rome in 1945 for meetings at the Vatican, *The New York Times,* March 23, 1945, p. 1, *The New York Times,* March 25, 1945, p. 23

62. O'Dwyer, *Beyond the Golden Door*, p. 193-208, *The New York Times,* January 31, 1945, p. 23, *The New York Times,* February 17, 1945, p. 11

63. O'Dwyer, *Beyond the Golden Door*, p. 179, 200; O'Dwyer also worked with the Swedish government in aiding Raoul Wallenberg. Wallenberg, like Count Bernadotte, became a victim of inexplicably grotesque malevolence a short while later.

64. Ibid, p. 197 mentions the Unitarian Services Committee.

65. O'Dwyer, *Beyond the Golden Door*, Chapters 29 and 30; O'Dwyer as 100th Mayor from *The New York Times,* January 30, 1987, B8

66. Ibid, Chapter 34

67. Ibid, p. 294,336; her father fought in the Spanish-American War at the turn of the century; *The New York Times,* December 21, 1949, p. 1, "Mayor Weds Miss Simpson and They Sail on Honeymoon."

68. *The New York Times,* April 20, 1950, p. 31, "Mayor's Wife Makes Official Debut at Needlework Show for the Blind," The O'Dwyers' arrival in Mexico, *Time*, November 27, 1950 and *Quick*, October 16, 1950.

69. *The New York Times,* August 15, 1950, p. 1, "Naming of O'Dwyer as Envoy to Mexico is Held Imminent;" *The New York Times,* August 16, 1950, p. 27 "Truman 'Sold'Job to Him, Mayor Says;" *The New York Times,* August 18, 1950, p. 13, "Mexico Hails O'Dwyer;" *The New York Times,* August 31, 1950, p. 32, "Mayor to Bid City 'Farewell' Today;" *The New York Times,* September 2, 1950, p. 9, "City's New First Lady is Deluged by Good Wishes From Every Side;" a couple of other odd things. A tourist returned from Mexico with smallpox in 1947 resulting in a frantic effort to inoculate the entire population of New York City. U.S. President Truman and President Aleman of Mexico traveled to New York to be publicly vaccinated, from O'Dwyer, *Beyond the Golden Door*, p. 325-326; O'Dwyer vacationed in Mexico in 1949, *Beyond the Golden Door*, p. 311; shortly following O'Dwyer's resignation as mayor, the police commissioner resigned and was replaced by Thomas Murphy, the Assistant U.S. Attorney who had convicted Alger Hiss, *New York Times*, September 26, 1950, p. 1.

70. Interview with Samuel A. Montague, Independence, Missouri, October 30, 1992, Truman Library. Viewed at www.trumanlibrary.org/oralhist/montague.htm.

71. David McCullough, *Truman*, Simon and Schuster, New York City, 1992, p. 632-633; O'Dwyer, *Beyond the Golden Door*, p. 354

72. Walsh, *Public Enemies*, p. 211-224

73. Ibid

74. The 97th Mayor of New York City, Jimmy Walker, did resign during hearings but was not hired by the federal government.

75. *Encyclopedia Brittanica*, 1957 edition, vol. 21, p. 140-141, depicts Spain's international ostracism following World War II. It was denounced at the U.N., unrecognized by the U.S. until December, 1950 (which means it was unrecognized at the time O'Dwyer was appointed). Mexico recognized a Republican government-in-exile in August, 1945. Shortly after the war, an international conference among the war's victors, at which Spain was not represented, demanded Spain remove troops from Tangier; the 102nd Mayor of New York City, Robert Wagner, became Columbia's U.S. Ambassador to Spain and Ambassador to the Vatican.

76. *The New York Times,* August 18, 1950, p. 13, "Mexico Hails O'Dwyer." O'Dwyer did speak Spanish fluently, which doesn't fully explain the enthusiasm over his presence; also, O'Dwyer. *Beyond the Golden Door*, p. 362, 409

77. O'Dwyer, *Beyond the Golden Door*, p. 354; Walsh, *Public Enemies*; a Cuernavaca divorce decree noted in *The New York Times,* August 11, 1953, p. 15.

78. O'Dwyer, *Beyond the Golden Door*, p. 354, Walsh, *Public Enemies*

79. Walsh, *Public Enemies*, p. 234

80. She appeared in "Brigadoon" on Broadway in 1957 according to IBDB.com and in the film *The Pusher* (1960) according to IMDb.com; there was a guest appearance on *Naked City* in 1959 according to IMDb.com; a role on *Kraft Television Theatre* noted in *The New York Times,* September 22, 1955, p. 34; theater performances in Pennsylvania noted in *The New York Times,* August 5, 1956, p. x3; a stage role in Cincinnati noted in *The New York Times,* May 29, 1955, p.36; an advertisement in *The New York Times,* March 1, 1955, p. 9 claims she appeared on panel show "Let's Take Sides" on WABC-TV in New York City; *Modesto Bee and News Herald* April 19, 1959 notes an appearance on *You'll Never Get Rich*; *The New York Times,* September 16, 1970, p. 95 notes a guest appearance on the *Joe Franklin Show*.

81. O'Dwyer, *Beyond the Golden Door*, p. 417-421

82. Ibid, p. 408; "Chicago Daily Tribune," July 18, 1957, p. B7, "Hundreds Flee to Mexico."

83. *The New York Times,* July 25, 1945, p. 1

Chapter 11

1. Heym, *Nachruf*, p. 185-186

2. see Franklin Folsom, *Days of Anger, Days of Hope*, University of Colorado, Niwot (Colorado), 1994

3. Heym, *Nachruf*, p. 187-193; corroborated in FOIA file on Stefan Heym in both FBI and Army records.

4. War Department, Military Intelligence Division, Report of Harold M. Robinson, May 19, 1943, p. 2; Interview with proprietor of New Union Press (name deleted), May 13, 1943 both Prompt Press and New Union Press occupied the same premises and may have had the same management.

5. War Department, Miltary Intelligence Division, Report of Harold M. Robinson, May 19, 1943, p. 2; Interview, President of the Herald Square Press (name deleted), May 14, 1943; Heym, *Nachruf*, p. 193 notes he earned $30 per week "fixum;" the proprietor claimed Heym earned $60 per week. Commission earnings could account for the difference.

6. "Memorandum for the officer in charge," May 6, 1943, by Harold M. Robinson, p. 2; interviewee who worked for publisher of *Hostages* cited as saying Heym was paid $20 per week as editor of the *Volksecho*.

7. Interview with proprietor of *New Union Press*, May 13. 1943; Interview, President of the Herald Square Press, May 14, 1943 and Robinson's notes also in Army section of FOIA file.

8. Interview with proprietor of *New Union Press*, May 13, 1943; Erwin Piscator Papers, Special Collections/Morris Library, Southern Illinois University, Carbondale contain a letter written by Stefan Heym to the New School for Social Research, dated October 31, 1940, making an offer of printing services. It is not clear that a transaction occurred from the single letter.

9. Interview with proprietor of *New Union Press*, May 13, 1943 and Interview with President of Herald Square Press, May 14, 1943.

10. Heym, *Nachruf*, p. 174

11. War Department, Military Intelligence Division, May 19, 1943, Report of Harold M. Robinson, p. 3

12. Ibid

13. Ibid and Heym, *Nachruf*, p. 193

14. See note 11.

15. Heym, *Nachruf*, p. 194-196, 206

16. Bruno Frei, *Hanussen, ein Bericht, mit einem Vorwort von Egon Erwin Kisch*, S. Brant Verlag, Strassburg, 1934; Heym claimed to have already begun work on *Deadline* in a July, 1939 letter to Erwin Piscator. Erwin Piscator Papers, Special Collections/Morris Library, Southern Illinois University, Carbondale.

17. Heym, *Nachruf*, p. 59-60

18. Bruno Frei, *Die Papiersaebel*, S. Fischer, Frankfurt am Main, 1972

19. Frei, *Die Papiersaebel*, p. 235; Lion Feuchtwanger, *Briefwechsel mit Freunden: 1933-1958*, Aufbau, Berlin, 1991, vol. 2, p. 185 mentions several KPD writers including Frei in Casablanca.

20. *See* Kiessling, *Brucken nach Mexiko*, p. 353

21. Will Schaber, who also remembered Heym's early days as a writer, spent the postwar era west of the Iron Curtain. Schaber also contributed to the *Prager Tagblatt* contemporaneously with Heym and later resided in New York. Will Schaber, *Profile der Zeit*, Edition Isele, Eggingen, 1992, p. 316

22. see Reinhardt, *Crime Without Punishment*

23. see Weiskopf, *Unter Fremden Himmeln*; Rosenfeld's role mentioned in Albert Norden, *Ereignisse und Erlebtes*, Dietz, Berlin, 1981

24. Phillip Daub, Albert Schreiner, Horst Baerensprung, Max Scheer, Hans Marchwitza, Max Schroeder, Norden, and Weiskopf had emigrated to New York City since the demise of the *Volksecho*. The contingent in Mexico included Katz, Kisch, Abusch, Frei, Bodo Uhse, and Anna Seghers. Heyms FOIA files though over 500 pages long are far from complete. Much information is deleted, even on the pages released. Much has not been released. Notations on records of files indicate much has also been discarded as the FBI does not consider itself a repository of information but merely complies with the law in releasing records it has retained.

25. Cazden, *German Exile Literature in America*, p. 46; Brandl, *That Good Old Fool Uncle Sam*, p. 16; Institut fuer Zeitgeschichte, Munich Fb 224 and Fb 225 show that Rosenfeld and the Overseas News Agency were approved of by the Office of War Information. See memoirs of Max Scheer regarding the Overseas News Agency.

26. Heintz, *Index des "Freien/Neuen Deutschland"*; Rosenfeld's contribution to *El Libro Negro del Terror Nazi in Europa* noted in, Kiessling, *Brucken Nach Mexiko*, p. 349

27. "Hefte zur DDR-Geschichte," Nr. 25, p. 38, article by Wolfgang Kiessling; Pohle, *Das mexikanische Exil*

28. Pohle, *Das mexikanische Exil*, p. 221, 230; Kiessling, *Partner im "Narren-paradies*," p. 198-199; "Hefte zur DDR-Geschichte," Nr. 25, p. 38, 64, article by Wolfgang Kiessling, Rosenfeld was in contact to an assistant to Otto Katz named George Stibi.

29. *Hammond Times*, Hammond, Indiana, October 30, 1942, p. 13, a "Central Press" wire service article. Pierre Cot, former French aviation minister, now known to have been a Soviet agent, was also present.

30. Rosenfeld's daughter Hilde was also a veteran communist by this point. She spent exile in Mexico and resided in the DDR following the war.

31. Reinhardt, *Crime Without Punishment*, p. 100-106; Heym, *Nachruf*, p. 238, 242-245 notes Heym's own familiarity with the background check done by the CIC. The Army's background investigation of Heym's took place at approximately the same time as Rosenfeld's remark.

Chapter 12

1. Helmut Pfanner, *Exile in New York* is helpful but doesn't scrutinize communist affiliations closely enough.

2. Gustav Regler, *Gustav Regler, Dokumente und Analysen*, Saarbrucker Druckerei, Saarbrucken, 1985

3. Bodo Uhse, F.C. Weiskopf, *Briefwechsel 1942-1948*, Aufbau, Berlin, 1990 a letter of March 27, 1944 by Weiskopf mentions Heym; Anna Seghers, Wieland Herzfelde, *Gewohnliches und Gefaehrliches Leben*, Luchterhand, Darmstadt, 1986; Herzfelde's philatelic shop in Manhattan is noted in Heym, *Nachruf*, p. 225. Herzfelde was earlier head of publishing firm Malik Verlag, a Muenzenberg subsidiary.

4. *Deutsches Volksecho,* October 9, 1937, *Deutsches Volksecho,* June 24, 1939

5. Stephan, *Im Visier des FBI*, p. 483; Kiessling, *Partner im "Narrenparadies,"* p. 248

6. "Exil," 1981, Nr. 1, p. 72, "Alfred Kantorowicz in franzosische Exil"; according to Caute, *The Fellow Travellers*, p. 142, L.A.W. was founded at the first American Writers Conference convened at the Mecca Temple in New York City in April, 1935.

7. Stephan, *Im Visier des FBI*, p. 483; Archives Nationales, Paris, F 7 15132 note of June 14, 1939, "Lieber Paul"-- signed "Kanto" (probably Paul Merker and Alfred Kantorowicz) mentions Kisch was in New York earlier in the year for a World's Fair exhibit opening. He may have been along on one of Katz' "fundraising" jaunts; Kiessling, *Partner im "Narrenparadies,"* p. 246 noted an August 1939 return to Paris. A July 30, 1939 entry in Bodo Uhse's diary notes a visit to Katz' apartment in Los Angeles.

8. "Philologica Pragensia," 1970, Nr. 2 article by Josef Polacek who is, the author recalls, a distant cousin of Egon Kisch.

9. Alexander Abusch, *Mit Offenen Visier*, Dietz, Berlin, 1986, p. 31

10. Pfanner, *Exile in New York* notes Bruno Kisch in New York City from 1938. Guido Kisch edited "Historica Judaica" in New York City from 1938 to 1940.

11. Kiessling, *Partner im "Narrenparadies,"* p. 243, 248; Katz was described as a French patriot in a review of "J'accuse" in the *Los Angeles Times*, September 22, 1940, p. C6. The *Los Angeles Times* had earlier described Breda as a "German refugee" on April 1, 1936, p. A20. Later André Simone became the "Czechoslovakian Red Writer" who denounced a U.S.-Vatican plot against the Soviet Union in the *Los Angeles Times*, August 3, 1949, p. 8; Katz had written a column for Prague's "Rude Pravo" titled "The Vatican Fifth Column."

12. *Spione und Verschworer in Spanien* was written as Franz Spielhagen. There was an actual 19th century German novelist named Friedrich Spielhagen;

according to Archives Nationales, Paris, F 7 15131, Otto Katz was officially an executive of Editions du Carrefour which published *The Brown Book of the Hitler Terror* and *The White Book of the Executions of June 30, 1934*; *The New York Times* once listed a book by Rudolf Breda in its "Books Published Today" section on March 23, 1936, p. 17 shortly before the blackamoor began his Hollywood scam. Katz, incidentally, spent much of 1930-1933 in the Soviet Union as a film executive; see *Film und Revolutionaere Arbeiterbewegung in Deutschland 1918-1932*, Berlin, 1975, vol. II, p. 233, Gross, *Willi Muenzenberg*(German version), p. 470

13 Stephan, *Im Visier des FBI*, p. 413, Reinhardt, *Crime Without Punishment*, p. 81

14. Heym, *Nachruf*, p. 217

15. Kiessling, *Partner im "Narrenparadies,"* p. 258; Schroeter had been in Mexico since January 1940. Schroeter and Begun resided there for the rest of their lives. Begun was interviewed by Kiessling in Mexico in 1981. She gave October 1940 as the time she, Gisela and Egon Kisch, and Ilse and Otto Katz resettled. Other sources are less precise; Wolfgang Kiessling, *Exil in Lateinamerika*, Reclam, Leipzig, 1980, p. 195 notes Hilde Rosenfeld Neumann as traveling to Mexico at nearly the same time as Begun, Kisch, and Katz.

16. Faligot, Kauffer, *Histoire Mondial de Renseignement*, p. 437 and Ralph de Toledano, *Lament for a Generation*, Farrar, Straus and Cudahy, New York City, 1960, p. 55

17. The radio program mentioned in Kiessling, *Brucken nach Mexiko*, p. 352-353

18. see Pohle, *Das mexikanische Exil*, especially p. 80, 234, 315-322, 456; Kiessling, *Brucken nach Mexico*, p. 352; "Hefte zur DDR-Geschichte," Nr. 25, p. 56 article by Wolfgang Kiessling.

19. Stephan, *Im Visier des FBI*, p. 491

20. Gross, *Willi Muenzenberg*(German version), p. 312, 472; Katz worked at the press bureau of the Czechoslovakian government-in-exile following the defeat of Republican Spain.

21. Alfred Kantorowicz, *Deutsches Tagebuch*, Kindler Verlag, Munich, 1959, p. 111; noted in a letter by Kantorowicz to Lion Feuchtwanger of February 26, 1946, Feuchtwanger, *Briefwechsel mit Freunden*; Stephan, *Im Visier des FBI*, p. 491 notes departure of the *Queen Elizabeth* on February 23, 1946, while p. 486 notes George Shaw, American Consul in Mexico, wrote that Kisch was an agent of the GPU in a letter to the U.S. Secretary of State of August 1941; "Frankfurter Rundschau," April 29, 1984, p. 22 by Edward Goldstucker on Egon Kisch's 100th birthday, noted a luncheon held by communists in Prague on April 4, 1946 for the return of Kisch and Katz; the return of other communists is noted in *The New York Times*, July 22, 1946, p. 5

22. see Uhse, Weiskopf, *Briefwechsel* and Warren Miller, *Transatlantic Liners at War*, David & Charles, Newton Abbot, 1985; *The New York Times,* March 9, 1946, p. 5 "Brief Mystery Fire Perils Queen Elizabeth, Sabotage Hinted," *The New York Times,* March 13, 1946, p. 48 "After the Fire," *The New York Times,* March 14, 1946, p. 7 "Fire Guard for Queen Elizabeth"

Chapter 13

1. FBI Summary of File, August 23, 1950, p. 88-89, 97, Main File No. 100-142236 "Aufbau," October 30, 1942, p. 13 is cited in the report. An informant passed on a circular of "Die Tribuene" to the FBI that announced a meeting at Hunter College in Manhattan on May 18, 1942. Stefan Heym was reported on the letterhead as "in charge of publications."

2. Heym, *Nachruf,* p. 206

3. FOIA Army File, Report of Harold M. Robinson, May 13, 1943 and interview of May 6, 1943; Pfeffer's name, presuming it is Pfeffer who the FBI spoke to as agent for the *Hostages* book deal, is deleted throughout. The literary agent claimed he introduced *Hostages* to the story editor at Paramount Pictures and that he sold Portuguese, Spanish, Swedish, and Hebrew rights to the book. He was also familiar with Heym's play, *Hanussen.*

4. Report of Harold M. Robinson, May 15, 1943, Interview with eastern story editor of Paramount Pictures of May 5, 1943; May Mann's syndicated "Going Hollywood" column stated "Paramount will film *Hostages,* a novel by Stefan Heym, 29-year-old former resident of Germany" before the novel was published. See *The Ogden Standard-Examiner*, Ogden, Utah, July 27, 1942, p. 7

5. Report of Harold M. Robinson, May 15, 1943, interview with a representative of G.P. Putnam's Sons; In the summary, Robinson states Putnam's printed 25,000 copies of *Hostages* in its first printing, the largest run it had ever granted a first novel.

6. *Chicago Daily Sun-Times,* April 16, 1953, "Stefan Heym Quits U. S., Joins Reds" found in FOIA file, FBI section

7. FOIA file, Army section; Stefan Heym, *Beitraege zur ein Biographie*, Kindler Verlag, Munich, 1973

8. Ads for *Hostages* in *The New York Times,* October 18, 1942, p. BR12, *The New York Times,* October 21, 1942, p. 19, *The New York Times,* November 16, 1942, p. 17, *The New York Times,* November 22, 1942, p. BR21; interview with Bennett Cerf noted in *The New York Times,* December 30, 1942, p. 39 on WQXR 1550 at 5 P.M.

9. *The New York Times,* March 27, 1943, p. 27 notes the program was scheduled for 3:30-3:45 P.M. on WEVD 1330; *The New York Times,* July 9, 1943, p. 35

on WWRL 1600; *The New York Times,* August 3, 1943, p. 35 on WINS 1000; *The New York Times,* August 28, 1943, p. 23 on WBNX 1380; Schildkraut had been in the U.S. since silent film days and was not a refugee from fascism. His memoir, as told to Leo Lania, is *My Father and I*, Viking Press, New York City, 1959. Lania was an early communist who went to primary school with Karl Frank and the Eislers. He claimed to have been the correspondent who first reported the Treaty of Rapallo; see Leo Lania, *Today We are Brothers*, Houghton Mifflin, Boston, 1942, esp. p. 54-55

10. Heym, *Nachruf*, p. 209-213; Gertrude lived at 244 East 15th Street. The couple met in late 1941 or early 1942. Army Intelligence interviewed her on May 13, 1943. Her maiden name, Peltryn, is mentioned several times in the FOIA material including Washington Report, June 4, 1952, p. 1, File No. 100-142236, WFO 100-25528 which also states her place of birth as Tremont, Pennsylvania.

11. *The Daily Hayward Review*, Hayward, California, April 4, 1938, p. 3, April 5, 1938, p. 3, April 13, 1938, p. 3 and several other days in the same month; *The Ogden Standard-Examiner*, June 1, 1939, p. 12; "Chief Advertiser," Perry, Iowa, September 25, 1941; "Barnacle Bill" by Gertrude Gelbin, "Star and Sentinel," Gettysburg, Pennsylvania, May 9, 1942, p. 3, "We Were Dancing"; the articles were found via newspaperarchive.com; the earliest such treatments found were dated April 4, 1938 and the latest on October 31, 1942. Since the story summaries were syndicated, they must have also appeared in many other newspapers; FBI Confidential Report, May 16, 1949, p. 2, File No. 100-89165JF notes the *Daily Worker*, January 23, 1943, p. 5 noted Gertrude Gelbin was Secretary of the Screen Publicists Guild, New York Local 114 UOPWA.

12. Heym, *Nachruf*, p. 455, 663; Heym stated explicitly that she was a member of the CPUSA and called the Communist Party "her party."

13. Brysac, *Resisting Hitler*, p. 216-220

14. Ibid; Kuczynski was in New York in 1938 on behalf of the Communist Party and was given money by Alfred Stern. It is quite possible he also visited the *Volksecho* office. When Kuczynski was interned in England in 1939, Martha Dodd's plea to President Roosevelt helped win his release. Kuczynski also worked with Sergei Bessonov, the Harnacks' controller, in Berlin; also Andrew, Gordievski, *KGB The Inside Story*, p. 313-314; Robert Williams, *Klaus Fuchs Atom Spy*, Harvard University, Cambridge (Massachusetts), 1957; one document in the FBI file indicates Helmut Flieg edited a student publication in Chemnitz to which Klaus Fuchs contributed an article, "Supplemental Correlation Summary," June 18, 1968, p. 7; the same document states Heym was active in a communist student union in Leipzig which is not noted elsewhere. The FBI report did not indicate that the FBI possessed or even viewed the publication which Heym is supposed to have edited, but only that an unnamed informer

claimed that Klaus Fuchs contributed to a publication of which Heym is said to have been editor.

15. Heym, *Nachruf*, p. 203-204

16. Ibid, p. 226

17. *Washington Evening Star*, February 4, 1943, copy of clipping in FBI file.

18. Heym, *Nachruf*, p. 230; 6AM at the Hotel Endicott, 100 West 82nd Street.

19. *The New York Times,* February 15, 1943, p. 18; both Papanek and Hurban were Slovaks. Papanek was removed from his post as Ambassador to the U.N. following the communist coup and the suspicious death of Masaryk in 1948. Heym was one of the coup's supporters.

20. Ibid

21. *The New York Times,* January 3, 1942, p. 4, "Term 'United Nations' Selected by Roosevelt;" *The New York Times,* January 4, 1942, p. E1

22. There was a daily feature titled "United Nations" on page 2 of *The New York Times* during the war period; *The New York Times,* January 5, 1942, p. 2, "Accord is Open to All Axis Foes;" *The New York Times,* January 11, 1942, p. E3, "United Nations Begin to Unify Their Strength;" *The New York Times,* January 26, 1942, p. 2, "Japanese Press Their Widespread Drives Against the United Nations; *The New York Times*, December 15, 1942, p. 2, "Bolivia is Placed in State of Siege Strike in Tin Mines Brings Step to Keep Up Output for United Nations;" *The New York Times,* April 12, 1942, p. E5, "Offensive Actions by Both Axis and United Nations are Indicated;" *The New York Times,* July 6, 1942, p. 18, "United Nations Song Cheered in Capital;" *The New York Times,* July 4, 1943, p. 5, "United Nations Aircraft 3-Fold Above Axis Output;" *The New York Times,* February 2, 1943, p. 1, "Churchill and Aides Visit Turkey and Cement United Nations Tie;" *The New York Times,* February 6, 1943, p. 4, "Senegalese Forces Pledged to Allies; Boisson Lists Troops as He Offers 'Everything' in West Africa to United Nations"

23. *The New York Times,* February 16, 1943, p. 22, "Women to Hold Rally"

24. *Nachruf*, p. 402 notes they married in Maryland; "Kontakte," Nr. 6, June, 1953 Hans Habe noted he first met Heym in a "hush-hush" camp in Maryland. One FBI report says he "resided" in Maryland in 1943 or 1944; uncorroborated is a report in the *Gettysburg Times*, Gettysburg, Pennsylvania, February 17, 1966, p. 6 that Heym had been stationed at Camp Sharpe in Gettysburg and Gertrude Gelbin stayed at a local hotel while visiting.

25. "Washington Report," June 4, 1952, p. 1, File No. 100-142236, WFO 100-25528

26. Heym's *The Eyes of Reason* was dedicated to Gertrude Gelbin under her pseudonym. Gertrude had a son by her previous husband. "New York Office Report," February 7, 1952, p. 5-6, NY100-89165 states that David Gelbin was

affiliated with "American Youth for Democracy" in 1943, which had been cited as a communist organization by the Attorney General.

27. Elsa Primo Flieg Fuchs was born in 1892. According to FBI records, she became an American citizen in 1947; Heym, *Nachruf*, p. 201-203

28. Confidential Report, New York Office, May 16, 1948, p. 4, NY100-89165JF

29. War Department, "Summary of Information," October 6, 1947, p. 2, "inducted into the United States Army on 11 March 1943 at Fort Dix, N.J." Heym's name was legally changed in April, 1943. He became an American citizen in May.

30. FBI Summary of File, August 23, 1950, p. 111, Main File No. 100-142236 citing 61-7566-4624

31. Heym, *Nachruf*, p. 234

32. Ibid, p. 231-241; also mentioned in interviews in the Army section of FOIA file.

33. Report of Harold Robinson, May, 19, 1943. Most of the FOIA Army file consists of interviews with former co-workers or acquaintances. Evidently, no *Volksecho* employees were interviewed.

Chapter 14

1 *The New York Times,* November 14, 1942, p. 14; in the category of unrealized film projects, Martha Dodd sold the film rights to her late father's diary to 20th Century Fox. The picture was cast and Otto Preminger was hired to direct, but it was never completed. Preminger, incidentally, was son of the Austrian equivalent of Attorney General who served during the period of the Redl tragedy. This fact would have been more interesting had "Through Embassy Eyes" been completed. Preminger's father also once indicted Eduard Benes; see Otto Preminger, *Preminger an Autobiography*, Doubleday, Garden City (New York), 1977, especially p. 23-26; also Brysac, *Resisting Hitler*, p. 136, 395; *The New York Times,* March 20, 1943, p. 11; Anne Baxter was to play Martha Dodd according to the *Los Angeles Times*, May 15, 1943, p. 13 article by Edwin Schallert.

2. Schwartz, *Hollywood Writers Wars* notes Cole as vice president of the guild in 1943; IMDb.com notes Cole as president of the guild in 1944-1945.

3. Lester Cole, *Hollywood Red*, Ramparts, Palo Alto, 1981, p. 191-192

4. See IMDb.com; two such *President's Mystery* features were made during Franklin Delano Roosevelt's first term. The first family's involvement in motion pictures isn't noted very often. Son James Roosevelt produced *Pastor Hall* (1940) based on a work by Ernst Toller.

5. G. Edward White, *Alger Hiss's Looking Glass Wars*, Oxford University Press, Oxford, 2004, p. 205-206

6. Kiessling, *Partner im "Narrenparadies,"* p. 240-250 and Koch, *Double Lives,* especially p. 75, provide information on Katz' early years.

7. Reinhard Mueller, *Die Saeuberung,* p. 160, 574 and see Rheinhardt, *Crime Without Punishment.*

8. Bernard Dick, *Hellman in Hollywood,* Fairleigh Dickinson University, Rutherford (New Jersey), 1982; Joan Mellen, *Hellman and Hammett,* Harper Collins, New York City, 1996; Koch, *Double Lives*(1994 edition), p. 80

9. Bodo Uhse, *Reise und Tagebucher,* Aufbau, Berlin, 1981, p. 466 entry for July 30, 1939, Uhse with Kisch in New York City, p. 471, leaves Santa Monica for Mexico in March 1940, p. 496; Heintz, *Index des "Freien/Neues Deutschland" (Mexico) 1941-1946*; Alma Neumann, *Always Straight Ahead,* p. 77 states that during the Spanish Civil War, Uhse interrogated prisoners who were subsequently shot.

10. Stephan, *Im Visier des FBI,* p. 196-197

11. see Koch, *Double Lives.*

12. Brecht-Katz/Simone correspondence in Bertolt Brecht, *Letters, 1913-1956,* Routledge, New York City, 1990, p.258, 450; Uhse, Weiskopf, *Briefwechsel 1942-1948,* letter from Weiskopf to Uhse relates that Brecht and Lion Feuchtwanger wrote a film script based on Feuchtwanger's *Simone.*

13. see IMDb.com, Leslie Halliwell, *The Filmgoers Companion,* 4th Edition, Avon Books, New York City, 1975, p. 633 lists *Hostages* as her last film and her second to last five years earlier.

14. see IMDb.com and *Halliwell's Filmgoers Companion,* 12th Edition, Harper, New York City, 1997, p. 459

15. Abusch, *Der Deckname,* p. 353 notes Katz and Kisch knew Peter Lorre in Paris in 1934. Likely, they had been acquainted earlier in Berlin.

16. see IMDb.com

Chapter 15

1. Heym, *Nachruf,* p. 227-230

2. *The New York Times,* March 14, 1943, p. BR24

3. *The New York Times,* October 5, 1944, p. 21, *The New York Times,* October 18, 1944, p. 19, Review by Orville Prescott

4. FBI Summary of File, August 23, 1950, p. 113, Main File No. 100-142236, citing 61-7559-2-5421

5. The December, 1943 "El Libro Libre" circular was given to the FBI by the office of censorship.

6. FBI Summary of File, August 23, 1950, p. 117, Main File No. 100-142236, citing 65-48817-3

7. Heintz, *Indes des Freien/Neues Deutschland*, Heym was mentioned in the KPD's Mexico City paper in May and April 1943 and June 1944.

8. *The New York Times,* December 3, 1944, p. 11ff; *The New York Times,* September 10, 1944, p. 9ff, "I am only a Little Man"

9. *The New York Times,* December 3, 1944, Sunday Magazine.

10. *The New York Times,* January 20, 1946, p. 81

11. Heym, *Nachruf*, p. 391-399 it is mentioned that he wrote and was paid for another article which was not published.

12. *The New York Times,* January 2, 1971, p. 17; *The New York Times,* May 24, 1973, p. 45, *The New York Times,* March 23, 1975, p. 232; Adolf Ochs who acquired the newspaper in 1896 was, at the time, owner of the *Chattanooga Times.* "The Chattanooga Choo-Choo" was the only success of the Stern-Morros record company.

13. Emil Franzel, *Gegen den Wind der Zeit*, Aufstieg Verlag, Munich, 1983, p. 478; *International P.E.N. a World Association of Writers*, Zentrum deutschsprachiger Autoren in Ausland, London, 1968, p. 36

14. Franzel, *Gegen den Wind der Zeit*, p. 478

15. Kim Kyong-Kun, *Die Neue Zeitung in Dienste der Reeducation fuer die deutsche Bevolkerung 1945-1946*, dissertation, 1974, p. 191

16. "Kontakte," Nr. 6, June, 1953, p. 10-11, "Abschied von Stefan Heym"

17. Heym, *Nachruf*, p. 402

18. "Kontakte," Nr. 6, June, 1953, p. 10-11

19. Kim, *Die Neue Zeitung*, p. 35

20. Peter Wyden, *Stella*, Simon and Schuster, New York City, 1992, picture #41; Weidenreich/Wyden is noted in Heym, *Nachruf*, p. 374, 422; Ibid, p. 44

21. Gerhard Frey, publisher, *Prominente ohne Maske*, FZ Verlag, Munich, 2001, p. 86

22. Paul Serant, Giampaolo Pansa and Giorgio Pisano are among the few authors to broach the subject.

23. Mueller, *Die Saeuberung*, p. 236

24. Statement of Helen Konieczny, p. 14

25. In English, "Shot While Attempting to Escape," this is supposed to have been one of the standard excuses the Nazis gave when someone was shot in a concentration camp. Knowledge of Stalin's much broader internment and liquidation system was successfully suppressed by the communists, partly because of their relentless accusations. Walter Schoenstedt, *Auf der Flucht Erschossen*, Strassburg, Editions du Carrefour, 1934

26. Abusch, *Der Deckname*, p. 327

27. Walter Schoenstedt, translated by Maxim Neumark, *In Praise of Life*, Farrar and Rinehart, New York City, 1938; Walter Schoenstedt, translated by Richard Winston, *The Cradle Builder*, Farrar and Rinehart, New York City, 1940

28. Archives Nationales, Paris, F 7 15132

29. Erika Mann, *Escape to Life*, Houghton Mifflin, Boston, 1939, p. 299-300

30. Ibid and *Lowell Sun*, Lowell, Massachusetts, June 11, 1938, p. 5; *Oshkosh Northwestern,* Oshkosh, Wisconsin, February 14, 1940, p. 5; *The Daily Times-News*, Burlington, North Carolina, March 7, 1939, p. 10; *New Castle News*, New Castle, Pennsylvania, December 11, 1937, p. 2; *The New York Times,* June 5, 1939, p. 22 "Exiles' Woes Move Writers' Congress; *The Hartford Courant*, Hartford, Connecticut, January 24, 1938, p. 15 "Schoenstedt Nazi Fugitive Speaks Here," January 25, 1938, p. 1 "Urges Nazi Propaganda Suppression," February 16, 1941, p. 10 "Ex-German Journalist Enters Army," and January 30, 1945, p. 4 "Schoenstedt Promoted;" Brandl, *That Good Old Fool Uncle Sam*, p. 14

31. Exilarchiv, Deutsche Bibliothek, Frankfurt am Main, Nachlass Wilhelm Sternfeld, EB 75/177

32. In e.g., John Spalek, *Guide to the Archival Materials of the German-Speaking Emigration to the United States after 1933*, University of Virginia, Charlottesville, 1978; Schoenstedt's papers are stored in an American university library and are not cited anywhere; a photo of Schoenstedt was published in Folsom, *Days of Anger.*

33. He was republished by Guhl and Oberbauverlag; his children's book *Kampfende Jugend* was displayed in the lobby of the Deutsche Bibliothek in Frankfurt am Main in 1999 as part of an exhibit on DDR children's books.

Chapter 16

1. Demetz, *After the Fires*, p. 384

2. "Die Neue Zeitung," October 18, 1945, p. 1; De Villemarest, *Le coup d'Etat de Markus Wolf*, p. 111 claims the O.S.S. responsible for Heym being named editor in charge; Kim, *Die Neue Zeitung*, p. 32 says Robert Murphy, whom Gibarti contacted in France in 1939, was the American political advisor. To be clear, there has not been any evidence uncovered showing that Murphy cooperated with Gibarti.

3. Heym, *Nachruf*, p. 390; a document in Heym's FBI file claims he was also editor of a newspaper located in Essen, Germany called the *Ruhrzeit*. Possibly, the paper only reprinted articles from the main paper in Munich, at least at that time.

4. The November 8, 1945 and November 15, 1945 editions are without Heym's byline.

5. "Neues Zeitung," October 28, 1945, p. 2

6. The *Preussische Allgemeine Zeitung* publishes weekly from Hamburg and still regularly carries individual accounts of the brutal repressions inflicted on

German civilians, often women and children, in areas that had been populated and first Christianized by Germans since the 13th century.

7. *Neues Zeitung*, October 25, 1945, p. 3; on titles banned by the Allies; see *Preussische Allgemeine Zeitung*, April 8, 2006, p. 20 "Alliierte verboten mehr als die Nazis"

Chapter 17

1. Heym, *Nachruf*, p. 391-399

2. Ibid, p. 394-398

3. Ibid, p. 406-407

4. Ibid, p. 405

5. *The New York Times,* August 22, 1944, p. 20 on divorce of Myrna Loy, of Hollywood and the U.N.; *The New York Times,* January 10, 1950, p. 32 on Emerson-Roosevelt divorce, also in January 18, 1950, p. 33; *The New York Times,* April 23, 1949, p. 10 on divorce action of Paulette Goddard; *The New York Times,* March 23, 1947, p. SM17, "Hollywood Invades Mexico" by Frank Nugent; *The New York Times,* November 7, 1949, p. 33 "Universal filming movie with James Mason and Marta Toren in Cuernavaca;" *The New York Times,* August 11, 1953, p. 15 reporting on O'Dwyer divorce decree.

6. Kiessling, *Partner im "Narrenparadies,"* p. 304-309, p. 323-325; Seghers, Herzfelde, *Gewohnliches und Gefaehrliches Leben*, p. 203 quoting the *New Yorker Staatszeitung*, February 5, 1946, stated Heym attended or was scheduled to attend a meeting of the Aurora Verlag at the Ottendorfer Branch of the New York Public Library. Weiskopf and Budzislawski are also named. If Heym was yet in New York at this date, he was in town contemporaneously with Kisch and Katz/Simone; Archives Nationales, Paris, F 7 15132 for messages signed "PM."

7. Heym, *Nachruf*, p. 408-409

8. Ibid, p. 408-410

9. William Buckley, Brent Bozell, *McCarthy and his Enemies*, Henry Regnery Company, Chicago, 1954, p. 9-10

10. Ibid

11. Ibid, p. 32-34

12. Ibid, p. 145-146

13. Ibid, p. 35

14. Heym, *Nachruf*, p. 409-410

15. *The New York Times,* June 1, 1946, p. 3

16. *The New York Times,* October 19, 1946, p. 18; referred to in Heym, *Nachruf*, p. 411-412

17. *The New York Times,* November 27, 1946, p. 27; Heym's involvement noted in *Publisher's Weekly*, December 7, 1946 according to the FBI file.

18. *New York Journal American*, October 22, 1946, "Red Plot to Rule Writers Aided by Reich Communist" cited in Stefan Heym's FBI file.

19. *The Post Standard,* Syracuse, New York, February 19, 1947, p. 1 and February 20, 1947, p. 2

20. Heym, *Beitraege zur eine Biographie* shows a bestseller list with *The Crusaders* in the top 10; Heym, *Nachruf*, Ch. 20 claims that a delay at his publisher gave *The Naked and the Dead* and *The Young Lions* a six-week head start and adversely affected the sales of *The Crusaders.*

21. The Italian song was recorded by Edoardo Vianello while another tune titled "Dondolo" was recorded in German by Rex Gildo, one of Germany's most popular singers of the postwar era.

22. FBI Summary of File, August 23, 1950, p. 135, Main File No. 100-142236; citing 61-4478-A citing the *Daily Worker*, April 7, 1948; *Chicago Daily Tribune*, August 15, 1949, p. 15 "List 84 in U.S. Behind Mexican 'Peace' Rally" by Jules Dubois notes Heym, Thomas Mann, Martha Dodd , Henry Wallace and Vito Marcantonio as supporters. Also noted as supporters of the conference are David Alfaro Siqueiros and Lombardo Toledano. Toledano was often involved in Otto Katz' projects while Katz was in Mexico; some of Heym's public appearances are noted in *The Hartford Courant*, Hartford, Connecticut, March 11, 1948, p. 17 "Heym Talks in Behalf of Jewish Appeal Fund;" April 3, 1948, p. 11, September, 9, 1948, p. 17 "Book Forum Will Attract Five Authors as Guests;" and September 18, 1948, p. 8; Heym noted as a luncheon speaker in *The Washington Post*, March 24, 1948, p. B6 "Women's Division Hears Plea for Jewish Fund;" Gertrude Gelbin, as Valerie Stone, is mentioned as a speaker in *The Evening Observer*, Dunkirk, New York, April 20, 1948, p. 8; *The Nebraska State Journal*, Lincoln, Nebraska, May 9, 1949, p. 1; *The Hartford Courant*, November 19, 1949, p. 10 "Jewish Women Open Fund Raising Campaign;" *The Galveston News*," Galveston, Texas, April 30, 1950, p. 7 "Valerie Stone To Talk Here" with a photograph.

23. Letter from the FBI's New York office to the Director, July 2, 1951, File Nr. noted on letter NY 62-8988 and 100-89165 the letter notes Budenz informed on Heym on June 19, 1951; Louis Budenz, *Men Without Faces*, Harper, New York City, 1950

24. Undated attachment to letter above. File Nr. 100-142236-24; Koch, *Double Lives*, p. 222

25. *The New York Times,* July 11, 1951, p. 1, "$875,000 Bail Asked for Indicted Reds," *The New York Times,* April 30, 1952, p. 10,"Budenz Names 9 at 16 Reds Trial;" *The New York Times*, May 6, 1952, p. 15, "Budenz Identifies Reds'

Documents;" *The New York Times*, January 22, 1953, p. 1, "All 13 Convicted in Red Trial," *The New York Times,* February 3, 1953, p. 1

26. *The New York Times,* July 13, 1984, p. 2 carried Heym's receipt of his FBI files as a news story. It is reasonable to presume that since the Budenz material was declassified in 1982, it was included in the 1984 release.

27. FBI, Confidential Report from New York City, May 16, 1949, NY File No. 100-89165 JF; FBI Office Memorandum From: SAC New York To: Director, FBI, May 28, 1949, File No. 100-142236; the departure from Halifax due to a strike in New York is noted in Heym, *Nachruf*; a public appearance is noted in *The Washington Post*, June 8, 1948, p. 5.

28. Heym, *Nachruf*, p. 432

29. see Ella Winter, *And not to Yield*, Claud Cockburn, *Crossing the Line*, Mac-Gibbon and Kee, London, 1959 and Folsom, *Days of Anger*

30. Abusch, *Mit Offenen Visier*, p. 235; Uhse, *Gesammelte Werke*, Vol. 6, has an oddly titled chapter heading, "Egon Erwin Kisch Werk und Leben 1948-1959;" Katz spoke at the funeral, see Madrasch-Groschopp, *Die Weltbuehne*, p. 70; if Kisch was not really dead, his funeral may have been as a mockery of the Masaryk funeral a month earlier.

31. Heym, *Nachruf*, p. 438

32. Brandt *et al*, *Karrieren Eines Aussenseiters*, p. 168; if he was recovering from a car accident, he likely had broken bones. Strangely, according to *Nachruf*, Heym was suffering from a broken rib and a broken toe when he reported to Prague.

33. Kiessling, *Partner in "Narrenparadies,"* p. 141-143

34. John Loftus, Mark Aarons, *The Secret War Against the Jews*, St. Martin's Press, New York City, 1994, p. 551 citing Richard Deacon, *The Israeli Secret Service*, Sphere, London, 1979

35. Brandt *et al*, *Karrieren Eines Aussenseiters*, p. 192, the same work, on p. 77, notes Bauer had met Hermann Field, Noel Field's brother, in 1939.

36. Heym, *Nachruf*, p. 451-452

37. Gross, *Willi Muenzenberg*(German version) mentions Katz-Clementis friendship; see "Communisme," Paris, Nr. 6, 1984, p. 47-53 "Le Pouvoir Communiste en Tchecoslovaquie et la Naissance de l'Etat d'Israel;" Loftus, Aarons, *The Secret War Against the Jews*, Chapter 9; see also Eli Sacharov, *Out of the Limelight*, Gefen, Hewlett (New York), 2004

38. Leonard Slater, *The Pledge*, Pocket Books, New York City, 1971

39. Stephan, *Im Visier des FBI*, p. 486 notes that President Cardenas received a contingent of KPD Germans including Egon Kisch, citing a Spanish language newspaper in Los Angeles; see Pohle, *Das mexikanisches Exil* and works of Wolfgang Kiessling about the exiles in Mexico.

40. Karel Kaplan, *Report on the Murder of the General Secretary*, Ohio University, Columbus, 1990; Kiessling, *Partner im "Narrenparadies,"* p. 249-250; *The New York Times,* November 23, 1952, p. 1; *The New York Times,* November 28, 1952, p. 1; if the postwar communist purges didn't make sense, it was dismayingly because they weren't intended to make sense. The returning exiles from Moscow, Pieck in the DDR, Gottwald in Prague, Dimitrov in Bulgaria, merely copied the system of accusations followed by extreme punishment which they had seen implemented in Moscow in the late 1930s. Noel Field served as a focal point because he knew so many communists who had been exiled in Western Europe. Also, casting Field as the evil imperialist contradicted statements made in the U.S. that he was a communist who was close to Alger Hiss. It rebuked Hiss' accusers with a very emphatic, if baseless, denial. Noel Field was sent to prison in the East Bloc during the affair and was released at nearly the same time Alger Hiss was released from prison in Pennsylvania. Hiss himself seemed to believe Field was released on the exact same day. See *Commentary,* April 1993, "Alger Hiss Guilty as Charged." Weinstein, *Perjury,* p. 527 and Kiessling, *Partner im "Narrenparadies,"* p. 24 show that they were released eight days apart, if both are accurate. Field lived in Budapest in the manner of someone who was in favor with the authorities following his release. The most thorough available examination of Noel Field is Flora Lewis, *Red Pawn*, Doubleday, Garden City, 1965.

41. Heym, *Nachruf*, p. 516f

42. Kiessling, *Partner im "Narrenparadies,"* p. 129

43. Ibid, p. 145-147 describes her questioning once the storm was over.

Chapter 18

1. As noted before, the *S.S. DeGrasse* did not arrive until April.

2. "Review of the Scientific and Cultural Conference for World Peace arranged by the National Council of the Arts, Sciences and Professions and held in New York City on March 25, 26 and 27, 1949," prepared and released by the Committee on Un-American Activities, U.S. House of Representatives, Washington, District of Columbia, April 19, 1949

3. Ibid; Heym, *Nachruf*, p. 436 Donald Ogden Stewart, a Hollywood screenwriter, was also a sponsor of the event. He is described as a friend of Gertrude's. Heym, Gelbin, and Stewart had stayed in the same hotel in Paris during the trip of 1948-1949. Stewart was a participant in the Katz "Breda" flimflam; see Koch, *Double Lives*; Gertrude was not mentioned by HUAC in connection with the conference of March, 1949; The Sterns' affiliation with ASP noted also in *Time,* September 2, 1957, p. 17

4. "Review of the Scientific and Cultural Conference," p. 3-5; *The New York Times,* March 26, 1949, p. 1, article by Richard Parke.

5. "Review of the Scientific and Cultural Conference," p. 7, 19, 34, 35, 56, 58

6. Ibid, p. 54; Heym, *Nachruf,* p. 221, 457

7. "Review of the Scientific and Cultural Conference," p. 2

8. Ibid

9. *The New York Times,* June 1, 1946, p. 3, "Case Bill's Defeat Urged by Committee;" FBI Summary of File, August 23, 1950, p. 159, 160, Main File No. 100-142236 citing 100-356137-604

10. FBI Summary of File, August 23, 1950, p. 159, Main File No. 100-142236, citing 100-356137-604

11. FBI Summary of File, August 23, 1950, p. 164, Main File No.100-142236; New York Office Report, February 7, 1952, p. 8, NY 100-89165, states "the National Council of Arts, Sciences and Professions is cited as 'one of the most important communist front organizations in the country'" by the California Committee on Un-American Activities report of March 23, 1949, p. 698.

12. New York Office Report, February 7, 1952, p. 9, NY 100-89165

13. The conference made the front page of *The New York Times* each day of the last week of March 1949.

14. "Review of the Scientific and Cultural Conference," p. 57-60

15. Heym, *Nachruf,* p. 461-462

16. New York Office Report, February 7, 1952, p. 7, NY 100-89165, citing the *Daily Worker,* July 29, 1949, p. 5; another FBI report cites Cuban communist newspaper *Hoy,* August 12, 1949; Heym did not attend the conference.

17. Heym, *Nachruf,* p. 461; *The New York Times,* May 1, 1950, p. 23 "Arts Council Sees U.S. Curbing Films"

18. Heym, *Nachruf,* p. 461-462 Odets was from Philadelphia.

19. Ibid, p. 419-420; Joseph Schildkraut, as told to Leo Lania, *My Father and I,* Viking Press, New York City, 1959, p. 210 Schildkraut, who worked with Heym in the radio-play based on *Hostages,* once co-starred with Luise Rainer in a Viennese staging of Dreiser's *An American Tragedy,* produced by Erwin Piscator.

20. New York Office Report, February 7, 1952, p. 8, NY 100-89165, citing "Worker," July 17, 1949, p. 2 "Worker" was the Sunday edition of the *Daily Worker.*

21. FBI Summary of File, August 23, 1950, p. 149, Main File No. 100-142236 citing 100-138754-544; New York Report, February 7, 1952, NY 100-89165 citing *Daily Worker,* September 13, 1949, p. 14; Heym, *Nachruf,* p. 462

22. Summary of File, August 23, 1950, p. 154, Main File No. 100-142236 citing 61-7558-476 citing *New York Herald Tribune,* November 21, 1949; New York Office Report, February 7, 1952, p. 4, NY. 100-89165 citing *Daily Compass,* October 5, 1949.

23. New York Office Report, February 7, 1952, p. 10, NY 100-89165

24. *The New York Times,* November 3, 1948, p. 1, "Marcantonio Wins by a Narrow Margin" article notes it was Marcantonio's first campaign on the A.L.P. line alone; *The New York Times,* October 23, 1948, p. 6 "Communists Aid Wallace Communists Also Support A.L.P. Candidate Simon Gerson for City Council"

25. *The New York Times,* May 17, 1949, p. 23 "New Tabloid Bows In"

26. Information from the catalogue of the New York Public Library

27. Heym, *Nachruf,* p. 464-465 mentions *Daily Compass* but without noting its slogan or that *The Crusaders* was serialized in it. I.F. Stone is called an "old friend from the *Volksecho* era."

28. *The New York Times,* May 17, 1949, p. 23

29. FBI FOIA File citing "Counterattack," October 28, 1949

30. Department of Justice, Legal Attaché, London, England to Director, FBI by Secret Air Courier, June 1, 1953 letter notes that the State Department advised the U.S. Embassy in London that Heym was a suspected Comintern agent and communist propagandist on June 8, 1949

31. Heym, *Nachruf,* p. 485-486; a further detail from this period is that Heym and Gelbin appeared together on the radio show "Algonquin Roundtable" on March 3, 1950 according to *The New York Times,* March 3, 1950, p.44.

32. A statement on FBI letterhead of Heym and Gelbin's passport histories, Unsigned, Three Pages, April 4, 1966, Washington; a 1952 FBI report stated that the latest information from the passport office noted Heym's travel documents expired in August 1950, but did not have or did not include information regarding the renewal.

33. Office Memorandum, New York Office to Director, January 8, 1953, 100-142236 the name of the storage company is stated. The name of the individual to whom Heym delegated power of attorney over his possessions in New York is deleted; News stories from East Germany stating that Leo Bauer and Hans Teubner were being demoted due to acquaintanceships with Noel Field began appearing in American newspapers on September 1, 1950. Recall that Bauer and Teubner were from Chemnitz. See *Daily Independent Journal*, San Rafael, California, September 1, 1950, p. 4; *Edwardsville Intelligencer*, Edwardsville, Illinois, September 1, 1950, p. 1; *The Lowell Sun*, Lowell, Massachusetts, September 1, 1950; *The News*, Frederick, Maryland, September 1, 1950; *The Post Standard,* Syracuse, New York, September 2, 1950; *The Joplin Globe*, Joplin, Missouri, September 2, 1950; *The New York Times,* September 2, 1950, p. 1, 7 "German Reds Oust Notables in Purge" by Kathleen McLaughlin; *Chicago Daily Tribune*, September 2, 1950, p. B8 "Report Arrest of Six Purged German Aids;" It seems a reasonable supposition that Heym left the U.S. to avoid possible exposure by domestic

authorities. Bauer was also mentioned by Drew Pearson in columns in 1951 and 1952. *The Washington Post*, March 17, 1951, p. B15 "Links to Field Mystery Cited" and November 29, 1952, p. 25 "Field's Role Feared in Red Trials." Lewis, *Red Pawn*, p. 219, says Bauer's detention had already been noted in a West Berlin newspaper on August 24, 1950; *Time,* September 11, 1950, "Foul Nest" referred to Heym's former classmate as "dark, sneering Leo Bauer, boss of Radio Berlin."

34. Heym, *Nachruf*, p. 473

35. Ibid, p. 151, 512 mentions the two meetings with Lohr thirteen to fourteen years apart.

36. *The New York Times,* January 14, 1951, BR5; *The New York Times,* February 1, 1951, p. 23; *The New York Times,* February 11, 1951, p. 186; Stefan Heym, *The Eyes of Reason*, Little, Brown, Boston, 1951; *Los Angeles Times*, November 19, 1950, p. 13 "U.S. Russian Welfare Race Proposed" AP article notes Heym was one of twelve Americans elected to the conference's 101-member presidium. While four Americans were elected as absentee members of the presidium, it is made clear that Heym was present in Warsaw. The article does not refer to Heym's speech.

Chapter 19

1. New York Office Report, February 7, 1952, p. 3, File No. 100-89165 the article is from the February 18, 1951 edition according to the report

2. Heym, *Nachruf*, p. 469 the very last sentence of Chapter 21

4. The U.S. Embassy, Prague, to Department of State, Washington, August 31, 1951; D.L. Nicholson, Chief, Division of Security, State Department to J. Edgar Hoover, Director, FBI, September 19, 1951; Heym attended a ceremony at the National Theater in Prague on August 22, 1951.

4. *The New York Times,* April 16, 1953, p. 14, the FBI files had clippings from *The New York Herald Tribune*, *Washington News*, and *Chicago Daily Sun Times;* Air Tel, April 16, 1953, File No. 100-25528 American authorities in Berlin, apparently unaware that Heym's defection had been brewing, request more information on Heym.

5. Stefan Heym, *Beitraege zur eine Biographie*, Kindler, Munich, 1973 it is a collection of material on Heym without page numbers.

6. Poretsky, *Our Own People*, p. 1-3

7. In addition to Poretsky, Kern, *A Death in Washington* and Koch, *Double Lives* (1994 edition) also discuss the case of Reiss. Koch claimed Noel Field admitted, even boasted of, involvement in the murder in Switzerland, where Field was connected with the League of Nations. Kern only notes that Field was known to Reiss as an agent.

8. Department of the Army, letter to FBI, October 27, 1953 signed by Colonel Perry, Chief, Security Division

9. State Department to Berlin, March 15, 1966, WFO 100-25528

10. *The New York Times,* May 6, 1953, p. 22 "Wechsler Gives List to McCarthy"

11. Ibid

12. John Edgar Hoover to Legal Attache, London, via Air Pouch replying to a letter of June 1, 1953 asking for verification of Heym's identity.

13. "Der Spiegel," Nr. 13, 1994, p. 228f; Heym, *Nachruf*

14. See Heym, *Offen Gesagt* and Heym, *Im Kopf Sauber*

15. "Der Spiegel," Nr. 13, 1994, p. 229

16. Stefan Heym, *Keine Angst von Russlands Baeren*, Brucken Verlag, Dusseldorf, 1955, p. 28 noted

17. Heym, *Offen Gesagt*, Verlag Volk und Welt, Berlin, 1957, p. 37 citing the *West Berliner Morgenpost*, January 12, 1955 and *Neue Zeitung*, January 11, 1955

18. Heym, *Beitraege zur eine Biographie*, Heym received the DM 10,000 Heinrich Mann Prize signed by Becher in 1953. Heym received the DM 50,000 German National Prize signed by Pieck in 1959.

19. *The Washington Post*, March 17, 1961, p. A18 "Reds Plan Film on Tower Sinking"

20. Stefan Heym, "Collin," L. Stuart, Secaucus (New Jersey), 1980

21. Stefan Heym, "Radek," C. Bertelsmann, Munich, 1995

Chapter 20

1. Mueller, *Die Akte Wehners*, including p. 318-319, 372-375

2. Ibid, p. 49 Wehner was "Polsek" or Politburo Secretary for the locality. Leo Flieg was Politburo Secretary for the KPD nationally.

3. *Deutsches Volksecho*, December 31, 1938, p. 7; Thompson, *The Political Odyssey of Herbert Wehner*, incl. p. 67;Wehner wanted information gathered on Nazis in the U.S. Wehner also compiled economic statistics from Germany. It is not possible to determine whether it was the data used in Heym's 1936 article in *The Nation*.

4. Mueller, *Die Akte Wehners*, p. 301 notes Kisch's help in gaining release of Lotte Wehner. Each of Wehner's three wives was named Lotte. See also, Soell, *Der Junge Wehner* and Wehner, *Zeugnis*, p. 333, 373

5. Thompson, *The Political Odyssey of Herbert Wehner*, p. 39 and other biographies of Wehner. Also, Nathan Steinberger, *Berlin, Moskau, Kolyma und Zuruck*, ID Archiv, Berlin, 1996; "Europaeische Ideen," Nr. 79, 1992

6. "Europaeische Ideen," 1992, Nr. 79, p. 208; Mueller, *Die Akte Wehners*, p. 63, 212-216, 234

7. Mueller, *Die Akte Wehners*, p. 66 in Saarbrücken with Honnecker; Klaus Vater, *Herbert Wehner*, Bertelsmann, Munich, 1978, p. 67 in Prague with Ulbricht; von Loewenstein, *Towards the Further Shore*, p. 197

8. Brandt *et al*, *Karrieren eines Aussenseiters*, p. 57, 63, 67, 297

Chapter 21

1. The bombing and subsequent events in Bulgaria were on the front page of *The New York Times* each day from April 17 to April 26, 1925, also *The New York Times,* April 16, 1925, p. 3; *Havre Daily Promoter*, Havre, Montana, April 26, 1925; *Port Arthur News*, Port Arthur, Texas, April 17, 1925; *Bridgeport Telegram* Bridgeport, Connecticut, April 18, 1925, p. 1

2. *The New York Times,* July 16, 1927, p. 1 "Red Riots Bathe Vienna in Bloodshed;" *The New York Times,* July 17, 1927, p. 1; *The New York Times,* July 18, 1927, p. 1; *Bridgeport Telegram*, July 19, 1927, p. 1; *Syracuse Herald*, Syracuse, New York, July 17, 1927, p. 3

3. President McKinley, Henry Frick, Mayor Cermak of Chicago (in the physical presence of President-elect Roosevelt) and likely, President John Fitzgerald Kennedy were shot by leftists. Lee Harvey Oswald lived in the U.S.S.R. and openly demonstrated for Castro's Cuba.

4. Thompson, *The Political Odyssey of Herbert Wehner*, p. 34 notes the Nazis and KPD voted the same way in 94 of 102 votes in the Reichstag between 1930 and 1932. The Berlin public transportation strike of 1931 is another case where the two sides cooperated.

5. Dallin, *Soviet Espionage*, p. 93; Pastor, *Willi Budich*

6. Pastor, *Willi Budich*

7. Dallin, *Soviet Espionage*, p. 93

8. Buber-Neumann, *Von Potsdam nach Moskau*

9. Heym, *Nachruf*, p. 68; "Exil," Nr. 1, 1989, p. 66 article by Josef Polacek; according to Groth, *The Road to New York*, p. 128, Kisch was forced to cancel a speech by the authorities in Prague in December 1933; According to *Le Monde Diplomatique*, October 1995, "Stefan Heym, un socialiste à visage très humain" by Brigitte Paetzold, Heym once said, "I saw the Reichstag Fire with my own eyes" ("'J'ai vu l'incendie du Reichstag de mes propres yeux'"). The article was read via the internet at www.monde-diplomatique.fr/1995/10/PATZOLD/1856.

10. Tobias, *The Reichstag Fire*, p. 93; also Hays, *City Lawyer*, p. 342; Torgler dined at an Aschinger's restaurant earlier in the night, see R. John Pritchard, *Reichstag Fire Ashes of Democracy*, Ballantine Books, New York City, 1972, p. 130; Heym lived above an Aschinger's restaurant, see Heym, *Nachruf*, p. 64. However, Aschinger's was a chain with several addresses in Berlin, so it shouldn't be

presumed that Torgler was present at the building in which Heym/Flieg resided. Witnesses from the restaurant testified at the trial, see Pritchard, above.

11. As noted earlier, Rosenfeld had a courtroom victory against Hitler in June 1932. Rosenfeld was stripped of his citizenship in March 1934, noted in the *Prager Tagblatt*, March 30, 1934, p. 1. Max Seydewitz, Oskar Maria Graf, and Hermann Remmele were among those banished at the same time.

12. How does one maintain the popular image of Nazi courts as kangaroo courts and have the defendants acquitted unless there was collusion between the Nazis and communists.

13. *Die Zeit*, October 28, 1948; Torgler wrote a series of articles for the October 21, October 28, November 4 and November 11, 1948 issues.

14. Friends of Karl Otto Paetel, *Don Quixote in Miniatur*, Privatdruck, p. 27

15. Koch, *Double Lives*(2004 edition), p. 138-139

16. Harry Wilde, *Theodor Plivier, Nullpunkt der Freiheit*, Kurt Desch, Munich, 1965, p. 317; Wilde also wrote a book on Van der Lubbe, *Rinus van der Lubbe, Doodstraf voor een Provo* in 1967

17. Pritchard, *The Reichstag Fire*, p. 50, 63-65

18. Wilde, *Theodor Plivier*, p. 310; "Rheinische Merkur," "Merkur Plus," Nr. 2, 2000, p. 30 states Kisch was in Gheel in the Netherlands or Belgium, with Dutch Muenzenberg writer Nico Rost in the early exile period, probably while Otto Katz was in the Netherlands also. Frei, *Die Papiersaebel*, p. 184, affirms that Katz actually traveled to Breda. In the author's opinion, communists often used investigations and accusations to protect themselves from the same. If the supposedly independent press even accepts that one has standing to investigate or accuse, it is automatically accepted that the investigator or accuser is not himself guilty. Wilde, in *Theodor Plivier,* notes Soviet-Swedish-Jewish banker Olof Aschberg financed a publishing house in Holland with Plivier as its head during exile. A defender might claim Plivier was never a communist. However, he was always on good terms with the Stalinists and survived the war in the Soviet Union, possibly the only writer who wasn't openly affiliated with the party to do so; see Pike, *German Writers in Soviet Exile* or *Prolegomena*

19. Wilde, *Theodor Plivier*, p. 329

20. Titled *Rinus van der Lubbe Doodstraf voor een Provo*, Last also wrote *Kruisgang der Jeugd* on Van der Lubbe in 1939

21. Pritchard, *Reichstag Fire Ashes of Democracy*, p. 62

22. Friedrich Stampfer, *Erfahrungen und Erkenntnisse*, Verlag fuer Politik und Wissenschaft, Koeln, 1957, p. 264; John Fuegi, *Brecht and Company*, Grove Press, New York City, 1994, p. 281

23. Fuegi, *Brecht and Company*, p. 289

24. Ibid, p. 429

25. Nikolai Tolstoy, *Stalin's Secret War*, J. Cape, London, 1981, p. 87

26. Hubert von Loewenstein, *Was war die Deutsche Widerstandsbewegung*, Grafes, Bad Godesberg, 1965, p. 22; other anecdotes that support the thesis that the Soviet Union wanted Hitler in power can be found as follows, Isaac Deutscher, *The Prophet Outcast*, Oxford University, New York City, 1963, p. 138; Jan Valtin, *Out of the Night*, Alliance Book Corporation, New York City, 1941, p. 420; Nollau, *Die Internationale*, p. 109; Ernst Heinrich Meyer-Stiens, *Opfer Wofur?*, p. 33; Eggebrecht, *Der halbe Weg*, p. 175; Marlen, *Earl Browder*, p. 120 notes Heinz Neumann spoke at an October 1930 Nazi meeting on same dais as Josef Goebbels. At the time, Neumann was the German closest to Stalin; p. 126 notes bank credits to Moscow in early part of Hitler's rule citing newspaper accounts; *Der Spiegel*, Nr. 12, 1993, p. 196 shows Walter Ulbricht and Goebbels on the same stage in 1931.

27. Tobias, *Reichstag Fire*, p. 199

28. Ibid

Chapter 22

1. "Der Weisse Traum" (1943), "Hundstage" (1944), "Leuchtende Schatten" (1945), "Glaube an Mich" (1946), "Das Unsterbliche Antlitz" (1947), "Liebe Nach Noten" (1947)

2. see Geza von Cziffra, *Im Wartesaal des Ruehms*, Luebbe, Bergische-Gladbach, 1985 Roth died on May 27, 1939. Yes, the publisher's name is ironic. Von Cziffra also wrote a biography of Roth.

3. Alma Neuman, *Always Straight Ahead*, Louisiana University, Baton Rouge, 1993, p. 100

4. Seghers, *Gewohnliches und gefaehrliches Leben*, p. 46, 195 October 2, 1942 is the date given for the letter. According to Marcel Reich-Ranicki, *Doppelte Boden*, p. 121, she suffered psychological trauma and couldn't speak for some time. Reich-Ranicki was, however, not personally in Mexico; *The New York Times*, June 26, 1943, p. 11 "Anna Seghers Hit by Auto in Mexico; Anti-Nazi German Author is Knocked Down on Her Way to Give Lecture in Capital," also June 27, 1943, p. 28, July 3, 1943, p. 5, July 8, 1943, p. 21, August 19, 1943, p. 17

5. Markus Patka, *Der Rasende Reporter*, Aufbau, Berlin, 1998, p. 260-261

6. Toller died on May 22, 1939, see *The New York Times*, May 23, 1939, p. 3; *The New York Times*, May 27, 1939, p. 22; *The New York Times*, May 28, 1939, p. G6

7. see Wolfgang Fruehwald, John Spalek, *Der Fall Toller*, Hanser, Munich, 1979; Richard Dove, *He was a German*, Libris, London, 1990

8. see Koch, *Double Lives* (1994 edition), Chapter 11

9. Dove, *He was a German*, p. 261 also Fruehwald, *Der Fall Toller*, p. 24

10. Dove, *He was a German*

11. Ibid, p. 262

12. Riess, *Das war ein Leben!*, p. 257

13. *Deutsches Volkecho*, May 27, 1939 and *Deutsches Volksecho,* June 3, 1939 covered the death and funeral of Ernst Toller; *Deutsches Volksecho,* January 14, 1939, p. 5 displays both the first installment of series of articles by Riess and an article on Toller.

14. Koch, *Double Lives*(1994 edition), p. 93-94

15. Weinstein, *Perjury*, p. xix, 322-323; Weinstein, *The Haunted Wood*, p. 46

16. Heym, *Nazis in USA*, p. 17; Fischer, Maslow, *Abtruennig Wider Willen*, p. 495 states assessments of Katz as a quadruple agent were approximately correct. Koch, *Double Lives*, p. 89, 95, 120-121 supports the view that Katz sometimes acted as a Nazi agent.

17. *The Nation*, February 7, 1942, p. 163-164 "OGPU at Work," by Richard Rovere; Gorkin, *El Revolucionario Professional*, p. 17 claims five attempted murders by the GPU in Mexico in 1941.

18. *The Nation*, February 28, 1942, p. 267 the letter, which refers to Katz as André Simone, was also signed by Ludwig Renn, Anna Seghers, several leftist members of Mexico's parliament, and Lombardo Toledano, a union leader who was close to Katz in Mexico; Stephan, *Im Visier des FBI*, p. 345 on Kisch instructing Weiskopf on how to 'attack' Gustav Regler; *Freies Deutschland*, Mexico City, February 1942 "Ein Held unser Zeit" also Ernest Bloch, "Verrat und Veraeter," January 1942; "Commonweal," March 1944 noted Gorkin, Serge, and Pivert were subjected to a search warrant. The dissidents were able to publish a pamphlet titled "La GPU Prepara un Nueva Crimen" which denounced Katz and Kisch. Some of the controversy was due to accusations that the Stalinists were involved in Trotsky's murder in Mexico in 1940. It was later proven that the Soviet NKVD or GPU was indeed guilty. Katz and Kisch weren't personally in Mexico until a few months after the death of Trotsky, which means they weren't directly responsible, but also that they couldn't be absolutely sure that local Stalinists were innocent.

19. Reinhardt, *Crime Without Punishment*, p. 106

20. Ibid, p. 80; Pohle, *Das mexikanishes Exil*, p. 307 corroborates the presence of Katz at the gathering claimed by Reinhardt. Even the number of guests stated roughly agree as Reinhardt wrote there were 'about 200' and Pohle stated 'over 200'; the murder was on the front page of *The New York Times,* January 12, 13 and 14 of 1943.

21. see Dorothy Gallagher, *All the Right Enemies*, Rutgers University Press, New Brunswick (New Jersey), 1988; *The New York Times,* January 14, 1943, p. 1

"Ex-Convict Seized in Tresca Murder;" *The New York Times,* January 18, 1943, p. 16 "1,000 Police Hunt Clue in Tresca Case"

22. *The New York Times,* March 11, 1948, p. 1, 2, 26 on Masaryk's death. The communists called it a suicide in the first news releases.; on Papanek, *The New York Times,* March 11, 1948, p. 1, 2; *The New York Times,* March 12, 1948, p. 13 by A. M. Rosenthal; Papanek also demanded an investigation immediately, oddly by the U.N. Security Council; *The New York Times,* March 14,1948, p. 1 by George Barrett "Prague Dismisses Chief Envoy in U.N.;" *The New York Times,* March 16, 1948 by A. M. Rosenthal, "U. N. Accepts Czech as new Delegate" shows the communists wasted little time in finding a replacement; Adolf Hoffmeister, the former caricaturist mentioned in *Nachruf,* was also a communist appointee, succeeding Jindrich Nosek who resigned; see *The New York Times,* March 25, 1948, p. 9 "Czech Envoy Resigns as a Protest"

23. see Mario Passi, *Vittorio Vidali,* Edizioni Studio Tesi, Triest, 1991, p. VII, 12f; Gallagher, *All the Right Enemies,* p. 138; *The New York Times,* April 30, 1927, p. 3 "To Plead Sormenti's Case; Darrow and Hays to Ask Davis not to Deport Anti-Fascist;" Malkin, *Return to my Father's House* contains anecdotes of Vidali in New York City in the 1920s where he operated as Enea Sormenti.

24. Gallagher, *All the Right Enemies,* p. 155 citing Herb Mathews

25. see for example, Hugh Thomas, *The Spanish Civil War*, Harper, New York City, 1961

26. Most accounts of Mella's death claim Vidali's involvement, though it is not absolutely proven. Another Cuban said to have been killed by Vidali is Sandalio Junco, who founded Cuba's rival Trotskyite party.

27. Pohle, *Das mexikanisches Exil*, p. 72; Pino Cacucci, *Tina*, Interno Giallo, Milan, 1997, p. 308-310 see also p. 313; note an odd continuity. Mella was killed, allegedly by Vidali, while in the company of Modotti. Modotti died of a heart attack in the company of Vidali in a taxi. Victor Serge died of a heart attack in a taxi in 1947. Vidali had returned to Triest before Serge's death. Reinhardt, *Crime Without Punishment* describes several other suspicious incidents in Mexico while Vidali and Katz were present.

28. Kiessling, *Partner in 'Narrenparadies'*, p. 200-202; Gallagher, *All the Right Enemies*, p. 169;

29. see Ralph de Toledano, *Lament for a Generation*, Farrar, Straus and Cudahy, New York City, 1960; Tresca also wrote of seeing Vidali to Marcel Pivert according to Cacucci, *Tina*, p. 312

30. Romerstein, Levchenko, *The KGB Against the "Main Enemy*," p. 140-141 also notes that Tresca's "Il Martello" carried a front page broadside against Vidali on May 14, 1942

31. Passi, *Vittorio Vidali*, p. 46-47; Gallagher, *All the Right Enemies*, p. 255

32. Cacucci, *Tina*, p. 298ff

33. see Karel Bartosek, *Les Aveux des Archives*, Seuil, Paris, 1996; the Triest CP did not merge with the Italian CP, led by Togliatti, until 1957 according to Passi, *Vittorio Vidali*. Incidentally, Togliatti's son-in-law, Mario Montagnana, also spent the war years in Mexico and saw a lot of Vidali and the KPD exiles.

34. Karel Bartosek, *Les Aveux des Archives*, Seuil, Paris, 1996

35. *Time,* September 6, 1948, p. 22; Vidali made the front page of *The New York Times* on August 24, 1948 and May 29, 1956.

36. Passi, *Vittorio Vidali*, p. 46-47

37. Ibid

38. Ibid; syndicated columnist Victor Reisel noted Vidali's connection to the WFTU in *Lima News*, Lima, Ohio, September 11, 1955, p. 14-C; Vidali was called by his nickname the "Jaguar."

39. Malkin, *Return to my Father's House*, p. 192-193; Malkin claims Vidali was wanted for murder in Italy in the 1920s.

40. McMeekin, *The Red Millionaire*, p. 135, 330-331; "Barnard Bulletin," November 22, 1917, p. 4 notes Poyntz was a 1907 graduate.

41. *The New York Times,* December 18, 1937, p. 19; *The New York Times,* December 19, 1937, p. 35; *The New York Times,* December 19, 1937, p. 35; *The New Times*, February 8, 1938, p. 1 both Tresca and Poyntz named on front page title heading; *The New York Times,* February 9, 1938, p. 10; *The New York Times,* February 22, 1938, p. 11; *Syracuse Herald*, Syracuse, New York, December 18, 1937, p. 2 includes a photograph of Poyntz.

42. *Walla Walla Union Bulletin*, Walla Walla, Washington, May 10, 1949 notes Poyntz disappeared June 5, 1937 and declared legally dead in 1944. Article appeared following testimony of Paul Crouch, an ex-communist newspaper writer who claimed Poyntz was murdered and thrown into the East River. Also in *The New York Times,* May 10, 1949, p. 4; George Sokolsky wrote in his syndicated column that she was kidnapped on 57th Street and taken away on a Soviet freighter; *Newark Advocate*, Newark, Ohio, June 2, 1956; also see De Toledano, *Day of Reckoning* and Reinhardt, *Crime Without Punishment*

43. De Toledano, *Lament for a Generation*

44. Kern, *A Death in Washington*, p. 382-383, 470; Hathaway (1892-1941) was mentioned in *Time* in the October 31, 1938 and April 15, 1940 issues. Some of his booklet titles are "Communists in the Textile Strike" 1934, "The People vs. the Supreme Court" 1937, and "Collective Security, the Road to Peace" 1938

45. Kern, *A Death in Washington*, p. 382-383, 470

46. Ibid. Kern notes the slayings and their publicity helped make Jan Valtin, *Out of the Night,* a bestseller. Krebs had once been head of VEGAAR, the organization which is purported to have lost Heym's manuscript, as noted in his letter

to Becher in 1936. According to Pike, *Prolegomena*, others had similar difficulties with VEGAAR.

47. *The New York Times,* May 7, 1941, p. 1 "Anti-Nazi Editor Slain in Capital"

48. *Syracuse Herald Journal*, Syracuse, New York, June 12, 1949; *Mount Pleasant News*, Mount Pleasant, Iowa, June 12, 1949, p. 2; *Edwardsville Intelligencer*, Edwardsville, Illinois, October 14, 1961

49. *Walla Walla Union Bulletin*, Walla Walla, Washington, October 21, 1948, p. 5; *The Washington Post*, October 21, 1948, p. 1, B1 and October 22, 1948, p. 1; *Los Angeles Times*, October 22, 1948, p. 15 "Attorney's Fall Ruled Suicide"

50. Drew Pearson noted Smith's death in a column in March 1951. Pearson was not generally considered an anti-communist, *The Daily Register*, Harrisburg, Illinois, March 17, 1951; Pearson also claimed Harry Dexter White's death, a few days before White was scheduled to testify at an investigation, was caused by an overdose of digitalis and not mere heart failure. Smith also mentioned in *Edwardsville Intelligencer*, October 14, 1961 by Lyle C. Wilson.

51. Allen Weinstein, *Perjury*, noted Smith's death among several incidents which involved figures near the Hiss case but did not expound on the tragedies. The deaths of White and Duggan are noted as well as the heart attack of Sumner Welles, which occurred shortly after contacting Mayor O'Dwyer in regard to Duggan's fall; Bert and Peter Andrews', *A Tragedy of History*, notes the suicide or murder and that Smith had been employed at the Department of Justice for approximately thirty-four years but also does not discuss the matter further; John Chabot Smith, *Alger Hiss the True Story*, notes Smith's testimony but omits that he died about two months later; Chambers, *Witness*, notes Smith's testimony and death but added little except to note "Justice Department officials have said in my hearing that his reasons were purely personal;" The Earl Jowitt, *The Strange Case of Alger Hiss*, states that Chambers stated that Smith's reasons, presuming suicide, were "according to his information, 'purely personal;'" Alger Hiss, *In the Court of Public Opinion*, noted Smith's testimony but excluded mention of his death; Fred Cook, *The Unfinished Story of Alger Hiss*, omitted any mention of Smith; Meyer Zeligs, *Friendship and Fratricide*, omitted mention of Smith; Edward White, *Alger Hiss's Looking-Glass Wars*, also omitted mention of Smith; Sam Tanenhaus, *Whittaker Chambers*, p. 284, 573 citing a newspaper article which had not previously resurfaced, mentions that Smith's widow was sure that the death was not due to suicide. Again, however, the matter is only the subject of one short paragraph. Note that Smith supposedly committed suicide at a place he had been employed for over thirty years and no note was found. The supposition that he behaved so extremely while involved in the Hiss case without his behavior being due to his involvement seems farfetched; *The New York Times,* December 21, 1948, p. 1, *The New York*

Times, December 22, 1948, p. 1, 3, *The New York Times,* December 27, 1948, p. 1, 13

52. Leftist accounts of the incident almost always omit the detail of the shoe. *Chicago Daily Tribune,* December 22, 1948, p. 18 notes the "overshoe" but theorizes Duggan was surprised as he was preparing to leave the office. *The Tribune* was one of the newspapers opining that the string of unexplained deaths were related. See *Chicago Daily Tribune* on the dates of May 25, 1949, p. 16, June 12, 1949, p. 1, December 13, 1949, p. 3 by Walter Trohan, April 1, 1951, p. 31, November 14, 1952, p. 2, November 16, 1952, p. 24 and April 15, 1954, p. 10 by Walter Trohan. Several other incidents are noted in these articles which seem to have been entirely forgotten.

53. *The Post Standard,* Syracuse, New York, May 23, 1949, p. 1 "Forrestal Ends Life"

54. Ibid. Loftus, Arons, *The Secret War* implies Forrestal's alleged anti-semitism was connected to his psychological difficulties. Other authors to deal with the Forrestal question are Cornell Simpson and Arnold Rogow. The information that Forrestal was called Vincent as a youth is from Forrestal, *The Forrestal Diaries,* edited by Walter Millis. Also strange is that while Toller died in the Mayflower Hotel in New York City, Gertrude Gelbin gave a speech at the Mayflower Hotel in Washington on May 24, 1949 according to *The Washington Post,* May 17, 1949, p. B4 and May 25,1949, p. B4.

Post Script

1. Gehring, Hansjorg *Amerikanische Literaturpolitik in Deutschland* (Deutsche Verlags-Anstalt, Stuttgart, 1976, p.101
2. Cohn, Roy, *McCarthy*
3. *Nachruf,* p.428
4. Habe, Hans, *Our Love Affair with Germany,* p. 94

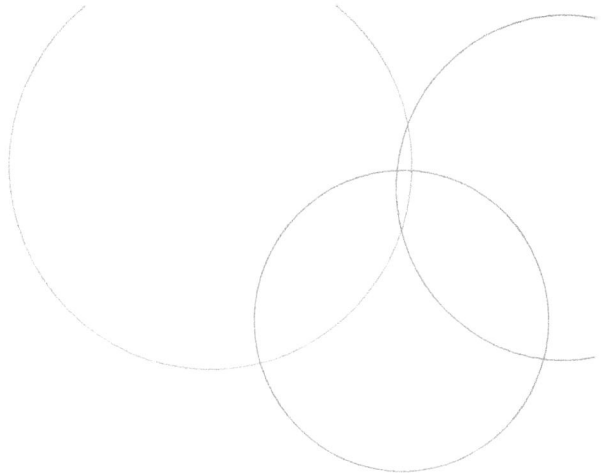

ABOUT THE AUTHOR

Hubert Veneman was born on August 6, 1961 to immigrant parents from Germany, then living in Flushing, New York. He graduated in 1978 from West Lake High School in Thornwood, New York. Hubert obtained a Bachelor of Business Administration from Drexel University, where he was accepted as a fraternity member of Tau Kappa Epsilon. He later studied law at Brooklyn Law, New York. He completed his formal studies by earning a Master of Business Administration from the University of Miami.

Hubert was a resident of the New York Metropolitan area for most of his life. During these years, his employment included managing, and subsequently owning, one of his family's several German-style bakeries. He also was employed as a paralegal with a Manhattan, New York firm.

Hubert was well travelled and spent time in Canada and Europe, mostly in Holland, where he connected with family members and those who shared his interests.

As Hubert's interests were widespread, he could be considered a Renaissance man. He attained either fluency or a strong knowledge of six languages: English, German, Italian, French, Spanish and Dutch. Another major avocation was European history (hence the writing of this book). He was also a follower of many professional sports.

Hubert died on November 20, 2019.

www.ingramcontent.com/pod-product-compliance
Lightning Source LLC
Chambersburg PA
CBHW022333280326

41934CB00006B/614